Governing Universities

SRHE and Open University Press Imprint
General Editor: Heather Eggins

Governing Universities

Changing the Culture?

Catherine Bargh,
Peter Scott and
David Smith

The Society for Research into Higher Education
& Open University Press

Published by SRHE and
Open University Press
Celtic Court
22 Ballmoor
Buckingham
MK18 1XW

and 1900 Frost Road, Suite 101
Bristol, PA 19007, USA

First Published 1996

A catalogue record of this book is available from the British Library

ISBN   0 335 19538 5 (pb)   0 335 19539 3 (hb)

Library of Congress Cataloging-in-Publication Data

Bargh, Catherine, 1960–
    Governing universities : changing the culture? / Catherine Bargh,
Peter Scott, David Smith.
        p. cm.
    Includes bibliographical references (p.   ) and index.
    ISBN 0–335–19539–3 (hardbound). — ISBN 0–335–19538–5 (pbk.)
    1. Universities and colleges—Great Britain—Administration.
2. College administrators—Great Britain. 3. Universities and
colleges—Great Britain—Sociological aspects. 4. Educational
change—Great Britain. 5. Educational surveys—Great Britain.
I. Scott. Peter, 1946– . II. Smith, David, 1955– . III. Title.
LB2341.8.G7835 1996
378′.1′00941—dc20   96–21853
                                                                      CIP

378·100941 BAR

Typeset by Graphicraft Typesetters Limited, Hong Kong
Printed in Great Britain by St Edmundsbury Press Ltd, Bury St Edmunds, Suffolk

971093067

Contents

Preface

This book is based on a research project into changing patterns of governance in higher education undertaken by the Centre for Policy Studies in Education at the University of Leeds. We are grateful to the School of Education for funding the cost of this project out of the research component of its grant.

We want to thank especially the members of the council of the University of Leeds and of the governing body of Leeds Metropolitan University and their respective chairs, Colonel Alan Roberts and Mr Leslie Silver, for agreeing to take part in a pilot study.

Our thanks go to all the council and governing body members who responded to our questionnaire survey. Particular thanks are due to the chairs and other lay governing body members, vice chancellors and other senior managers and registrars/secretaries in our four case-study universities for giving us so much of their time, and also for their invaluable advice.

Most of all, we want to thank our colleague Alison Moore, who provided us with constant support and help, and has a fair claim to be regarded as a fourth 'author'.

Catherine Bargh
Peter Scott
David Smith

1

University Governance:
the Historical and Policy
Context

The process of government, and the nature of governance, have again become urgent considerations in late twentieth-century Britain. In the eighteenth and nineteenth centuries, constitutional questions were passionately argued to-and-fro. The emergence of a powerful and organized state and development of progressively more democratic forms of government meant that these questions were at the heart of political debate and popular agitation. But for much of the present century they have lain dormant. It was complacently, and condescendingly, assumed that they had been settled for all time. The conventions – quasi-constitutional, legal and political – that governed the polity came to be regarded as 'the best of all possible worlds'. The conceit that the Westminster model – the sovereignty of Queen-in-Parliament, the rotation of two dominant parties of government, a neutral civil service – could not be substantially improved upon was reinforced by the establishment of the welfare state, and by the new post-war social order to which it gave rise. Issues of governance appeared to have been consigned to that fabled realm of Bagehot's 'dignified' constitution. Government had become a given.

In the last quarter of the twentieth century, this edifice of compromise, consensus and convention has collapsed. The sovereignty of Parliament has been challenged by new forms of constitutional agitation, notably the movement that began with Charter 88, and of legal activism, notably through the increasingly popular (and effective) mechanism of judicial review, and undermined by the weighty presence of the European Union and its agencies, both Commission and court. The nature of the state has been called into question, in practice, by the unravelling of the so-called post-war settlement of which the welfare state was the centre-piece and, in the ideological domain, by the revival of notions of a slimmed down neo-conservative state and of rival ideas of 'community' or 'civil society'. The historical personality of Britain as a nation state has even been thrown into doubt by the re-emergence of more ancient national principles in Scotland and Wales (The continuing trauma of Northern Ireland, of course, has continued to highlight the fragility of the United Kingdom) and, more subtly, by the development of multi-ethnic and multicultural communities in our transformed cities. The cumulative effect of these challenges has been to reignite interest in constitutional and governance issues. The terms on which we are governed, the legal and political frameworks in which ideas of allegiance and loyalty on the one hand and citizenship and participation on the other are constructed, are now more hotly contested than at any time in the past century. Government is no longer given.

A similar process has taken place in universities. In the nineteenth century, issues of governance were prominent. The corporations of booming Victorian cities competed to secure Royal Charters to found universities. Always vigorous, and often illuminating, debates took place on issues that are familiar today, as practical efforts were made to balance the 'ivory tower' idea of a university, essentially an Oxbridge model to which great prestige was attached (even by nineteenth-century entrepreneurs), with the 'professional' needs of an urban and industrial society. Local elites, civic and commercial, shouldered much of the responsibility for funding and even managing these fledgling universities. University councils were actively engaged in acquiring sites, employing architects and hiring professors. The government of universities was an active arena, not a 'dignified' domain.

In the present century, as in the wider state, issues of governance subsided. Structures, which had ceased to be 'efficient', solidified – and then atrophied. The legal, and conventional, framework in which universities operated appeared to have been settled. Meanwhile, the management initiative was seized by vice chancellors, registrars and professors, and the policy initiative by the national state. The increasing dependence of universities on national funding, already evident before 1939, accelerated after the war. The post-war expansion of higher education, especially after the publication of the Robbins Report in 1963, required the creation of planning structures, again national in scope. University councils, although still ruling their own individual institutional territories, were unable to influence these emerging debates. In the new funding and planning environments they had no standing. For a brief moment, which significantly coincided with the high tide of the post-1945 settlement in society at large, it seemed as if the new university order, in which councils and governing bodies[1] played a subordinate role, would prove to be permanent.

In the past two decades, that hope – or expectation – has proved to be an illusion. Two overarching trends – towards massification (the acceleration of the expansion begun in the Robbins era) and marketization (inter-institutional competition has intensified, university–state relations have been recast in contractual terms and private income streams have increased) – have created a new policy, and management, environment. In this new environment, issues of governance have re-emerged for two main reasons. First, governance has become contested terrain as university councils and governing bodies have been forced to reinterpret their responsibilities in more active terms at the very time when – and partly because of this activism

– their legitimacy has been questioned. This applies particularly to the 'new' universities. In the 1990s it is no longer possible, therefore, to regard the government of higher education institutions as a settled, and uncontroversial, matter. Second, the pressures of massification and marketization have tilted the balance of university business away from 'internal', essentially academic, issues to 'external' issues concerning institutional positioning, mission and even survival. These are issues which university councils, however reluctantly, are obliged to engage. The evolution of university government is discussed in the next section of this chapter.

In both the state and society, and within the more confined territory of higher education, government is no longer a given. Both the quasi-constitutional conventions and the ideological presumptions that sustained traditional patterns of government have been undermined and alternative, even radically different, arrangements suggested (Wilmott, 1993). At the same time, the increasing volatility of structures and environments, not least in higher education, have highlighted the importance of a 'governance culture' in organizational development (Osborne and Gaebler, 1993). The strategic significance of active governance has subsumed (and perhaps subverted) the custodial–constitutional ethos and functions of more traditional forms of government.

This shift highlights the second major theme, after the problematization of government, that informs this book and provoked the research on which it is based: the 'reform' of the public sector. Governance has again become a contested arena, not only because government is no longer a given, for reasons briefly sketched above, but because since 1979 those who govern the public, or quasi-public, sector – whether Cabinet ministers, senior civil servants, quangocrats, the directors of privatized utilities or members of university councils and governing bodies[2] – have used their authority, with enthusiasm or under instruction, to effect cultural change in the institutions for which they are responsible. The broad intention has been to replace a traditional public service ethos, and the allegedly unresponsive and inefficient administrative tradition which that ethos had sustained, by a 'business'-oriented ethos comprising an enterprise culture and a more assertive managerial style (Pierson, 1991).

This intention is evident across the wide territory of the welfare state. It has operated at two levels. The first is rhetorical. A new discourse has developed in which citizens have become clients and then have become customers. Key relationships between students and teachers or patients and doctors are now defined principally as market exchanges and only subordinately in terms of professional responsibilities. This marketization, however contrived, has been closely linked to the rise of managerialism, in turn intimately related to the emergence of the new 'governance culture'. The second level is substantive. New mechanisms have been established in the public sector, characterized on the one hand by organizational decentralization, even disaggregation, and on the other by the introduction of competitive funding regimes. Universities, or hospitals, are now expected to define themselves as discrete quasi-private 'businesses' and to compete against each other for reputation and funding, rather than regard themselves as public institutions within political, and planned, systems. The marketization and massification of higher education is discussed in the third section of this chapter. In the fourth, and final, section we return to the research project, first discussing the theoretical considerations that grow out of our examination of the historical and policy context and then describing the methods of enquiry which were chosen.

The development of university government

With the (important) exceptions of Oxford and Cambridge, the four ancient Scottish universities and the church colleges, British higher education institutions were established largely through lay endeavour. That endeavour took two main forms. The first, typical of the civic universities established in the nineteenth century, was an alliance between local political, professional, commercial and industrial elites, first to press for the grant of a Royal Charter and, when successful, to mobilize the resources required to establish a university. Motives were mixed: civic pride (it is no accident that campaigns to be chartered as cities and to found universities often ran in parallel); the development of 'expert' professions, especially medicine, law and engineering; the growth of local industry and commerce. Usually several false starts were made and delays were frequent. Almost 20 years of effort (1854 to 1872) were needed to establish the first college of the University of Wales (Ellis, 1972: 9–30), and 66 years elapsed between the foundation of the Liverpool Royal Institution in 1814 and the creation of the university (initially as part of the federal Victoria University) in 1881 (Kelly, 1981: 14–35).

The second form of lay endeavour, typical of the 'new' universities, was municipal enterprise. For example, the foundations of the University of East London were laid in two bursts of local government activism: in the 1890s, when West Ham council, which had been made into a county borough in 1889, established a college following the Technical Instruction Act of the same year; and between the wars when Essex county council founded the other two colleges, in Waltham Forest and Barking, that were later amalgamated to form first the polytechnic and then the university (Burgess *et al.*, 1995: 39–80). However, whichever form lay endeavour took, it was decisive. The two groups that came to dominate the twentieth-century university, the national state and its agencies and the academic profession (especially its senior layers), played subordinate roles. The former assisted by granting university charters, by establishing local government structures and, modestly, by contributing resources through direct grants to fledgling universities or by permitting councils to spend rate income on post-school education. The latter's contribution was largely made through the impact of charismatic individuals rather than the weight of an organized profession.

As a result, lay councils were the dominant organizations in the early universities. In the civic universities the composition of councils continued to reflect their 'founders', the alliances of local elites that had successfully pressed for their foundation. In the institutions which later formed the 'new' universities, governing bodies were overwhelmingly composed of their successful sponsors, local councillors. Not until after the First World War did the academic profession in the 'old' university sector, through senates, assert its claim to co-rule with lay-led councils. Only gradually did councils cede their powers over the supervision of academic staff and their responsibility for academic matters, and concentrate instead on financial and other administrative questions (Archer, 1979: 520). The Oxbridge model of academic self-government combined with the rising tide of professionalization to stimulate the autonomous ambitions of the academic profession. According to Halsey and Trow:

> They [academics] often had to engage in struggles with local trustees to establish the elements of academic freedom and institutional self-government which they held to be appropriate to their professional status and which many of them had brought to their new universities from the traditional academic guilds of Oxford and Cambridge. They quickly won academic freedom in practice, if not in formal constitutions.
> (Halsey and Trow, 1971: 149)

This pressure to establish academic guilds, strong in the civic and redbrick universities between the wars, intensified after 1945, when universities enjoyed unprecedented (and subsequently unparalleled) prestige as a result of their contribution to the war effort and to post-war reconstruction, and again in the 1960s, when the new universities were founded, stimulating a new Oxbridge diaspora, and the colleges of advanced technology were promoted to university status.

However, in the light of the long persistence of lay-dominated forms of university government and the more recent lay revival, two points are perhaps worth emphasizing, although they point to opposite conclusions. First, the consignment of councils, and in particular their lay element, to form the 'dignified' component of university constitutions and the elevation of senates (and/or vice chancellors) to become the 'efficient' component are comparatively recent phenomena. Neither process was complete before 1945 or, arguably, until the Robbins-induced and state-funded expansion that began in the 1960s. It is also important to recognize that until the mid-1960s most of the institutions that later formed the 'new' universities did not have properly constituted academic boards analogous to 'old' university senates. Governing bodies, and principals/directors, went largely unchallenged. It is misleading, therefore, to regard the unequal balance between 'dignified' council and 'efficient' senate, Halsey's 'donnish dominion' in the title of a later work (Halsey, 1992), as the norm from which the recently renewed emphasis on a stronger 'governance culture' is an exception. For most of the time, and in most institutions, lay control was the norm. Its reassertion, if that is an accurate account of recent shifts in university government, is perhaps best seen as a reversion to that norm.

Second, the civic universities were founded before the integrity of nineteenth-century intellectual culture had been completely undermined by the ceaseless sophistication of twentieth-century science and technology. Although a key instrument in the formation of professional society, the university was also the heir to older cultural norms. The gap between 'lay' and 'academic', today perceived as categorical, was then much narrower. The man of letters and the man of science survived, not yet displaced by the academic scholar and professional scientist. The dominant, and detailed, involvement of lay-dominated councils in matters that today would be seen as purely academic did not strike contemporaries as either perverse or anomalous. But there is no going back to a broad-church intellectual culture embracing both lay-generalist and academic-specialist constituencies. The professionalization of society and the academicization of the intellect are irreversible, despite their uneasy cohabitation with marketization and in the face of postmodern critiques of authority and expertise. Seen in this different light, increased lay involvement cannot be regarded as reversion to an earlier norm.

Since the 1960s, a radical shift appears to have taken place in both the conception and practice of university government. The dominance of the academic guild, perhaps more recently established than Halsey and Trow suggest, has been eroded. Other institutional elements have come (back?) into their own: professionalized administrations led by registrars, senior management teams headed by vice chancellors and, of course, university councils. But it has been a slow and gradual erosion, imperceptible at first. Initially, in the Robbins afterglow, the 'donnish dominion' was even strengthened. When the first wave of new universities was established on green-field campuses in the 1960s, governance was not a contested, or even much debated, issue. Courts and councils were created, as the 'dignified' components of their constitutions, on the existing model of the civic universities, although they tended to be smaller. The sprawl of civic dignitaries typical of older university councils was avoided. Their 'founders', after all, had not been local elites; their effective sponsor was the state.

Exceptionally, and momentarily, lay people may have played a key role in the establishment of the new universities as agitators and promoters. The local good and the great led deputations to the University Grants Committee to press their case and lobbied politicians (Shattock, 1994: 73–97). But once decisions had been reached about the location of the new universities, their influence dwindled (Warwick was perhaps an exception and was much criticized for what was then seen as intrusive lay/industrial involvement, notably in E. P. Thompson's (1969) book *Warwick University Ltd*). Formally the councils of the new universities were granted more restricted powers than those enjoyed by the councils of older universities. It was regarded as axiomatic that their 'efficient' government should be in academic hands, effectively a dual-control system of quasi-representative senates and central administrations presided over by vice chancellors (guided by registrars). Councils, and especially their lay members, were relegated to the margins of university government, their effective roles confined to acting as long-stop trustees of their universities, providing a powerful group of 'friends' and offering assistance on restricted topics, notably estates and (as the financial climate chilled) financial management.

At the same time, in the former polytechnics and colleges of higher education the question of governance was also regarded as essentially settled. The balance between lay – in this case municipal – control and academic self-government was different for historical reasons, but the trajectory of change appeared to be the same. The former was a declining interest; the latter a rising one. Again it was taken as axiomatic that if the binary system was to succeed, and the newly formed polytechnics and relabelled colleges of education were to be fully accepted as bona fide higher education institutions, they had to be granted a greater degree of academic self-government; hence the Weaver Report on academic boards (Department of Education and Science, 1965). Governing bodies, although more powerful than university councils, had to make room.

Any resistance to this displacement of governing bodies was hampered by their organizational weaknesses. Their integrity was compromised by the failure to establish sufficient 'distance' between them and their maintaining local authorities. They were large and inchoate. Some local education authorities struggled to maintain a tight political grip over governing bodies by appointing only councillors to the positions they controlled; others adopted more liberal policies, nominating sympathetic supporters less amenable to the party whip. Behind academic board and other staff governors loomed the presence of their trade unions.

Industrial members tended to be bewildered by what often appeared to them unproductive 'politics'. Despite these disadvantages, some polytechnic and college governing bodies managed to work well, bequeathing strong and flourishing institutions to their corporate successors. But the action was clearly elsewhere – in the new academic boards and burgeoning directorates, ancestors of today's senior management teams, or in the town halls.

Only in the 1980s was academic self-government openly challenged, although it had already been compromised during the 1970s by a combination of the increasing size and complexity of institutions, growing constraints on resources, the revolt against professorial cliques and the politicization provoked by student revolt. In the 'old' universities the key period was between 1981, when university budgets were sharply cut and lay members of councils sharply reminded that institutional success (or even survival) could no longer be taken for granted, and 1985, when the Jarratt Report on university efficiency was published (Committee of Vice Chancellors and Principals, 1985). Jarratt, like Robbins, has come subsequently to represent far more than it actually said. There is little in the report about university governance; its focus is on institutional management. Its 'headline' recommendation was that the vice chancellor should be recognized as the university's chief executive.

But Jarratt was a milestone in at least three senses. First, it introduced a new rhetoric into higher education. The language of business efficiency, more congenial to lay council members, was set against that of the 'donnish dominion', the classic discourse of senates. The former was destined to dominate. Second, Jarratt recommended that, where they had not already done so, councils and senates should form joint committees to oversee policy and resources and other key strategic activities. Although many universities had previously had joint council–senate committees, they tended to be on second-order subjects, such as honorary degrees. Even when the business of such committees was more central to the academic purposes of the university (for example, chair committees), lay members often took a recessive role. So Jarratt not only introduced a new language in which lay council members could discuss strategic issues; the report also suggested mechanisms through which their participation could become effective.

Third, Jarratt was part of a wider pattern of policy changes. The activism of the University Grants Committee (UGC) in its last days, when a tough planning regime was imposed on the universities (including the first round of research assessment); the establishment of the Universities Funding Council (UFC) in place of the UGC, with its ill-timed lurch towards contractual funding; the parallel establishment of the Polytechnics and Colleges Funding Council (PCFC), which triggered a powerful rivalry between the two bodies and sectors; the abandonment of the binary system at the beginning of the 1990s and the rapid growth and increasing heterogeneity of the university system – all these episodes focused attention on the role of university councils as the effective governing bodies of their institutions and ultimate arbiters of their fortunes. The demarcation (borrowed from Anthony Giddens, 1984, 1985) between 'allocative' resources, grudgingly conceded to be within the competence of councils, and 'authoritative' resources, the prerogative of the academic guild, was substantively eroded after the mid-1980s by these developments.

In the 'new' universities and colleges the key period was between 1983, when the National Advisory Body (NAB) was created, so heralding the beginning-of-the-end of local rule, and 1988, when the polytechnics were finally freed from the control of local education authorities and established as free-standing corporations. The creation of the NAB, a quasi-quango, although designed to modernize, and so preserve, local government rule of the polytechnics, unsettled the existing pattern of governance by highlighting its anomalies (and anachronisms?). In 1986, the NAB published a report on good management practice, in essence the equivalent of the Jarratt Report (National Advisory Body, 1986). Because of the political sensitivity of the topic, the report had almost nothing to say about governance. But, like Jarratt, it was an important episode in a dynamic process of disengagement from local government, which inevitably reopened the question of governance. It too introduced a new language of efficiency that was difficult to reconcile with the municipal tradition, although unlike Jarratt the NAB report stopped short of recommending positive (as opposed to platitudinous) remedies.

When the Education Reform Act finally cut the links between polytechnics and local education authorities (LEAs), therefore, a root-and-branch reform of institutional governance followed. It took effect at two levels. The first was symbolic, because the 'ownership' of the polytechnics and colleges was transferred, so creating an urgent need to create new institutional personalities. Fundamental issues of identity were raised. Governing bodies were thrust into the front line. The second level was practical. The newly incorporated institutions overnight became the owners of their buildings and employers of their staff. New mechanisms had to be established to manage these key activities. Key decisions had to be taken across a range of estates development, financial management, personnel and, in particular, industrial relations issues. Although many polytechnics had already developed strong senior management teams and significant progress had been made towards building a self-confident cadre of polytechnic administrators, expertise gaps were inevitably created by the forced evacuation of local authorities which governors, collectively and individually, had to help fill.

The centre-piece of this reform was the replacement of sprawling 'political' governing bodies of the LEA era by small 'executive' boards. The model was that of NHS trusts, Training and Enterprise Councils and other quangos established at very much the same time. The future of the polytechnics was placed in the hands of 'independent' governors, who, ministers hoped, would not 'go native' but instead become agents of culture change within the newly incorporated institutions, although in fact there was a significant degree of continuity between pre-1989 and post-1989 governing bodies. The tension between quasi-executive and representative cultures remained, even if the balance had been firmly tilted towards the former. In the first instance, 'independent' governors were chosen by the Secretary of State, which explained their much criticized political bias towards the Conservative Party and its business friends. Subsequently, in effect, they became self-perpetuating.

These arrangements for appointing 'independent' governors produced an accountability deficit which, it has been argued, contributed to recent episodes in which governors have fumbled their responsibilities. The most critical occurred at the University of Huddersfield in 1994, when the long-serving vice chancellor, Professor Ken Durrands, was obliged to resign following a staff and student revolt against the 'independent' governors' decision, supported by Professor Durrands, to exclude their representatives from the governing body. There have been other examples of governors' apparent failure to foresee, and defuse, institutional crises of confidence at Bournemouth and Portsmouth Universities. However, such episodes have been exceptional. In fact, the transformation of the former polytechnics from being LEA institutions, through the NAB interregnum and incorporation in 1988 to full university status after 1992, was remarkably trouble-free (although the external policy environment was generally favourable until, first, the 'consolidation' of student numbers in 1993 and, subsequently, budget cuts).

The experience of post-incorporation governance and the polytechnics/ 'new' universities suggests that a distinction needs to be drawn between institutional redefinition and reconfiguration, inescapably embracing far-reaching culture shifts and a baleful and counter-productive politicization. The development of 'new' university and college governing bodies is better explained in the context of the former than stigmatized as the latter. Important, and worrying, questions about accountability have been raised by the post-1988 arrangements for governing these institutions, which reflect the way in which 'independent' governors are appointed and, less surely, may influence their actions and attitudes. But they are best addressed as structural issues rather than in the language of conspiracy theory. The selection and appointment of governors is discussed in Chapter 4.

The 'governance culture' of the 'new' universities and colleges of higher education remains volatile. Recent developments have tended to soften the more abrasive, and adversarial, styles allegedly characteristic of the new governing bodies. First, the 'shock of the new' experienced in the turbulent aftermath of incorporation has faded. Institutions have settled down. Second, the events at Huddersfield, Portsmouth and Bournemouth have clearly had a sobering effect. The damage institutions are likely to suffer from full-scale confrontations has encouraged many 'independent' governors to reconsider their enthusiasm for enforced culture change. After the departure of Professor Durrands, staff and student governors were quickly reinstated.

Third, some 'independent' governors have gone partly 'native', because through more lengthy acquaintance with their institutions they have both greater respect for managers and staff and a fuller appreciation of the funding and other pressures on higher education than their erstwhile 'friends' in government. Fourth, the abandonment of the binary system, and elevation of the former polytechnics to university status, has encouraged 'new' university governors to conceive their responsibilities in different, and perhaps more dignified, terms. Labels count. To be the governor of a university is a different experience and suggests different associations from being the governor of a polytechnic. Titles, and language, matter too. Renamed vice chancellors and professors may invite an instinctive deference not accorded to directors and principal lecturers.

But the fifth, and probably decisive, reason has been the shift in the political climate, and public doctrine and policy, against what is seen as excessive marketization (the backlash against the NHS reforms, the unpopularity of the privatized water companies and opposition to the privatization of British Rail are perhaps the best examples) and, in particular, the decline in probity that is seen as a consequence of abandoning public service and professional values – in a word, 'sleaze'. This shift has been felt more sharply in the 'new' than the 'old' universities because their development has been more closely aligned with the thrust towards marketization, but its effects are felt across the whole system. Notions of responsiveness to, and involvement by, stakeholder communities have revived. As a result, the fierce emphasis on 'market' responsiveness and 'business' efficiency in the public sector, which dominated the political climate of the late 1980s, has been tempered.

There was little evidence of significant 'sleaze' in higher education. Nevertheless, this phenomenon, which most powerfully provoked the shift in political climate and led to the creation of the Committee on Standards in Public Life chaired by Lord Nolan (Committee on Standards in Public Life, 1995a), had an important impact on the 'governance culture' of universities in three respects. First, in the public mind, a strong link was established between 'sleaze' and lack of transparency. Closed corporations, which the governing bodies of 'new' universities at any rate superficially resembled, were seen as inherently more open to 'sleaze' than open and more representative bodies. Second, vice chancellors' salaries (and pay-offs) were linked to the excessive payments made to the directors of companies, especially privatized utilities. Third, more significant examples of impropriety have occurred in the further education sector, although the culprits have more often been senior managers than governors. Because the government of 'new' universities and colleges of higher education and that of further education colleges are organized on identical bases and according to the same principles, similar issues of openness, transparency and accountability have been raised in the context of higher education.

As a result, the Nolan Committee included university and college governing bodies among the agencies it wished to scrutinize, along with grant-maintained schools, Training and Enterprise Councils (and Local Enterprise Companies in Scotland) and housing associations. In a preliminary issues paper, the committee raised three topics: the appointment and accountability of board members; the role of boards in relations to officers and staff; and safeguards in respect of conflicts of interest (Committee on Standards in Public Life, 1995b). Although the third topic, 'sleaze', was less relevant to university governance for reasons discussed above, the first two had already been identified as key issues. In particular, the competing demands of accountability and confidentiality, and the proper demarcation of roles between governors and senior managers, had emerged as potential difficulties.

The ripples of Nolan spread out across higher education. The Committee of University Chairmen, assisted by the Higher Education Funding Council for England and the Funding Council for Wales, published in June 1995 a guide to members of governing bodies, elaborating earlier advice on good practice issued in December 1994 (Committee of University Chairmen, 1995). Its major themes were the need for transparency and openness in the conduct of governing body business and the importance of finding appropriate ways to involve the community. Although both 'old' and 'new' university chairs[3] separately formed loose club-like organizations more than a decade ago, their more active style and higher profile in the mid-1990s reflected three new factors. The first was the perceived need to put their house in order in the face of implied criticism from the Nolan Committee and others. The second was the establishment of a new body covering all university chairs, within which differences and similarities between 'governance cultures' could be explored. The third was recognition that issues of governance had become more central in the post-binary higher education system, and that university chairs should develop a stronger collective voice able to influence the national policy agenda.

In the post-Jarratt decade, the pattern of governance in the 'old' universities has not been marked by such radical disjuncture. Change has been more gradual. It was expected by some that, as the 'donnish dominion' crumbled, councils (and especially their lay members) should reassert themselves. This does not appear to have happened yet, or on the scale anticipated. Instead, power has flowed to senior management teams headed by vice chancellors in their post-Jarratt role as chief executives, or been drained away to external agencies, notably the funding councils. But among these competing centres of power and influence councils have come to represent a strategic arena. Chairs, vice chairs, treasurers and other key members have tended to be drawn into closer alliances with senior management, and have also begun to take more seriously their leadership responsibilities in relation to the external environment.

The significance of 'old' university councils, therefore, grew during the 1990s, albeit discreetly. This has been reflected in efforts to reduce the size of councils by shedding supposedly supernumerary members – often from neighbouring local authorities. (One of the paradoxes of the post-incorporation environment was that local authorities were much better represented on the councils of 'old' universities, for which they had never been responsible, than on the governing bodies of 'new' universities which they maintained up to 1989.) The probable effect has been to produce convergence between 'old' university councils and 'new' university and college governing bodies. The former tended to become more 'efficient' and the latter to become more 'dignified'.

Markets and mass higher education

Radical changes have taken place not only in the shape of the higher education system and the scale and character of institutions but in the links between universities and society, culture, science and innovation. These changes have transformed the environment of governance. Two overarching trends, massification and marketization, mentioned earlier in this chapter, provide an appropriate conceptual framework in which to consider the detailed changes that have taken place inside higher education, at the level of the system and of individual institutions. They explain a lot. But the modern university is not just bigger and market-oriented. More fundamental transformations are also under way.

There is general agreement among social analysts, cultural critics and political commentators that a new kind of society is emerging in the late twentieth century. Some describe it in terms of its most basic attributes:

acceleration (volatility as well as velocity), simultaneity (the extended present and 'glocalization') (Nowotny, 1994), complexity (in particular, non-linearity), risk (Beck, 1992) and reflexivity (Giddens, 1990). Others emphasize its ideological contours, for example by making assertions about the 'end of history' (Fukuyama, 1992); others again stress its socio-economic and technological dimensions, by constructing scenarios of post-Fordism or the 'learning society' (Amin, 1994); yet others highlight its cultural impact, by either spinning post-modern myths or analysing the ambiguous effects of globalization and individualization. The university, however, is implicated in all these accounts: as the source of novel intellectual discourses; as the producer of potent symbolic goods in a post-industrial economy; and as the agency for the reordering of social relations and redefinition of individual life chances and life styles.

The pervasive, and incestuous, nature of these linkages has led some to argue that the mass university is a new kind of institution, and that the development of mass higher education can only be properly understood as one of a series of modernizations of the late-modern world (Scott, 1995). The first is a political revolution characterized by the 'reform' of the welfare state, in particular the rise of quasi-contractual relations between 'customers' and 'contractors' within the public sector (Le Grand and Bartlett, 1993) and of what has been called an 'audit society' (Power, 1994). The impact of both ideas, contracts and audit, on relations between higher education and the state (and funding and research councils) over the past decade has been pronounced. The second is a socio-economic revolution, post-Fordism in the generic sense referred to above. In terms of inputs, the nature of demand for higher education has been transformed, as participation has risen to semi-compulsory levels. In output terms, new kinds of articulation have developed between higher education and the labour market and the economy generally. As a 'positional' good, the value of higher education to the individual has declined, while the restructuring of employment has eroded distinctively 'graduate' jobs – but at the same time, as a symbolic good, higher education has acquired a direct economic significance within the leisure-and-learning industry, a key sector of the post-industrial economy (Office of Science and Technology, 1995).

The third revolution has taken place in intellectual culture and in the innovation system. In the former there has been a slide into relativism and indeterminacy. Plural discourses are preferred to universal truths. Just as in the mid-nineteenth century (elite) cultural values were unbundled, in the late twentieth century cognitive values may be threatened with a similar fate. The consequences for the university, as the premier cognitive institution, are baleful, although ambiguously the university is also the primary source of this intellectual playfulness. In the latter, an ordered system of pure and applied science, technology transfer and product and service innovation is being replaced by a much fuzzier knowledge production system, in which producers are proliferating, old demarcations between scientists and users are increasingly elided and market initiatives are more decisive. This has been described as a paradigm shift from mode 1 to mode 2 (Gibbons *et al.*, 1994). To the extent that the prestige of the modern university has depended on its hegemony in science and, less certainly, technology, this shift is likely to compromise its status. But the mass university is a dominant node of the emerging innovation system, orchestrator of its epistemological eclecticism and heterogeneous stakeholders.

The particular evolution of British higher education during the past two decades, therefore, has to be set in the context of these larger transformations – of all higher education systems and of modern society. As has already been suggested, two overarching trends characterize this evolution: massification and marketization. The first embraces not simply the expansion of the system(s) and the increasing variety of institutions but also their growing size and complexity as organizations and the growing heterogeneity of their academic 'products', in terms of both teaching and research. Marketization denotes the development of a more competitive environment within higher education. This has two aspects: first, at the system level, government departments, funding councils and other agencies have developed strategic policies to build a 'market' culture and resource allocation systems designed to create quasi-markets; second, at the institutional level, more competitive values have been espoused and competitive behaviour has been stimulated between, and within, universities. Both reflect the wider marketization of public policy and public choices, which has been an important element within the political revolution referred to above.

The expansion of the system, institutional diversity, organizational complexity and academic heterogeneity, therefore, are the key components of massification. The growth of the higher education student population has been spectacular. It has risen from 324,000 at the time of the 1963 Robbins Report to more than 1.4 million – a growth rate of more than 500 per cent. In higher education the age participation increased, slowly at first, from less than 10 per cent in the 1960s to 17 per cent by the mid-1980s and, more rapidly and recently, to 32 per cent currently. An elite system has been transformed into a mass system, with levels of access rivalling those of continental Europe and North America. Low wastage rates have led to graduate production rates that now outstrip France and Germany.

The second component, institutional diversity, is equally significant. The number of universities has increased from 24 in the late 1950s, to 45 after the Robbins expansion had been completed and 93 following the abandonment of the binary system in 1992. In addition, there are 60 other higher education institutions, and over 400 further education colleges have some stake in higher education (one-in-ten higher education students are enrolled in further education colleges). The effect has been to highlight the diversity of institutions comprising the system. As long as the university sector comprised 45 institutions, all animated by analogous academic and professional values, all organized along similar collegial-administrative lines and all engaged in both teaching and research (although in different, and divergent, proportions), the university could plausibly be regarded as an identifiable ideal-type. Now that the sector comprises 93 universities with starkly divergent academic missions and managerial traditions (as well as different legal constitutions and governance arrangements), institutional personality has been eroded.

Diversity has another dimension. In place of a Britain-wide university system, three national higher education systems in England, Scotland and Wales have been created with their own funding councils (higher education in Northern Ireland was always administratively separate). The long-term effects of these new arrangements are difficult to predict. In the wider context of higher education it can be argued that the structure has actually been simplified. Three national systems have replaced four sub-systems: the British universities funded by the University Grants Committee; the English polytechnics and colleges funded through the National Advisory Body; non-university higher education in Wales funded through the Wales Advisory Body; and the Scottish central institutions directly funded by the Scottish Office Education Department. But although the detailed impact of this devolutionary arrangement on the actual diversity of higher education so far has been limited, the existence of three (four, if Northern Ireland is included) distinct policy domains is likely to have divergent long-term consequences.

The third component of massification is organizational complexity. At the time of Robbins the average British university had 2750 students – equivalent to a middle-sized college of higher education today. Many had far fewer. The average was pulled up by the federal University of London and Oxford and Cambridge, still in the early 1960s the next two largest universities. In 1995 the average university had well over 8000 full-time equivalent students. Several enrolled approaching 20,000. Although the scale of British universities remains modest by North American or continental European standards, a step-change has occurred, with profound consequences. The 'intimacy' of institutions, which until recently appeared the British universities' most characteristic quality, has been degraded; a far-reaching professionalization of administrative and academic services has taken place; and new management cultures and institutional norms have emerged.

The university has become a complex institution within which different organizational models coexist, often uneasily. It is rather like an archaeological site. In the lowest layer is the idea of the 'collegium' ruled by academic elders; in the next layer is the notion, popular in the 1960s, of the university as a political system in which issues of representation and participation were dominant; next up is the 'corporate' ideal that came into its own post-Jarratt and post-incorporation, and relied on line management bureaucracy; finally, on the surface, is the idea of the university as a creative organization, its separate 'businesses' orchestrated by a strategic centre. These different organizational models are closely related to the increasing scale and complexity of universities.

The fourth, and final, component of massification is the growing heterogeneity of student constituencies and academic 'products', which has been produced by a combination of the first two, growth and diversity. In higher education students are no longer predominantly 18- or 19-year-old school-leavers, although most full-time students in the 'old' universities continue to fall into that broad category. More than a quarter are now mature students. The number of part-time students has also increased sharply, especially among postgraduates. A significant number of students with non-standard qualifications is now admitted, after completing access or foundation programmes in local colleges or on the strength of work-based or prior, often experiential, learning.

As a result, universities offer a much wider range of academic 'products'. Novel subjects reflecting broader student constituencies and changing labour-market requirements have entered the higher education curriculum. These new subjects, and traditional academic disciplines, are delivered in novel ways – through modular structures and credit accumulation and transfer systems designed to maximize student choice. Older ideas of inter-disciplinarity, rooted in the notion of a liberal, and common, intellectual culture and popular in the first phase of post-war expansion during the 1960s, have been succeeded by new academic configurations, built around generic competences such as teamwork, problem-solving, communications skills and so on, or based on vocational affinities. Once-clear distinctions between undergraduate and postgraduate, initial and continuing, academic and vocational have been significantly eroded as a result. At the same time, the idea of 'research' has been stretched to embrace not only traditional scholarly and scientific production but activities such as 'action' research, technology transfer and so on. Again the effect has been to increase the number of research 'products' offered by universities and colleges.

The second overarching trend has been the growth of a more competitive environment in further and higher education – in a word, marketization. This has two aspects. The first is the development by the Department for Education and Employment and other departments, funding councils and agencies such as Training and Enterprise Councils (or Local Enterprise Companies in Scotland) of explicit policies to create quasi-markets in the allocation of resources and/or students; the second is the growth of a more competitive culture within, and between, institutions, partly as a direct result of these policies, partly because 'market' values and practices have been powerfully encouraged and partly as a result of the growing responsiveness of higher education, which has just been discussed.

At the level of national policy-making, marketization and massification were inextricably linked from the mid-1980s onwards. Until the mid-1980s the government's aims were to restrict student numbers and steer the system. Only in 1987 was there a switch to market-led growth, when the Secretary of State, Kenneth Baker, was able to secure the Treasury's agreement to renewed expansion, announced in a speech at Lancaster University in 1988. Between 1988 and 1993, universities and polytechnics were allowed to increase their income by recruiting more students than were covered by their core grant, and for whom they only received tuition fees. As a result, three conditions appeared to be satisfied. First, burgeoning social demand for higher education was met (and the matching political dividend collected?). Second, a 'market' in student choices was created, which was ideologically satisfying and would have been impossible within a system of planned student numbers. Third, unit costs in higher education were cut, which pleased the Treasury. Tuition fees were doubled to strengthen these 'market' effects.

However, the attractions of 'efficient expansion' had begun to fade by the early 1990s. The Treasury, ignoring (or, rather, taking for granted) the impressive 'efficiency gains' produced by this policy, worried about its uncapped obligation to pay fees on behalf of all the students that higher education institutions cared to admit. Moreover, evidence accumulated that the demand for places was not as intense as had been supposed. The policy of market-led growth was abandoned, although the costs squeeze and 'market' culture continued. First, tuition fees were cut, and then cut again, to reduce the incentive for institutions to recruit extra students. Finally, a fixed cap was imposed on student numbers. Under the policy of 'consolidation', which persists, each institution was allocated a MASN (maximum aggregate student number). If it overshot its MASN, or under-recruited, grant was deducted. With the reimposition of a system of planned student numbers, the thrust towards marketization weakened.

A similar pattern of waxing, and than waning, enthusiasm for 'market' policies was apparent at the intermediate level, that of the funding councils. The most celebrated attempt to establish a full-blown internal market was made by the Universities Funding Council chaired by Lord Chilver in 1989–90. Universities were encouraged to bid against each other for funded student places. Although indicative bid prices were suggested by the UFC, they were explicitly invited to make lower bids. The attempt failed, partly because the universities responded by creating an unofficial cartel and, with very few exceptions, declined to undercut the bid prices, and partly because the establishment of an internal market became entangled with a costs-reduction exercise (which was the government's more immediate priority). Nevertheless, this episode sensitized the universities to a more competitive culture.

At the same time, the new Polytechnics and Colleges Funding Council adopted more modest policies, which combined planning and market approaches. Institutions were guaranteed funding for the core of their work (minus the efficiency gains required by the government), where student numbers were effectively planned, and only had to bid at the margin for additional student places, the market element in the PCFC's methodology. The Higher Education Funding Council for England and the other two funding councils, which took over from the UFC and PCFC in 1992, leant to the latter's more gradualist approach rather than the former's overtly 'market' ambitions. The imposition of 'consolidation' soon afterwards left the funding councils with no choice but to revert to a system of centrally planned student numbers. A revolution in policy had taken place: in the late 1980s, government and funding council policies seemed to be moving rapidly towards a quasi-voucher system; in the 1990s, there was a return to central planning.

At the institutional level, where initial resistance to marketization (at any rate in the 'old' universities) had been most intense, the opposite happened. Resistance to markets was succeeded by acquiescence, which has been followed by grudging support. The government's decision to increase tuition fees in the late 1980s had powerful side-effects that outlived its reversal. Its psychological impact remained. Most universities continued to be growth-oriented, which entailed pragmatic if not ideological acceptance of a 'market' culture. All students came increasingly to be characterized as 'customers'. Fees paid by overseas students in particular represented a vital income stream in many higher education institutions. Other areas of university work, notably postgraduate and post-experience courses, also came to depend on the willingness of students (or their employers) to pay their own fees, although not always on a full-cost basis.

Even after the abandonment of 'efficient expansion', other government and funding council policies continued to encourage competitive behaviour among institutions. Research assessment, on the basis of which departments (more accurately, units of assessment) are ranked and funding is allocated, fuelled the competitive spirit in higher education. Teaching quality assessment, also undertaken by the funding councils, had a similar effect. The results of both kinds of assessment were routinely used to secure, or consolidate, market advantage. For example, the research assessment exercise created a lively 'transfer' market in active researchers and teaching quality assessment grades frequently featured in promotional material.

Both research and teaching quality assessment form part of a wider policy picture. The shift from an inner-directed and self-referential academic culture to more open and outer-directed regimes has had an important influence in reshaping institutional and professional attitudes towards the legitimacy, and feasibility, of competition. This growth of a grass-roots 'market' culture in higher education is perhaps more significant than the detailed policies of the government, funding councils and other agencies. These have been only one element in the massification and marketization of higher education, which has been driven by much more deeply rooted secular changes. National policy has been characterized by stop (1981 to 1986), go (1987 to 1992) and stop again (since 1992). The drive towards marketization has largely been contingent on this cycle of expansion and consolidation. The key consideration has always been to secure 'efficiency gains'.

But these inconsistencies and hesitancies of policy have been subsumed within a larger evolution of a 'market' culture inside institutions, which reflects the impact of the various components of massification on the inner life of higher education – the expansion of the system, institutional diversity, organizational complexity and academic heterogeneity – and also the fundamental transformations of political, socio-economic, intellectual and scientific life discussed at the beginning of this section. And it is in this institutional environment, rather than in the context of national policy, that the governance of universities and colleges needs to be analysed and reshaped.

The cumulative effect of massification and marketization has been to erode the demarcation between the allocative and authoritative domains, or 'external' issues, for which governing bodies have traditionally been responsible and 'internal' issues, the prerogative of the academic guild. This is apparent at the level of national policy-making, particularly in the evolution from an arm's length UGC to funding councils that 'steer' the system through mechanisms such as research and teaching quality assessment – in Giddens's terms 'authoritative' interventions – as well as through their decisions about the allocation of resources. But, as has been argued, the fuzziness between the allocative and the authoritative, the 'external' and the 'internal', is even more apparent at the institutional level, which is also the level at which governing bodies act.

This fuzziness has three components: conceptual, strategic and operational. The first is the reconceptualization of the university. It is no longer seen as an academic community, however hierarchical, but as a 'business' – or, more often, a set of 'businesses'. Clearly, lay governors possess a legitimacy in the latter context which they were denied when the 'donnish dominion' had yet to be challenged. Second, it has become much harder to distinguish clearly between academic and support functions, or at any rate categorically to insist that the latter are ineluctably subordinate to the former. As a result, strategic planning has become an integrated process which steers academic policy rather than being steered by it. Again, lay governors have added leverage. Third, functions once regarded as peripheral have become central to the political and academic economy of the modern university. Many of these are hybrid academic–service functions, such as continuing professional development or technology transfer. Yet again, this has increased the potential significance of the lay element in university government.

University governance in the context of public policy

This book attempts to explore the changing nature of university governance. Conceptually, governance is distinct from management. In operational terms, however, the issue of governance is intimately connected with wider debates about managerialism, collegiality and accountability. As has already been pointed out, universities, like other institutions in the public sector of the late twentieth century, have been caught up in the effects of reform policies which have shifted the frontiers of public and private sector enterprise. These reforms, in turn, echo deeper transformations of late twentieth-century society. In the wake of those reforms have come new emphases on quasi-markets, new systems of funding for public and private welfare provision, new methods of devolved control and, critically from the perspective of governance, new structures and expectations of accountability. Consequently, governing bodies, in universities no less than other areas of the public sector, are increasingly seen as strategic arenas of management and influence. Key members of such bodies have been drawn into senior management and are expected to play an increasingly significant role in leadership terms, particularly in relation to the external environment.

The perspectives on university governance offered in this book are based on a research project undertaken by the authors and funded by the University of Leeds. This research set out to explore the extent to which different types of higher educational institutions – 'old' universities, which are chartered or statutory corporations, and 'new' universities and colleges, which are higher education corporations established under the 1988 Education Reform Act – converge and/or diverge in their styles of governance. The focus on governance, a largely unexplored arena, was prompted by a broader interest in the political, organizational and cultural dimensions of the shift of British higher education from being an elite formation (although liberally extended in the 1960s) to becoming a recognizably mass system by the early 1990s. Accordingly, the project was designed to provide the necessary empirical data with which to assess the nature and impact of recent changes in the governance of higher education and to analyse the broader relationship between governance, management and institutional culture in a mass system.

The research proved to be timely in at least two respects. First, as has already been indicated, growing public concern about standards in public life led to the establishment of the Nolan Committee. The committee's subsequent decision to review local public spending bodies, including further and higher education institutions, proved that the governance of universities could no longer be regarded as a privileged domain isolated from the broader environment of public policy. Second, it quickly became clear that, to understand the policy dimensions of governance, the key changes in that environment, in particular the reconceptualization (and consequent reconfiguration) of public institutions according to the ideology of the New Right, had to be considered. Governing bodies, too, have been re-engineered, subtly so in the 'old' universities, more brazenly in the 'new' universities and colleges. In both cases they are seen in new structural, social and discursive settings. The different emphases of these settings need to be explored, as do the perceptions of them held by relevant players or actors.

Perceptions – of self and others, institutions and environments – emerged as a key element in the research. Understanding the role of the social actor, how we identify ourselves and others both as individuals and as citizens, was critical to the broader project of analysing the linkages between the massification of higher education and broader socio-economic transformations. As has already been emphasized, governance and governors need to be seen not just within the context of massification but within the broader external environment: new social formations, economic structures and political cultures. But there were clear-cut empirical questions. Who are the citizens who become governors? How diverse are their backgrounds? What drew them into university governance? What are their views about their institutions and the wider system of higher education? How do they define themselves both inside and outside their governing bodies? What skills and experience do they think they bring? How do they see their roles? But these questions, however significant in empirical terms, also need to be considered in the context of new, and often competing, discourses offered by the concepts of active citizenship, new management, quasi-markets, the state and civil society.

Recent public policy shifts in Britain and other developed countries have had a major impact on the culture of public sector institutions. The most important have already been discussed: the creation of quasi-markets in major areas of the welfare state; decentralization of decision-making; and the growth of a culture of competition. These policy shifts have led to a revolution in the management of public sector institutions. A new public sector culture has emerged that increasingly resembles the corporate culture of the private sector. In some cases, such as the privatization of public utilities or the contracting-out of public services, a straight switch from public to private sectors has taken place. In other cases, notably the NHS, vigorous attempts have been made to implant a corporate culture in a public service environment. In others again (universities may be an example), efforts to 'privatize' governance and management have been pursued more intermittently.

Two distinct but, in application, related concepts can be identified: the 'new' public management and the enterprise culture. Neither is unproblematic as an explanation for recent shifts in public policy. The new public manager, the key player in the reconfiguration of public sector institutions, remains a shadowy figure. According to one mundane and minimalist account, he or she merely employs leading-edge management styles and techniques to pursue largely unchanged public goals. But according to a second, more expansive and ideological, account, the 'new' public sector manager has many of the attributes and values of the private sector entrepreneur. The latter, of course, is the subject of a wide diversity of definitions and methodological approaches (Chell *et al.*, 1991). The cult of the entrepreneur, in turn, is linked to the process of managerialization, which, despite all the slipperiness of both its definition and its associated symbolism, has transformed old power relationships and patterns of control and accountability in the public sector (Clarke *et al.*, 1994).

Public governance has become embroiled in these management changes in two apparently contradictory ways. First, for the New Right, the governing bodies of public institutions are regarded as key arenas of change. 'Business' governors, in particular, occupy a central role in the enterprise culture, portrayed by its advocates as 'cultural change agents', inculcating their institutions with enhanced awareness of competitiveness and the need for excellence in management (Jessop, 1994). Here the emphasis is on stripping away the symbolic facades and old organizational structures that, allegedly, marginalized governing bodies' role. In their place 'efficient' responsibilities are substituted that embed within the public sector the imperatives of a 'market' culture, circumscribing older professional autonomies.

Second, the governing body has been identified as a means of ensuring high standards. In the private sector, growing concern with imperfections in the regulatory framework and some notorious corporate failures led to the formation of the committee on the financial aspects of corporate governance, the so-called Cadbury Committee (Cadbury, 1992). Its report emphasized the supervisory responsibilities of non-executive directors, a theme taken up by the Committee of University Chairmen in their 1994 good proactive advice. In the public sector, as has already been pointed out, similar concern led to the establishment of the Nolan Committee.

These alternative perceptions of the role and responsibilities of governors have exacerbated the existing confusion about the nature of governance, especially in the public sector. The New Right demands culture change, which suggests that governors should not be afraid to intervene in management. Cadbury and Nolan require governors to be more Olympian, intervening only to maintain high standards of conduct and eschewing meddling in management (which leads to potential conflicts of interest). The central question is whether governors should act as directors or trustees. Where should the emphasis of governance be placed: on the powers of governors to act in an entrepreneurial fashion, remaking their institutions in the image of the corporate rationalizer who is often benign but sometimes amoral in his or her calculations, or on the responsibilities of governors as trustees, dull but safe pairs of hands with which to entrust the spending of large sums of public money? This dilemma remains unresolved.

The universities have been caught up in the eddies of this turbulence. In the new universities, governors from 'business' backgrounds were favoured in the post-incorporation restructuring of governing bodies. This opened a new space for the participation of 'citizens' in the governance of universities – but only on the basis of three assumptions, all of which have been contested. First, certain citizens, primarily those whose social and cultural identities are aligned with a 'market' ideology, are the best placed to become governors or 'active' citizens. Second, those with industrial and commercial experience are most likely to possess the value positions, and perhaps political beliefs, needed to help institutions adapt to the new quasi-market environment. Third, entrepreneurial knowledge is equal, or superior, to expert or professional knowledge. In the complex world of university governance, only 'knowledgeable actors', to use Anthony Giddens's term, can operate effectively. Since the professional knowledge and, historically, the autonomy of academics are both extensive and, in the 'old' universities, entrenched, 'business' governors need to bring to their task alternative knowledge structures, if not academic then relevant managerial expertise.

These questions not only relate to theories of and debates about citizenship. They also raise fundamental issues about the purposes of universities and, in turn, the values which underpin their governance. The defence of academic autonomy, notions of the academic space and the wider relationship between the university and its communities have been set in a context of mounting threats to traditional academic freedoms and approaches to learning created by the drive for more applied and vocational education. Growing emphasis on the relevance of 'business' ideology values in university governance suggests that there is more at stake than simply whether governors are able to police standards of conduct, offer management advice or even set strategic directions. At stake also is the mission of the institutions, their basic purpose.

There may be clear fault lines between academic and lay people which can make a difference to how institutions are governed and institutional purposes defined and redefined. Governors may also adopt clearly defined roles based on their own knowledge, experience and value positions in order to provide alternative perspectives to the professional academics. To assess these possibilities, and their articulation with the reconfiguration of public institutions, requires detailed investigation of the backgrounds, value positions and political beliefs of lay governors, whether from the business community or elsewhere. The other side of the coin, of course, is that certain citizens may be considered not to possess the knowledge necessary to participate in university governance nor the appropriate value positions and political beliefs. These citizens, in practice, will be excluded from participating in university governance. Through an exploration of these issues in the empirical domain of university governance the theoretical debate about the nature of active citizenship may be advanced.

A key element in that exploration is to acquire a better understanding of how the formal and informal processes of appointment work in practice. The power of governing boards to select and reappoint members in their own image is an important element in the broader question: governance by whom for whom? It also raises two further issues. The first, raised by the Nolan Committee, is that governing boards, appointed in their own image, are likely to become closed to new (or different) ideas, so posing a threat to standards of conduct. The second arises from the broader debate about the growth in the number of quangos. How do recent changes in university governance relate to what some analysts of the development of quangos refer to as the 'new magistracy'? (Stewart *et al.*, 1992) If there is, how do university governing bodies attempt to make themselves accountable to the various constituencies interested in universities, whether as consumers or as taxpayers? These broader themes will be explored in subsequent chapters.

Important differences in governance persist between 'old' and 'new' universities. Most of the former are chartered corporations. There are a few exceptions. Some, such as the University of Wales, are statutory corporations; the London School of Economics is a company limited by guarantee; Oxford and Cambridge are governed by statutes although they do not possess charters (both are governed wholly by academics and, consequently, were excluded from the scope of this research). The standard pattern is for 'old' universities to be governed by a council (court in Scotland), the membership of which ranges in number from 25 to more than 60. Councils are broadly representative and are required to include staff and student representatives. They are presided over by a chair, who is generally pro-chancellor (or the chancellor's deputy). Academic matters, which tend to be defined in broad terms, are the prerogative of senates. In addition, most universities have courts, formally the supreme governing bodies, which are presided over by the chancellor, have wide memberships and largely ceremonial functions and meet infrequently (typically once a year). Significantly, membership of the university as a corporation extends to all staff and students.

In the 'new' universities (the former polytechnics, some former Scottish central institutions and two former colleges of higher education) and the colleges of higher education the governance framework was established by the Education Reform Act 1988 and the Further and Higher Education Act 1992. All are higher education corporations. Boards of governors are appointed under articles of government approved by the Secretary of State for Education. These boards are responsible for establishing the educational character and mission of their institutions. They are limited to a maximum of 24 and a minimum of 12 members. The majority is made up of 'independent' members. Boards are not required to include staff or student representatives, although all currently do. Academic affairs, much more narrowly defined than in the 'old' universities, are the responsibility of academic boards, equivalent to senates. None have courts, although some 'new' universities are considering establishing such bodies as community sounding-boards. A few have appointed chancellors. Significantly, membership of the corporation is confined to the members of the governing body.

Despite these important differences, 'old' university councils and 'new' university and college boards of governors both act as the governing body of the institution 'with ultimate responsibility for all the affairs of the institution' (Committee of University Chairmen, 1995: 3). Their primary responsibility is to ensure the proper conduct of public business. The Committee of University Chairmen has advised members of governing bodies of four guiding principles: first, that the governing body should observe 'the highest standards of integrity and objectivity'; second, that a policy of openness and transparency should be followed; third, that it be accountable for the stewardship of public funds; and fourth, value for money is ensured by delivering services in 'the most effective, efficient and economical way'. The key issue, however, is that the governance process has to ensure that the institution is operating within a framework of effective accountability (Committee of University Chairmen, 1995: 17).

The research project on which this book is based involved a large questionnaire survey of university governors and multi-site case study analysis, and was conducted over a 15-month period commencing in October 1993. The project was designed to explore the extent to which different types of higher educational institutions (that is, 'old' and 'new' universities and colleges of higher education) converge and/or diverge in their styles of governance. Three main objectives were identified:

1. To examine the composition of governing bodies throughout the higher education sector and assemble a basic demographic profile of university governors, and also to develop an understanding of the appointment and selection mechanisms employed by different institutions.
2. To investigate the role of the governing body/council and the substantive activities undertaken in performing that role. The intention was to begin to understand the dynamics of governance in action, establishing which governing bodies/councils are proactive or reactive in strategic leadership and decision-making.
3. To examine patterns of power relationships within university governance, specifically the triangular relationship between the governing body or council, the executive and the academic board or senate.

These objectives presented different methodological challenges. Some parts of the research were relatively easy to investigate empirically, such as demographic data. Others, however, notably power relations, which are difficult to establish in the field, were more difficult to investigate. As a result, both quantitative and qualitative research methods were employed, and these methods were undertaken in two separate phases. The former, undertaken through a questionnaire survey, was designed to provide some empirical breadth and enable some broad generalizations to be made about the nature of governance. The latter, undertaken by case study analysis based on semi-structured interviewing and limited observation, was intended to study governance processes in greater depth. Details of both questionnaire survey and case study investigation are given in Appendix 1.

This book on changing patterns of governance in higher education is also based on a broader consideration of the historical, political, constitutional and comparative context in which the government of higher education is situated. Its conclusions are inevitably partial and provisional, for at least two reasons. First, there is a lack of adequate conceptualizations of university governance. Many of the available theoretical frameworks have to be imported from adjacent, but not always appropriate, contexts. Our modest hope is that the research reported in this book will provide a foundation on which more sophisticated theoretical accounts can later be built.

Second, as has already been asserted, British higher education is more heterogeneous than is commonly supposed, in terms of both its historical roots and its future directions. An important aspect of that heterogeneity is that institutions differ markedly in their governance cultures. These differences reflect a multiplicity of factors, such as origin and historical development, position within the higher education 'market' and the stability of this position, the size and composition of its student body and the personalities, backgrounds and managerial styles of chief executives, senior managers and governing body members. The research attempts to uncover these influences and place them within a broader context. The next chapter considers the concepts, often contested, of governance and management in modern higher education systems. Chapters 3 and 4 focus on governors themselves – their backgrounds and perceptions of higher education and how they are appointed. Chapters 5, 6 and 7 look at governors in their organizational setting: the place of governing bodies in organizational structures, their role in institutional decision-making and key relationships with vice chancellors and others. Chapter 8 offers a comparative perspective, by discussing recent changes in governance cultures in the rest of the public (and the private) sector and in the government of universities in the rest of Europe and the United States. Finally, Chapter 9 summarizes the main conclusions and offers an agenda for future action.

Notes

1. The term governing body includes university council or board of governors and refers to the body with ultimate responsibility for the affairs of the institution.
2. The term member includes external (lay or independent) members and internal (academic and non-academic staff and student) members.
3. The term chair refers to the chairman, chairwoman or other person who chairs meetings of the governing body and its committees. The term 'chairman/men' is retained in quotations.

2

Governance and Management in Higher Education

The present chapter considers the concept and practice of governance within the specific context of universities as organizations. As we have suggested, universities, like other institutions in the public sector, have not been immune from wider changes in the external environment which have impacted directly and indirectly on higher education institutions. A period of rapid growth in the numbers of students in the system and the 'creation' of new universities, mainly the former polytechnics, have brought about major changes in the contours of the system of higher education. At the same time, a sense of uncertainty and volatility has been introduced by declining resources from the state relative to increased student numbers, by the development of new funding arrangements and methodologies and by the need to adapt to more diverse student constituencies as new qualification routes have been created.

Meanwhile, major shifts in the political environment have also occurred. The ascendancy of new ideologies, driven in the main by a government intent on 'rolling back the frontiers of the state' and pushed through often without consultation with the policy communities affected by radical reform and, frequently, in spite of protests about the effects of drastic changes (Becher and Kogan, 1992: 41), has attached a new set of values and imperatives to the notion of public sector education. Projected increases in capital from private sector investment sources, to replace what the Chancellor referred to in his 1995 budget speech as 'old-style public sector capital spending' on higher (and further) education, reflect the sort of thinking that has reshaped the system.

Underpinning these policy reforms in the public sector has been a pervasive government-led belief in the power of better management to effect change, a doctrine which has been termed 'managerialism' (Pollitt, 1990). The faith in the new public management is based on its power to deliver:

The efficient and disciplined use of resources, the achievement of value-for-money and increased productivity. All this to be achieved through

the use of systematic planning, organisation and control, the measurement of achievement against declared objectives, and often too in the
light of comparisons across institutions. The role of management is
considered vital to the realisation of those aims and the model of
management which informs this ideal is that of the large business
corporation.

(Middlehurst and Elton, 1992)

As far as the universities are concerned, borrowing corporate management
techniques and applying them to public sector management has coincided
with other, mainly government inspired, pressures. Demands that higher
education be linked more explicitly to the needs of the economy and its
labour market have risen alongside the introduction of policies designed to
curtail public expenditure. The expansion of higher education at reduced
units of resource has been 'policed' more vigilantly by government and its
agents via new funding mechanisms which have compelled universities to
compete in a quasi-market for state funds. These managerial mechanisms
revolve around assessments of the 'quality' of teaching and research by
committees appointed by the central funding agency, the results of which
feed through into funding.

Any attempt to understand the ascent of governance as a policy preoccupation, therefore, has to be seen in terms of these challenges to existing
arrangements. Our analysis in this chapter attempts to locate the issue of
governance within three specific themes. The first explores the tensions
between the academic endeavour and the professional values which underpin it, on the one hand, and the imposition of new managerialism, on the
other. The second seeks to understand the terrain of decision-making in
universities and the impact of recent reform policies on the organizational
images of universities. The third examines how institutional governance
articulates with the first two themes and sets out a framework for understanding the parameters of the governance process.

Professional versus managerial values

The academic endeavour: universities as communities of scholars

The nature of academic work is problematic. Advanced teaching and research, often at the outer edge of established understandings and knowledge bases, requires creativity and self-motivation and can frequently be
unpredictable and, at times, controversial. Those engaged in academic work
possess extensive and highly specialized knowledge bases acquired after
lengthy periods of education and training. Claims for professional expertise
rest on these foundations. Together these professional foundations and the
nature of the academic labour process itself pose twin problems of 'control'

over academic labour. Traditionally and by custom and practice, both authority and loyalty are derived from and owed to the profession – typically expressed in terms of 'disciplines' rather than institutions. It is also from this source that are derived associated claims for professional self-regulation and control by peers rather than 'managers'. Accordingly, the structures of control in the classic university have been mediated by professional claims for autonomy and academic freedom. Organizational structures have reflected these claims, with the academic disciplines, to which prime loyalty may be given rather than universities as institutions, arranged into departments which either singly or, as faculties, collectively provide the basic building blocks of university organization.

At the heart of these arrangements can be discerned a fundamental principle concerning the essential nature and *raison d'être* of higher education. This principle provides the justification behind notions of academic and institutional autonomy and the structural arrangements within the system devised to protect such notions. Becher and Kogan (1992) provide a succinct articulation of this principle:

> Higher education nurtures beliefs that the growth and transmission of knowledge are legitimate in themselves, not depending for their right to flourish on stated public demands; and that it is a proper function of academic institutions to act as centres of alternative opinions within the political system.

Such a principle allows for what Becher and Kogan term a 'contrafunctionalism' to the perceived needs and expectations of society. So although the higher education system changes as it influences and is influenced by its environment, it retains a 'critical edge' allowing for reflection and criticism of dominant value systems or political ideologies. This is the fundamental emancipatory function of higher education, a function endemic to the academic value system. It is achieved primarily through critical activities involving self-reflection and reasoned argument and is legitimized on the basis of equal rights within a community.

Arguments against the imposition of 'managerialism' on higher education centre on the fears that the main educational objectives – the development and transmission of knowledge – will become subordinated to central prescriptions based on a financial value system. Moreover, it is a system imported from the private sector, where objectives are constructed from the basic building blocks of the profit motive and market forces. Critics of this financial value system identify two facets of the academic enterprise which are incompatible with and resistant to subsumption under managerial imperatives.

The first is the intrinsically individualistic nature of knowledge generation. This gives rise to the collegial form of academic authority in universities. Collegial authority is based on the notion that individual scholars reaching a certain level of personal achievement in a subject area qualify for entrance into 'a guild arrangement in which the individual master has a personal domain within which he controls subordinates while the masters come together to exercise control over a larger territory of work' (Clark, 1983). The academic's authority is not derived from formal hierarchical positions with prespecified functions (known as bureaucratic authority), but from the quality of academic work – assessed by peers according to disciplinary criteria. Each discipline has its own caucus of individual experts concerned with the development and progression of specialist knowledge.

The second feature of the academic enterprise is the notion of participative decision-making. Professional academics who have reached a certain level of expertise and acclaim are qualified to enter the *demos*, where consensus over decisions is reached through consultation among equals. This collegiate or professional model of organization centres on notions of academic autonomy and 'cohesions based on a limited hierarchy of seniority and expertise, a common heritage and shared ideals' (Middlehurst, 1993). It accommodates the differentiation between the disciplines and the plurality of value systems found among the disciplines; and its central organizational feature is the committee system. In this context the vice chancellors are subordinate leaders of the academic *demos*, being described as 'first among equals' and having reached their position because others see them as embodying the groups aspirations and achievements (Middlehurst, 1993).

The collegiate model itself is not without flaws, however. First, it can be presented as conceptually naive, romantic even, since it underplays the extent of differences and competing interests arising from the diversity of members and disciplines. In periods of unfavourable economic conditions, conflict can arise over scarce resources, rendering the model inadequate for achieving interdisciplinary consensus (Middlehurst and Elton, 1992). Second, it can be seen as operationally dysfunctional because the bedrock of the model, the committee system, is frequently in tension with policy and strategy formation (Lee and Piper, 1988). Over-reliance on committees can be criticized for leading to delays in decision-making, impeding individual initiative and leadership and creating uncertainty over both the finality of decisions and responsibility for their implementation.

Managerialism: universities as bureaucracies

These conceptual and operational problems highlight important flaws in the collegiate organizational model which, some critics argue, impede effective decision-making in universities. The problem inherent to university management is the tension between disciplinary and institutional imperatives on the one hand and the respective forms of professional and bureaucratic authority on the other. The goals of the institution are frequently ambiguous and contested, producing conflict rather than cooperation, competition rather than compromise. Adopting the bureaucratic perspective allows for these tensions to be subsumed by managerial intervention designed to achieve control and coordination of the diverse and often irrational processes that comprise the academic endeavour. In the place of the equality of the *demos*, therefore, are substituted hierarchical authority relations intended to impose order or rationality on complexity and instability.

Empirically, the Jarratt Report (CVCP, 1985) addressed these tensions, highlighting professional self-interest as a specific problem when 'large and powerful academic departments together with individual academics ... sometimes see their academic discipline as more important than the long-term well-being of the university which houses them.' For Jarratt the detrimental effects of professional self-interest were to be avoided by reducing the influence of senate and enhancing the strength of council and vice chancellor. When combined with greater emphasis on corporate planning, the efficient and effective use of resources and clearer delegation of authority, Jarratt gave an important boost to the concept of universities as corporate enterprises.

Opponents of the shift towards the introduction of bureaucratic or managerialist values into higher education base their opposition on two arguments: first, that there are certain intrinsic qualities belonging to the academic enterprise which are incompatible with managerial values and systems; second, that the academic endeavour will inevitably be distorted and harmed by universities venturing into the entrepreneurial mode of managerialism. Clark (1983) argues that the academic is pluralistic by nature and the appropriate departmental procedures are developed logically and temporally after consideration of the varied structures of knowledge of different subject areas. Any attempt by the central planner to impose greater uniformity and coherence will prove detrimental to the academic endeavour. He argues that 'the variation in subject matter that is part and parcel of the system produces a need for extreme non-uniformity: in structure and procedure in policy and governance.'

A similar argument is developed by Becher and Kogan (1992), who stress that the individual nature of knowledge generation and exchange is ill-suited to the imposition of hierarchically distributed management objectives. Mechanistic management systems are further criticized by Jones (1986), who argues that the pursuit of quality assurance and accountability by such means leads to little more than pseudo effectiveness and efficiency. Managerialism does not operate at the interface where quality is the issue – with students and academic peers – and leads to the demoralization and demotivation of staff owing to the dilution of professional self-regulation. Concern for the impact of managerialism on staff has also been highlighted by the Council for Academic Autonomy in *Academic Democracy* (1995), which links the climate of managerialism to an erosion of academic democracy and a decline in openness and accountability.

These objections to the introduction of managerialist values into the university sector tend to be couched in polemical terms. They seem to view the dual requirements of management, for greater accountability, and professionals, for greater autonomy, as a zero-sum game. They provide rationales against perceived threats to the exercise of academic autonomy – which is deemed the crucial factor in sustaining a creative environment in which the primary goals of higher education can be achieved.

An alternative view is taken by Lee and Piper (1988), who argue that the introduction of 'executive' management will improve effective decision-making in universities. This argument is underpinned by an analytic distinction between 'commercial' and 'executive' management perspectives. The underlying orientations of the former are profit and market forces operating along clearly defined financial objectives. 'Executive' management 'requires the establishment of objectives, the development of plans and the relating of planning to resource allocation. Performance evaluation takes place against plans, corrective action is taken and plans are modified' (Lee and Piper, 1988: 117). The suggestion is that since Jarratt does not make explicit reference to privatisation or market forces, it advocates 'executive' rather than commercial management. The executive management perspective provides clear roles for management and the accountable body. Management is to ensure the achievement of set objectives, while the accountable body is responsible for determining the content of those objectives and the extent to which they have been achieved.

Universities as systems: political, cybernetic or entrepreneurial

For some commentators the internal organizational world of universities is inadequately captured in either the rationality which characterizes the bureaucratic model of organization or the consensus of professional values which underpins the collegial. For some, the potential for conflict generated by differences between disciplines and other groups within universities and, not least, the scramble for resources both internally and externally engaged in by these groups is the dominant characteristic of universities as organizations. Hence, a political perspective highlights clashes between various interest groups which compete for power and control over decision-making. In this interpretation of organizational dynamics the university is a deeply politicized institution – the 'political university' (Baldridge, 1971) – with complex and often deeply set subtexts of informal relationships and deal-making. These, rather than the formal tenets of constitutions and committees, are what really make the university tick. The outcome is less stable or regulated than the bureaucratic image, less amenable to control by hierarchical structures and certainly governed less by procedural norms than political bargaining and compromises.

The organizational imperatives created by the nature of academic work itself reinforce the tendencies towards conflict, particularly over posts and resources, and give rise to a conceptualization of universities as 'organized anarchies' (Cohen and March, 1974). The driving force of anarchy in this sense is the high discretion over the job task held by academics and so the extensive scope for autonomy within the labour process (Puxty *et al.*, 1994; Willmott, 1995). In this environment, clarity of organizational goals is elusive and the 'fit' between people and organizational structure extremely loose. Consequently, bureaucratic or corporate forms of control are, if not inappropriate, then certainly ineffective. The extensive scope for participation by labour in decision-making ensures that there is little that is crisp in decision-making terms and even less that is certain in organizational outcomes. Such a perspective holds a particular challenge for those who would wish to see managerial control of universities further enhanced. With the rise of managerialism there is, ironically, a greater need for reliance on bureaucratic structures and less willingness to tolerate an internal organizational world which does not conform to preset patterns and norms of behaviour. The notion of the managed academic springs to mind. To be sure, this is an oxymoron, yet in its internal focusing it offers to the exponents of managerialism rather greater prospect of success in the 'closed' internal world of the university than the 'management' of an increasingly volatile external environment.

The contradictions and tensions manifest in these perspectives, however, are made less explicit in models of organization which see the university in terms of cybernetic and entrepreneurial images. These perspectives use the metaphor of the institution as a dynamic system which comprises a number of interacting elements. In the cybernetic image, for instance, the university is projected as a flexible, adaptable and highly resilient institution capable of 'thinking' and reacting to changing environments (Morgan, 1986; Birnbaum, 1989). Here the organizational emphasis is on the various structures and processes which ensure that the university is self-correcting and in a state of internal balance. In this image the focus is on the internal systems of the university, ensuring that the institution 'learns' from the external environment and directs that learning in order to make appropriate adjustments according to agreed priorities.

The entrepreneurial image extends the metaphor of the university as a living organism, brain-like in its functioning, suggesting that its relationship with its communities is in a continuous process of adaptation and change. Here the driving (and democratizing, in Adam Smith's terms) force is the perfect operation of markets. To survive in organizational terms the university increasingly engages in a series of exchange and trading relationships. To the task of managing the internal organizational world of the university is added, therefore, the need to identify opportunities, develop trading relationships and compete effectively and efficiently. The orientation in this image is rather more the external than the internal environment of the university.

The key strategic actors in executing the policy agenda imposed by the external world, particularly in the entrepreneurial image, are the new managers. Their role is to ensure that the university interacts with the external world and to deliver change by deploying systems of strategic planning – vision and mission – and various tools of business control and manipulation.

In this image one would expect to find trenchant beliefs in the powers of the new public management to effect as well as control change, and with language and techniques borrowed from the market. Two recent changes within universities suggest that such beliefs may have taken hold. First is a general weakening of collective bargaining frameworks and the imposition of diluted employment contracts for university staff, particularly growing use of fixed-term contracts and part-time labour. Second is the rise of marketing to occupy a central role not just as a vehicle for sharpening promotion, public relations or advertising, but in effecting wider cultural changes within institutions. Arguably, the shift of organizational cultures of universities from overwhelmingly producer-centred to customer-centred is closely associated with the entrepreneurial image.

The entrepreneurial perspective clearly integrates the university with the wider reform imperative of recent public policy, which has sought to reconfigure national institutional arrangements on market lines, 'selling' the concept on the back of consumer-friendly attractions such as choice, quality and value for money. However, none of the perspectives or images outlined here is likely fully to describe universities as organizations. Instead we need to acknowledge the complexity and interconnectedness of the authority systems, administrative structures and leadership styles likely to be found in the various images of universities as organizations and try to relate these to the concept of institutional governance.

These organizational models present alternative perspectives on the 'social architecture' (Middlehurst, 1995: 81) of universities. In so doing they provide clues to the nature and dynamics of universities as organizations. However, it is also the case that, like all organizations, universities present a rich and often subtle combination of organizational characteristics which are influenced by the distinctive histories and cultures of each institution. These distinctions are important, for they mediate the apparent homogeneity of the models and perspectives outlined above. Critically, they also begin to help us to understand the often complex relationship between the organization and governance of institutions in day-to-day practice. In this sense, the organizational models and images associated with them can only take us so far. To be sure, they may illuminate some key features of organizational arrangements, but they may shed little light on others. In practice, therefore, it is necessary to look for elements of all the perspectives offered if we are to construct a comprehensive view of governance within specific organizational settings.

University decision-making and institutional governance

An understanding of the basic elements of the balance of power in universities has to be set within a broad context which acknowledges how that balance tracks back to the underpinning provided by competing authority

Figure 2.1   The balance of power in universities.

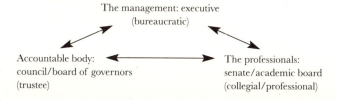

systems. Figure 2.1 presents a schematic description of the key decision-makers in universities and their sources of authority (indicated in parentheses). The balance of power in terms of decision-making depends upon the strength of allegiance between the 'management' and the 'professionals' or between the 'management' and the 'accountable body' (the governors). Governance in universities reflects the outcome of the contest between two alternative models of decision-making. First is the professional model, in which policy and strategic decisions lie firmly in the hands of the academic oligarchy and its subordinate leader (the vice chancellor). In this model decisions are determined largely by intellectual/educational objectives and consensus management. Second is the managerial model, in which the accountable body, as the executive body, and the senior management group impose centrally (government) driven imperatives, relating primarily to economic objectives such as efficiency and value for money, on to differentiated academic units. In this model, decisions are determined largely by managerialist conceptions of higher education.

In practice, of course, these disjunctives are not necessarily mutually exclusive. The informal 'flat' configuration of professional decision-making which devolves to horizontally arranged 'professional' units may frequently coexist with the formal hierarchy of bureaucratic decision-making, with its vertical arrangement of executive management. Nevertheless, they serve to conceptualize the nature of university decision-making and its articulation with the governance process.

How does the issue of governance relate to the balance of power? So far we have located our exploration of perspectives of universities as organizations in a literature developed largely by organizational theorists which is routinely recited by those concerned with understanding higher education and its institutions. Relevant though much of this thinking is to conceptualizing both the management and balance of power in universities, it can take us only so far in thinking about institutional governance. Governing bodies have a very definite organizational existence and in this sense take their place in conceptions of organization that might stress the rationality of bureaucracy, entrepreneurial images or concepts of loose coupling and organized anarchy. However, as Deem *et al.* (1995) have observed of school governing bodies, they also have an 'evanescent quality, that is best described as "now you see them, now you don't".' University governing bodies share this evanescence. They, too, are curious, in that they are statutory bodies, yet voluntary in character. Searching for a framework of explanation which assists us in the task of exploring the organizational characteristics of university governance led us, like other recent writers on educational policy (see, for example, Ball, 1994; Weiner, 1994; Deem *et al.*, 1995), to consider more recent theoretical perspectives on post-modern organizations.

This is not the place to enter debates about understanding educational policies either as text or as discourse. However, following Deem *et al.* (1995), we can conceive of university governing bodies as caught somewhere between modernity and post-modernity. Such bodies come from an age when roles and responsibilities were more symbolic than real, when governors were invariably chosen from the 'great and the good', when, to borrow the language of Bagehot, the 'dignified' as opposed to 'efficient' elements of governance were emphasized. As our analysis above has sought to emphasize, these old facades are increasingly challenged by new ideologies and value systems which have progressively introduced into the public services notions of quasi-markets, consumerism and the culture and practices of business and entrepreneurialism. As they do so, governing bodies have begun to shuffle from the dignified to the efficient in their orientation and role. The problem is analysing the extent of the 'shuffle', and the definitions of 'efficient' adopted, and understanding the organizational practices which have facilitated the reform of governance processes.

The concept of 'surveillance' (Foucault, 1977) is relevant, at least in part, to these tasks. Notions of autonomy and self-regulation, now favoured by government in its arrangements for public services once heavily under the tutelage of the state, national and local, rely heavily on 'surveillance' of the affairs of schools, colleges, hospitals and universities on behalf of the state (community?). This so-called steering at a distance (Ball, 1994) has two separate but related strands.

One is new managerialism, which we have discussed already. This has created tensions by replacing the traditional and once unchallenged 'modern' notions of a professionally-led education sector with a managerially-led system. In this system the sector's goals and framework of institutional action are defined centrally by government in terms of financial criteria or funding methodologies. Funding agencies, nominally independent of government but in practice closely connected, are appointed as regulators of the system. We may see such agencies as 'regulators as policemen' (Pearce and Tombs, 1990). Regulatory 'tools' include uniform systems of funding, in which recurrent funding is allocated according to a unit based system built on competitive assessment exercises. The new managers at the level of 'autonomous' institutions act as a second tier of the regulatory environment, controllers of the destiny of their institutions yet responsible to the funding agency (and Parliament) for carrying out the intentions of central government (on behalf of the community).

The second strand of 'distance steering' is provided by the governing bodies. Increasingly these are recruited to reflect business (employer?) interests, and their primary responsibility is to oversee institutional objectives.

In practice, this means to agree policy and strategy and to ensure that the institution is properly managed in order to fulfil its mission. Conceptually, therefore, governance is, or should be, quite distinct from management. A useful analogy is often drawn between a governing body and a steersman or commanding staff on the bridge of a ship – with a grip, firm or otherwise, on the helm. In operational terms, however, the issue of governance is intimately connected with the whole debate about managerialism, collegiality and accountability. In the new policy environment, governance sits somewhat uneasily between three constituencies. On the one hand are the imperatives and intentions of central government, whether they be for increasing participation in education, the achievement of training targets or ensuring value for money. On the other are the diverse and potentially conflicting interests of producers and consumers. Although governing bodies work directly with the producers, it has become axiomatic that producers' interests should be subordinated to consumers'. The former are expected to deliver their services in a framework of responsiveness, efficiency and quality, giving the latter the maximum in choice and opportunities for participation.

So the shift from dignified to efficient roles gives to governing bodies a clear monitoring or 'surveillance' task. In so doing it changes the relationship, or balance of power, within institutions and represents a challenge to notions of professional or collegial autonomy. Accountability once depended on such autonomy, with only a symbolic or dignified gubernatorial overview to ensure public confidence and credibility. New models of accountability have eroded the trust between professional and lay community which previously underpinned the system. Now accountability is defined much more rigorously in control terms. As the investigations of the Nolan Committee make clear, with control accountability there is no longer an unquestioning assumption that the autonomous professional should define and monitor standards of conduct. Instead, it is for governors, representing consumers and employers, to undertake this task. Indeed, the very existence of the Nolan investigations confirmed what might be termed a crisis of governance created primarily by the need to redefine standards of openness and accountability in the wake of the decline of professional autonomy and the vestiges of trust once ascribed to it.

Responsible to and, in the main, recruited from the external environment, governing bodies nevertheless spend their time inside the institutional environment. In this environment they are concerned essentially with organizational resources. But in what ways? To answer this it is useful to adopt Giddens's (1984, 1985) division of resources into two types. Allocative resources include land, buildings, capital and people. Authoritative resources are less tangible and might include culture, ideology, information and time. Authoritative resources necessarily involve surveillance and control of activities within the organization. Given what we have said of 'surveillance' as the monitoring and regulation required to be undertaken by governors in emergent new public organizations if 'steering at a distance' is to be achieved, we might expect to find governing bodies engaging rather more with authoritative resourcing issues than allocative. The evidence from schools, however, suggests that governors spend more time dealing with allocative than with authoritative resources (Deem *et al.*, 1995: 98). Indeed, in this setting governors appeared to find it difficult to deal with the latter resources, the researchers citing the scarcity of meetings, lack of independent 'normalizing' notions about what schools were supposed to be about and, critically, an inability by governors to penetrate professional control of the classroom and school generally. Faced with such obstacles, governors were thus forced to rely on indirect attempts to influence organizational culture, such as discretionary pay, appraisal systems and staff development schemes for teachers (Deem *et al.*, 1995: 99).

We shall return to this framework in subsequent chapters as we explore the engagement of university governors with organizational resources, both allocative and authoritative. At this stage it is sufficient to note that the relationship of the three elements in the balance of power – the executive, senate and governors – to these resources is critical to an understanding of the organizational challenges confronting the governance process. Defining the role of governance and devising suitable organizational practices to make it work are, arguably, the key tasks facing universities in the new era of tight accountability. As a final insight into these tasks we refer to a model of governance provided by Tricker (1984). For Tricker,

> The governance role is not concerned with running the business of the company, per se, but with giving overall direction to the enterprise, with overseeing and controlling the executive actions of management and with satisfying legitimate expectation for accountability and regulation by interests beyond corporate boundaries. If management is about running business, governance is about seeing that it is run properly.
> (Tricker, 1984: 6–7)

Tricker is primarily concerned to develop a 'collaborative model' of corporate governance, which he contrasts to outmoded 'classical models'. Governance of corporate enterprise in the commercial sector relies on the notion of capital as the legitimation of authority. The collaborative model provides a more fluid framework for governance as a political process that allows for participation of different dimensions of influence: owners, directors and management (including, when sufficiently enhanced at corporate level, labour).

The collaborative model outlines four dimensions of corporate governance. These are shown schematically in Figure 2.2. The key dimensions of governance encapsulated in this model can be seen as the main roles of the governing body. Two of them – 'direction' and 'executive management' – potentially overlap with management's role. The extent to which these two dimensions in particular encompass the main roles of governing bodies in universities is a principal focus of the case studies which follow. The collaborative model provides a valuable tool of analysis. First, it allows us to elaborate the responsibilities of councils/governing bodies against a background

Figure 2.2   Dimensions of governance. *Source*: Tricker (1984: 174).

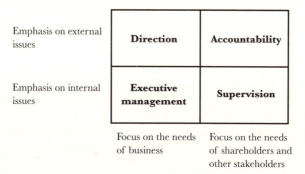

of greater conceptual clarity. Second, it draws attention to the degree of convergence or divergence found between the ideal/typical governance model and the reality of practice in the case study institutions. Our empirical investigations, therefore, attempt to establish clear accounts of how governing bodies are selected, the roles they perform and, critically, the relationships between governing bodies and other key players in universities, notably executive management and academic bodies.

Conclusion

In this chapter we have focused on the transformations of many areas of the public sector, which have created a turbulent environment of instability and uncertainty within higher education. We have suggested that new values and ideologies that have accompanied doctrines of consumerism, quasi-markets, competition, managerialism and accountability have created a number of organizational challenges for universities. By seeking to achieve greater accountability of professionals to consumers, new managerialism in particular confronts some of the traditional ideals not only about the nature of the academic endeavour but also about the wider issue of control and management structures.

It was argued that two facets of the academic labour process – the nature of knowledge generation and the notion of participative decision-making – were particularly intractable in a new regime of managerialism. More specifically, the emergence of managerialism in the governance and direction of universities may be interpreted as evidence of a lack of trust between government and universities. Critics see the government's emphasis on the need to find a 'bottom line' in order to improve the product and lower unit costs as evidence of lack of trust in the universities' ability to assess critically their activities and improve upon them (Trow, 1993: 4). In such a turbulent climate, the traditional dependence on collegial rule and referential professional values declines, to be replaced, increasingly, by the establishment of audit and assessment systems.

The implications of these challenges were traced out in terms of how the balance of power and competing authority systems within universities relate to their social architecture as organizations. Several alternative perspectives on these organizational arrangements were considered with a view to understanding where and how institutional governance engaged with organization and management. It was argued that the ascent of governance as a policy preoccupation across the public services needs to be seen against the backdrop of anxieties and turmoil created by fundamental changes in the way in which those services are financed, organized, managed and delivered. The development of executive agencies and the increase in the numbers of non-departmental public bodies have focused attention on the sensible conduct of public business and arrangements for securing both the honest handling of public money and the promotion of efficiency and value for money (Committee of Public Accounts, 1994: v). Governance has come to be seen as central to the drive to make the public service sector and its professionals more efficient, effective and, transparently, accountable.

How governance is conceptualized and operationalized within universities, therefore, is closely connected to changing organizational and symbolic arrangements within the host society. Since the role of universities in terms of both advanced teaching and research is held to be a critical component of industrial restructuring, the arrangements devised for directing and controlling their organizational existence and their articulation with the broader imperatives of the host society and its economy are held to be highly significant. Although the exploration of university governance which follows seeks to provide an empirical account of the organizational practices uncovered by our research, the intention throughout is to try and relate these to both the theoretical and contextual environments currently being shaped by broader social, political and cultural changes.

3

The Governors: Backgrounds and Perceptions of Higher Education

The debate about the power balance between professionals, managers and governors, explored in the previous chapter, needs to be set in a broader social and policy context. Governing bodies, like those in schools and hospitals, provide opportunities for lay persons to participate in key decisions about the future direction and well-being of the organization. However, we have seen how the government and management of universities have followed different evolutionary patterns, with the power and influence of academic, managerial and lay elements on governing bodies changing over time. There is certainly nothing new about lay elements claiming control and influence over university councils, even if those claims were to be marginalized, supplanted even, by the rise of the donnish dominion during the twentieth century. Yet in the recent development of the framework of governance once again there are substantial claims being made on behalf of lay governance, initiated not by the governors themselves but by the state.

The rise in the state's interest and intervention in higher education as a means of advancing the development of advanced knowledge and technique is well chronicled, yet in its implications, arguably, only hazily understood. For much of the century that interest was accommodated by a tacit compromise between control and autonomy, with the professional academic community undertaking to 'manage' universities, so that, in theory at least, academic freedom was preserved while the state's legitimate interest in receiving a 'return' for its investment, in the form of knowledge advancement and the production of well educated graduates, was also served. Throughout the era of the post-war political-economic settlement, this arrangement remained largely in place. Despite claims for professional expertise and academic autonomy, however, the hand of the state, directly or indirectly, on the funding 'tiller' of the system was always at work shaping the overall size and development of the system of higher education. But while the influence remained largely benign, the accommodation generally worked and took its place as one of the building blocks of the welfare state. Higher education remained rationed but to those able to participate in the system the state had offered its benevolent hand. Under these arrangements the idea of universities as self-governing communities of academics became firmly entrenched in the ideology of the post-war political-economic settlement, an idea undisturbed by successive governments of both left and right. Inside the universities, the practices of governance reflected the power of the donnish dominion, with lay influence in government and management largely reduced to a supervisory role.

In the 1980s, however, the old order began to crumble as government began to redefine the frontiers of state economic activity. Whether seen as a response to the fiscal crisis of the state, emerging global economic pressures or the ascendancy of New Right politics, the emergence of the reform policies of this period challenged many traditional assumptions and arrangements for the organization and delivery of public sector services. Out of this process emerged the notion of markets, or quasi-markets, to replace portions, the exact amount to be determined, of the welfare state. At the same time, as global economic pressures began to press on existing economic arrangements, so the state began to link the training of students ever more explicitly to the needs of the skills base of the workforce. Radical policies designed to deration higher education added to the pressures, as did subsequent 'consolidation' of the expansionary forces unleashed. For universities, the outcome has been the need to participate in the drive to make education and its institutions more business-like in their operations, to think strategically about mission and management and to reorder the hierarchy of decision-making about the efficient and effective use of resources. In this policy environment lay new rationales for the participation of lay elements in the performance of universities.

Two facets of old relationships were no longer required, or trusted, under the impact of quasi-markets. The first was the organization and management of the organizations by the professionals themselves. This tenet of welfare provision was under attack across the public sector as a whole, and the universities could not expect immunity from the new disciplines. The second was the notion of social citizenship, in which people act as clients to a paternalist state in a system of universal welfare entitlement. In its place emerged, and are still emerging, new concepts of citizenship, variously proposed and claimed by right and left in politics, in which a relationship to markets provides a more coherent and efficient methodology for ensuring the provision of public services. Rather than clients, people act as consumers empowered by the exercise of choice, which, in turn, holds the key to ensuring 'democratic' provision. Ownership and control of public services, of which higher education is but one, can no longer be left solely in the hands of the professionals who have vested interests in organizing things in particular ways, usually of greater utility to the producer than the customer. The answer, in the market-based scenario, is to give more control to consumers, to ensure responsiveness to the market and so, in the process, to 'empower' citizens. The emerging concept of citizenship which sits alongside these perspectives requires that citizens be given a greater voice in the services they consume. It is in the latter requirement that governing bodies offer their greatest source of attraction in securing greater accountability to the community.

These ideas are not without contradictions, however. For one, realigning governing bodies to ensure that organizations act in accordance with market-based realities has meant refocusing on traditions of lay participation in local service provision. Yet the origins of lay participation have more to do with the emergence of the liberal democratic state and, later, the welfare state, than they do with post-modern conceptions of consumers and citizens. Promoting the cause of active citizenship, therefore, has meant grafting on to pre-existing conceptions of governance new meanings and values with a view to subsuming the running of what remain local public spending bodies into a broader set of state-led imperatives. The latter, of course, are the antithesis of earlier conceptions of governance drawn from nineteenth-century perspectives of the liberal state. In the renaissance of lay governance, however, the managerial perspective holds that the governing body acts as the essential channel of communication between the 'external' world of consumers and policy and the 'internal' professional world of service deliverers. The essential task of the governing body is to ensure that the latter provide what is required – where, when, how and at what cost – by the former.

The burden of governance in quasi-markets, then, is not just to ensure the participation of active citizens in local public institutions, but to engage with broader problems of reconfiguring state welfare provision and the cultures associated with post-war political-economic settlements, notably state intervention and state dependency. Two levels of analysis are suggested by this analysis. The first is conceptual and concerns the 'fit' between university governance and the broad context of social and policy reform imperatives. The extent to which the culture of university governance replicates that of business organizations is highly relevant here. It relates both to the process of university governance itself and to its wider articulation with the analytical perspectives offered by new managerialism. The second is operational and concerns the sort of citizens involved in university governance. This relates to issues of 'surveillance', accountability and which citizens are best placed to ensure that the professionals are adequately monitored and accountable to the lay community and its consumers.

The remaining chapters of the book attempt to draw out the interconnections between these two layers of analysis. In this chapter we focus on the university governors themselves. We examine their social and cultural identities, the sort of experiences they bring to the task of governance and the reasons why some lay citizens seek to become 'active' as university governors. We also consider the views governors, particularly from the lay community, hold about university organizations and the broader system of higher education. How governors are selected, the organizational procedures adopted for their appointment and the roles they actually perform are the subjects of subsequent chapters. The rest of this chapter is arranged in two sections. The first examines the composition of university governing bodies and the reasons for becoming governors. The second considers the views of the university system held by university governors.

The composition of governing bodies

Age and gender

In this section we address the question: 'who are the members of council and governing bodies?' In answering this question we establish a demographic profile of members' characteristics, detailing their age, gender, ethnic origin, voting propensity and educational and professional backgrounds. Data for this profile are drawn from our survey of university governors, which, it will be recalled, explored differences between institutional type and external (lay or independent) and internal (academic and non-academic staff and students) members. Initially, we present simple frequencies of the demographic variables for which data were collected. Subsequent sub-sections consider in further depth the differences between institutional type and internal/external membership.

Across the higher education sector, the majority (70 per cent) of university governors were aged between 46 and 65. Old universities had a slightly higher age profile, with the largest proportion of members being between 56 and 65, while in the new universities and colleges the largest proportion of members were between 46 and 55. An even larger proportion of all members, 82 per cent, were male, although there was no relationship between gender and type of member or type of institution. The substantial under-representation of women (18 per cent) on university governing bodies in both old and new universities is consistent with an earlier study of governing body membership in the then polytechnics, which also found that just 17 per cent of the total membership were women (Bastin, 1990). At the time of this earlier study, the Equal Opportunities Commission had voiced its concern over the small proportion of women being appointed as independent members to the (then) Department of Education and Science (DES). However, the DES was reluctant to interfere with the 'self-regulatory' affairs of each institution and the results of our study confirm that during the past five years little or no progress has been made in rectifying the huge gender imbalance on university governing bodies.

Ethnicity

Gender was not the only factor in exclusion from university governance. Our survey also revealed that representation from ethnic minority groups was minimal, being under 2 per cent of the total membership for the whole sector. In other words, fractionally over 98 per cent of all members were white. This compares to a proportion of 5 per cent of the total population recorded in the 1991 census as being members of 'ethnic minorities'. Again, no significant differences were found between type of member or institution.

The barriers to participation in university governance created by both gender and ethnicity would appear to be considerable. However, exclusion on these grounds is by no means confined to higher education. A recent study of further education, for example, found that the proportions of women on governing bodies of both colleges of further education and sixth-form colleges in 1995 were only slightly higher than in universities, at 22 and 26 per cent respectively (Graystone, 1995). The same study reported a similar under-representation of black and Asian members on further education boards, with over 97 per cent of governors being described as white (Graystone, 1995). In school governance, women are not under-represented in comparison to the population as a whole, although the proportion of black or Asian school governors is around the same as both further and higher education (Keys and Fernandes, 1990).

Educational background and occupation

In addition to being highly skewed in favour of white males in the 46–65 age range, participation in university governance is also heavily weighted by two further obstacles reflective of broader social-class based inequalities. The first is educational background. The survey found that the largest proportion of governors were qualified to first degree level. A smaller proportion possessed qualifications at sub-degree level, while virtually none admitted to having no formal educational qualifications. For internal members, excluding of course student governors, this is hardly surprising given the strong association between high academic achievement and entry to virtually all grades of the university teaching and research profession. However, the association between high educational achievement and governing body membership was also found for lay members. Certainly the largest proportion of lay members in both old and new universities were also qualified to first degree, although internal members in old universities were more likely to have doctorates. Interestingly, in the new universities internal members were more likely to have master's degrees than doctorates.

The second inequality in participation is indicated by occupational background. The latter, of course, is strongly associated with educational achievement and given expression by the strong representation on university governing bodies of lay members from professional and managerial backgrounds. The largest proportion (40 per cent) were from a professional background and the second largest (35 per cent) from industry. Almost one-fifth of external members had commercial backgrounds and the same proportion had local authority experience. Only 4 per cent had backgrounds in the voluntary sector and an even smaller proportion (2 per cent) were from the trade unions.[1] New universities and colleges of higher education had a greater proportion of external members with commercial and professional backgrounds, while the old universities had a greater proportion of external members with local authority backgrounds. Overall, over half (55 per cent) of the members were in full-time employment, but the second largest proportion, consisting of one-fifth of the members, were retired. Old universities had more members who were retired or in part-time employment than new universities and colleges of higher education; however, new universities had more self-employed members.

These findings present a fairly clear profile of the citizens engaged in the practice of university governance. Those participating are most likely to be drawn from a narrow section of society. Briefly the majority of members were white, male, aged between 46 and 65 and full-time professionals who had qualified to at least first degree level. These findings indicate the forms of both material and cultural resources required to be a university governor under present arrangements. Time is obviously a vital resource, its prominence suggested by the large number of retired members active as governors. And time is probably linked to money, since being a governor remains voluntary and unpaid (except for expenses). But 'cultural capital' (Bourdieu, 1971) is also emphasized by the survey, since both educational qualification and occupational background imply at least some experience or knowledge of the system of higher education and, with it, perhaps, possession of self-confidence born of shared values and language.

Participation in other arenas

Significantly, perhaps, our survey established that those participating in university governance were also likely to be involved in other public decision-making arenas. Governors in the sample population were asked to indicate whether at present they were members of other public bodies. The results are presented in Table 3.1.

Over half (56 per cent) of the respondents indicated that they were currently members of other public bodies. One-third of these respondents were currently members of schools and one-quarter were members of HE institutions. Almost one-fifth of these respondents were members of local authorities, one-tenth were currently members of NHS trusts and just under one-tenth were members of Training and Enterprise Councils.

Examination of these categories by institutional type reveals certain differences.[2] The most notable difference was found in local authority membership. In the old universities a quarter of these respondents (currently members of other public bodies) belonged to local authorities, compared with only 13 per cent of new university and 17 per cent of college respondents. New universities were likely to have a greater proportion of members belonging to NHS trusts than old universities and colleges. Both new universities and colleges had higher proportions of members belonging to Training and Enterprise Councils than old universities.

Table 3.1 Present membership of other public bodies (percentages)

Public bodies	Type of institution			
	Old university	New university	HE college	Total
School	36.9	28.4	30.0	32.8
Other (specified)	26.2	28.4	23.3	26.7
Local authority	25.4	12.7	16.7	19.5
Regional health authority	2.3	2.9	3.3	2.7
District health authority	3.1	2.9	6.7	3.4
NHS trust	9.2	12.7	6.7	10.3
Training and Enterprise Council	5.4	14.7	13.3	9.9
Funding council	1.5	3.9	6.7	3.1
Urban development corporation	2.3	2.9	3.3	2.7
Other HE institution	23.1	26.5	26.7	24.8
FE College	8.5	9.8	6.7	8.8
Total number	130	102	30	262

Note: percentages do not total 100 per cent as respondents could indicate membership of more than one public body.

The strong likelihood that university governors are also members of other public bodies provides two further insights into not just the image of the university governor but the broader concept of active citizenship. First, it implies that vestiges of nineteenth-century conceptions of 'active citizenship' remain: in terms of occupational background and position within the social order, the Victorian 'man of property' would probably not be out of place on the governing body of the late twentieth-century university. Second, setting our survey findings in the context of the 'active citizens' debate gives rise to serious doubts about notions of participatory democracy and self-development raised by the restructuring of governing bodies across swathes of the public sector. On the basis of the survey of university governors alone it could be argued not only that such bodies are likely to be unrepresentative of the broader population which they purport to act on behalf of, but that in their operations they are likely to be articulated with certain sets of value positions and to espouse cultures associated with particular social and occupational backgrounds.

Political affiliations

Certainly the strong representation of certain social categories among university governors implies a number of consequences to the ways in which the governing bodies may actually operate. If governing bodies are perceived as political institutions which grapple with often complex decisions about resource allocation, then it is legitimate to consider the values and cultures which might underpin governors' contributions to debates and eventual decision-making. As a first and tentative step towards beginning to understand the value positions which, implicitly or explicitly, inform the ways in which governors perceive their task and, in turn, how governing bodies operate, we asked our sample population of governors how they had voted in the 1992 general election. We appreciate that this is a relatively crude proxy for the more complex range of values governors actually adopt and the cultures with which they most strongly associate. However, at the very least we felt that the results would allow us to uncover any distinctive patterns and contrasts between institutional types and categories of members.

Although nearly a fifth of respondents (19 per cent) refused to answer this question, the remaining responses suggest that the largest proportion of governors (43 per cent) supported the Conservative Party at the last election. Those voting Labour were the next largest group at 28 per cent, and members voting for the Liberal Democrats comprised a slightly smaller proportion of respondents (22 per cent). Apart from the three main parties, just over 1 per cent of members voted for other parties, while nearly 6 per cent did not exercise their right to vote.

Voting patterns between the three main parties were then examined. Such an examination necessitated the exclusion of all respondents who had not voted for the three main parties. No significant differences were found between voting patterns of members of the three types of institution. However, differences in voting patterns between types of member were detected. Lay members were much more likely to vote Conservative than internal members (a 41 per cent difference). Internal members, on the other hand, were much more likely to have voted for the Labour Party (51 per cent), with the Liberal Democrats as the second most popular party among internal members (30 per cent). Lay members had voted equally between Labour and Liberal Democrat (both 21 per cent). These political inclinations are shown in Figure 3.1.

In order to examine further the relationship between voting pattern and type of member, we compared types of member from the same institution (results are shown in Figures 3.2 and 3.3). When eliminating the influence of 'type of institution' from the relationship we find that the differences decrease slightly in the old universities, but that these differences are exaggerated in the new universities. (Cell numbers were too small in the higher education colleges to obtain reliable significance tests).

The overall voting patterns for types of members in old universities remained very similar to those of the original relationship. The reduction in differences between members was due mostly to internal members having a greater propensity to vote Liberal Democrat and Conservative (although Labour still attracted the most support among this group). Moreover, the number of lay members voting Conservative slightly reduced in favour of Liberal Democrats. However, in the new universities we find the opposite effect: greater proportions of internal members voted Labour, and similarly

Figure 3.1 Voting patterns (three main parties), by type of member.

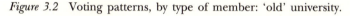

Pearson chi-square 0.00000, d.f.2, correlation 0.390, no. 371.

Figure 3.2 Voting patterns, by type of member: 'old' university.

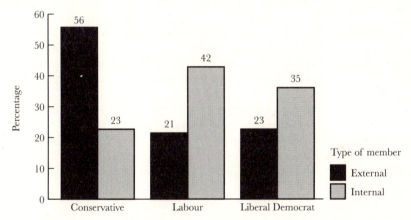

Pearson chi-square 0.00002, d.f.2, correlation 0.331, no. 197.

greater proportions of independent members voted Conservative (see Figure 3.3).

Thus, in the new universities, there appears to be a strong polarity in voting patterns between lay or independent governors, who are mostly Conservative voters, and internal or academic governors, who are mostly Labour voters. Voting distinctions between lay and internal members are also apparent in the old universities, although the polarity is of a lesser magnitude, owing mainly to internal members being more inclined than their counterparts in the new universities to vote Conservative and Liberal Democrat.

Figure 3.3   Voting patterns, by type of member: 'new' university.

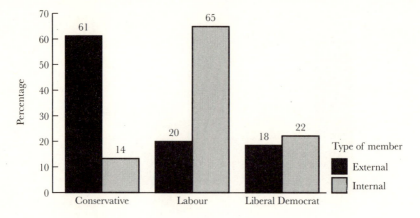

Pearson chi-square 0.00000, d.f.2, correlation 0.465, no. 135.

Reasons for becoming governors

Given the nature of decision-making processes in any large organization, it is difficult to establish any clear linkages between the political inclinations of participants and how the task of governance is actually performed. However, the polarity in voting patterns between external and internal members is repeated in the evidence drawn from the survey about what motivates individuals to participate in university governors. Respondents were asked to rank, in order of most influential, a list of potential reasons for becoming a member of a university/college council or governing body. A ranking order was achieved by obtaining mean scores for each reason and ordering them in ascending order (since the ranking scores were from 1, most influential, to 7, least). Non-parametric tests also indicated that external and internal members thought of these reasons in different orders of influence (see Appendix 2 for graphical representation of means scores of reasons by member). Table 3.2 gives the separate mean scores for external and internal members and the respective rankings obtained from these scores.

If we examine the first three most influential reasons for both groups, then, apart from both types of members construing 'the role as important' as the most influential reason, lay or external members were more likely to perceive the most influential reasons for becoming a governor as being related to their own personal attributes – which they believed were sufficient to perform the role. Internal members, in contrast, were more likely to perceive 'political' reasons as their prime motivation. The suggestion is that internal members see their representational (being elected) and participatory (contributing to changing the institution) functions as being most

Table 3.2 Ranking of reasons for becoming a member by type of member

External members			Internal members		
Ranking	*Reason*	*Mean score*	*Ranking*	*Reason*	*Mean score*
1st	Thought the role important	2.13	1st	Thought the role important	2.19
Equal 2nd	Had necessary skills	2.67	Equal 2nd	Other	2.86
	Relevant previous experience	2.71		Wished to contribute to changing institution	2.89
3rd	Wished to contribute to changing the institution	4.01	3rd	Had necessary skills	3.07
Equal 4th	Maintain ethos of institution	4.68	4th	Relevant previous experience	3.32
	Time to do the job	4.71	5th	Maintain ethos of institution	3.79
	Other	4.71	6th	Time to do the job	5.92

Respondents were asked to specify other reasons. The majority of internal members listed the fact that they had been elected for the role, while external members were most likely to specify the fact that they had been asked to become a member.

influential. Of course, the light shed by the survey on the motivations of governors may only dimly illuminate the range of factors involved. In school governance, for example, it has been suggested that the main reason for becoming a governor was because someone had asked them (Deem *et al.*, 1995: 59). Our own survey found some evidence to support this view. But it is unlikely that, given the considerable personal investment in terms of time and other resources given to the task of governance by what remain as volunteers, simply being asked would be unlikely to sustain interest and commitment to the task over even medium periods of time. It is far more likely, as Table 3.2 indicates, that members are likely to be motivated by more sophisticated assumptions about why they should be involved and what particular contribution they can make to the governance process.

Views of higher education

Although only recently a significant feature of other areas of the British education system, site-based management has long been accorded to universities and is inextricably bound up in notions of academic freedom, autonomy and control. Unlike in schools, for example, there is no strong tradition or framework of direct central control of either the curriculum or management of the old universities. While the former polytechnics developed under local authority tutelage, institutional management was essentially site-based. Under recent reforms the nominal tutelage of the local authorities has been removed entirely. In higher education institutions, therefore, governing bodies have always been involved in site-based management. This has given to governing bodies considerable freedom to develop institutional policy in individual directions, even though, historically, universities have been characterized by a considerable degree of convergence.

Engaging in site-based management requires considerable expertise and knowledge of not just institutional requirements, but the wider integration of the university within the higher education system. However, access to this expertise and, in particular, knowledge of the internal workings of the institution is characterized by asymmetry between professionals and lay persons. Professional knowledge tends to be the preserve of senior managers and academics on the governing body and those external members who happen to be employed in education. Technical knowledge about the particular university and the wider higher education system will, inevitably perhaps, be acquired through socialization as much as by practice. This form of knowledge, or 'practical consciousness' as Giddens (1984) calls it, is encountered in the practice and discourse of the craft. There may be a tendency, therefore, for this knowledge to be imbued with certain values and philosophies associated with the professional practitioner.

Yet given the social, professional and cultural backgrounds of lay governors it would be unwise to assume ignorance of the higher education system or any inevitability of values and philosophies of education at odds with those of the professional. As we have stressed, the system is, in any case, undergoing a period of rapid change which is undermining and, in some cases, overturning once deeply entrenched practices and assumptions. Rather than suggesting that lay governors will have a more limited knowledge of higher education, it is probably more accurate to portray that knowledge as different. That knowledge may well be fed by different sources and it may not always be appropriate or relevant to the task of performing the role of governor. Nevertheless, we felt it would be difficult, perhaps impossible, to quantify the extent of governor knowledge. We knew from talking to governors that many from the lay community were highly informed, while some were prepared to admit to knowledge gaps. A more fruitful course, therefore, was to attempt to ascertain the views held by governors, from both internal and external backgrounds, of the broader higher education system within which their institutions operate. Although governors have not participated (with a few exceptions) in the construction of the broader framework, their views on certain key parameters of the framework and possible changes to them are highly relevant to understanding institutional responses in the wake of policy reform. This led us to ask governors a range of questions on topical issues confronting their institutions, either directly

Figure 3.4 System of higher education preferred, by type of institution.

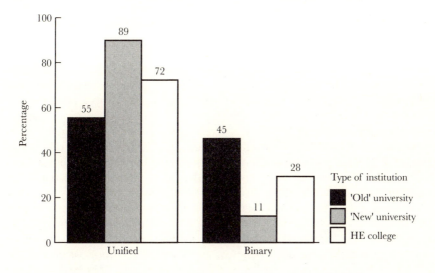

Pearson chi-square 0.00000, d.f.2, correlation 0.352, no. missing 20, no. 474.

or indirectly. The results of our questioning are tested for statistically significant differences between types of member and institution.

Systems of higher education

Respondents were asked to indicate which system of higher education they preferred. Two choices, historically based, were offered: first, a unified system, whereby all higher educational institutions are funded on the same basis by a single agency; second, a binary system, in which institutions are funded by different systems and the higher education sector is subdivided into universities, polytechnics and central institutions. Overall, governors were most likely to favour a unified system of higher education; over two-thirds of respondents opted for this system as opposed to 30 per cent who chose a binary system.

Similar preference patterns were found with both external and internal members. However, significant differences were found between members of different types of institution. Although the largest proportion of old university members still favoured a unified system, 45 per cent remained in favour of a binary divide. These figures contrast sharply with new universities and colleges of higher education, in that almost all new universities members and over 70 per cent of higher education college members favoured a unified system (see Figure 3.4).

Degree programme

Respondents were asked to chose between two types of degree programme structure: either modularization of higher education courses and credit accumulation and transfer systems (CATS) or the traditional pattern of three- or four-year single honours degree. The overall majority of respondents (57 per cent) favoured modularization and CATs, while 40 per cent favoured traditional degree programmes. A small minority of governors (3 per cent) refused to view these as exclusive options and favoured both.

Percentages differed by 20 per cent between external members, who were more likely to favour modularization and CATS, and internal members, the largest proportion of whom preferred traditional programmes. Differential preferences were also found between members of the three types of institution. Members of old universities were more likely to favour traditional programmes than members of the new universities and colleges the majority of whom favoured modularization (details in Appendix 2). The main (and only significant) differences found between members within institutions were in old universities, where internal members preferred traditional programmes and the lay members were equally split between both options. (No significant differences were found between members of the new universities and cell numbers for colleges of higher education precluded the use of significance tests.)

Academic year

Preferences were also sought over whether respondents did or did not favour an extended academic year. Overall preferences were fairly balanced, with those against being a slightly larger proportion at 51 per cent as opposed to those in favour at 48 per cent. A few respondents (1 per cent) did not like this exclusive dichotomized choice and indicated both positive and negative replies. As might be expected, overall differences between types of member were quite stark. Over 80 per cent of internal members, as opposed to about a third of external members, were against an extension – a difference between types of member of almost 50 per cent. When we examined the differences between members within types of institution, it was found that the strength of relationship between 'attitudes towards an extended academic year' and 'type of member' was slightly weakened in the old universities and colleges, while being strengthened in the new universities. This latter condition is mainly owing to independent governors in new universities having a greater likelihood than their counterparts of favouring extension to the academic year. Figures 3.5, 3.6 and 3.7 demonstrate that both external and internal members of new universities were more likely than their counterparts to favour an extension – although the majority of internal members remained against extension. Members of old university councils were more likely than their counterparts in the colleges

Figure 3.5 Extended academic year, by type of member: 'old' university.

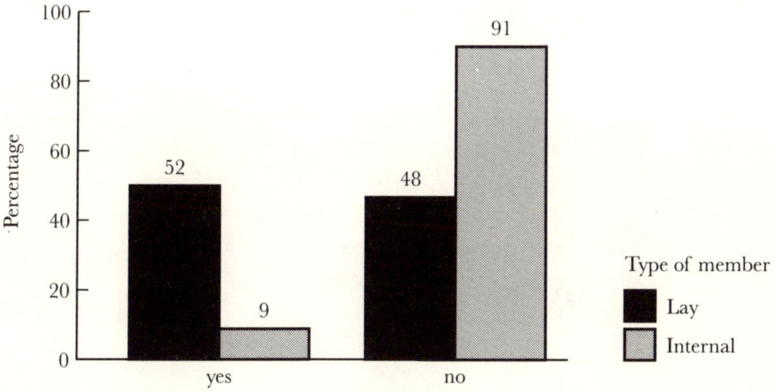

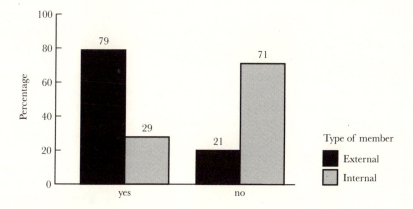

Pearson chi-square 0.00000, d.f. 1, correlation 0.436, total no. 238.

Figure 3.6 Extended academic year, by type of member: 'new' university.

Pearson chi-square 0.00000, d.f. 1, correlation 0.465, total no. 176.

and new universities to be against an extension; however, just over half of external members preferred this option.

Teaching and research in higher education

High on the list of concerns within higher education are the funding arrangements and relative balance of teaching and research activities. Competition between institutions for both students and research funds has been

Figure 3.7   Extended academic year, by type of member: higher education college.

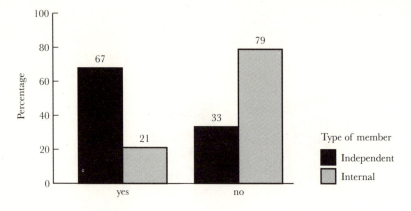

Pearson chi-square 0.00395, d.f.1, correlation 0.407, total no. 50.

encouraged by reforms to funding methodologies and fears for survival heightened by cuts imposed by government in both teaching and research budgets. Given the prominence of these issues and the need to develop sound institutional strategies to make the most of present and future resources, it was decided to investigate governors' views on a range of alternative approaches towards teaching and research issues. Respondents were asked to indicate the extent to which they agreed or disagreed with five policy statements appertaining to research and teaching within the sector.[3] A summary of the responses is given in Table 3.3.

All higher education institutions should engage in research
There was strong support among governors for research activity spread across the sector as a whole. Overall, the majority (almost two thirds) of respondents agreed with this statement. A relationship was found between the strength of attitude towards this statement and types of member. Although the majority of both types of member agreed with the statement, internal members were more likely than external members to agree. A majority of governors from the three types of institution also agreed that 'all higher education institutions should engage in research'. However, council members of old universities were more likely than their counterparts to disagree (for details see Appendix 2).

   A relationship was also found between attitudes towards this statement and political affiliation. Although the largest proportion of respondents from each party agreed with research being conducted in all higher education institutions, those voting Conservative in the last general election were more likely to disagree (42 per cent) than those voting Labour (21 per cent) or Liberal Democrat (24 per cent).

Table 3.3 Respondents' opinions regarding teaching and research (percentages)

	Strongly agree	Agree	No opinion	Disagree	Strongly disagree	Total number
All HE institutions should engage in research	29.6	35.5	2.7	24.8	7.4	487
Separate 'research universities' should be established	6.4	14.4	5.2	39.7	34.3	484
Some universities should be exclusively teaching institutions	5.5	23.7	5.6	40.3	24.9	486
All academic staff should be actively involved in research	10.1	28.0	9.7	43.6	8.6	486
The majority of staff should concentrate exclusively on teaching	2.3	25.2	7.5	46.0	19.0	480

Separate 'research universities' should be established
Overall, nearly three-quarters of all respondents disagreed that separate 'research universities' should be established. There were no significant differences between members from the three sectors. However, internal members were more likely than external members to disagree strongly with this statement.

Some universities should be exclusively teaching-institutions
Two-thirds of all respondents disagreed with the statement that some universities should be exclusively teaching institutions. Members from all types of institution disagreed with this statement. However, members from new universities were more likely to disagree than their counterparts from other institutions. Both external and internal members disagreed with the statement, but strength of opinion differed (by 20 per cent), in that internal members were more likely than external members to disagree strongly.

The relationship between attitudes towards this statement and political affiliations (to the three main parties) was also examined. Although the majority of all members voting for these three parties disagreed that some universities should be exclusively teaching institutions, those voting Labour or Liberal Democrat in the last general election were more likely than Conservative voters to disagree.

All academic staff should be actively involved in research
Just over half of all respondents disagreed with this statement, while almost 40 per cent agreed that all academics should be involved with research.

Again, a polarity between types of member was found. Just over half of the academics agreed, whereas nearly 60 per cent of external members disagreed with all staff undertaking research. Differences were also detected between types of institution. No doubt owing to the higher representation of lay/independent members in the sample, the majority of members from old and new universities disagreed with all staff engaging in research. However, unsurprisingly, members of higher education colleges – with a proportionately similar sample configuration – were equally divided (40 per cent for and 40 per cent against) and were more likely than their counterparts to have no opinion on the matter. Differences in attitude to all staff being engaged in research were also found between voters for the three main political parties. The majority (60 per cent) of Conservative voters were in disagreement, while the greatest proportion of both Labour and Liberal Democrat voters agreed that all academic staff should engage in research.

The majority of staff should concentrate exclusively on teaching
Almost two-thirds of all governors disagreed with this statement. Both internal and external members were more likely to disagree than agree. However, internal members (80 per cent) were more likely than external members (58 per cent) to disagree. The greatest proportion of members from each type of institution disagreed with the majority of staff concentrating on teaching. However, old university members were more likely than their counterparts to disagree and members of higher education colleges were almost equally divided on the issue (49 per cent in disagreement and 45 per cent in agreement). The greatest proportion of members from all three main political parties disagreed with the majority of staff concentrating on teaching. Those members voting Labour and Liberal Democrat were more likely than those voting Conservative to disagree.

Funding universities

Governors were asked to circle their preferred positions on a 1–5 scale indicating how they think universities should be funded: from 'predominantly by taxes' to 'significantly more private funding'. Overall, 60 per cent of all respondents were evidently in favour of maintaining predominant reliance on state funding (i.e. those members favouring scale items 1 (27 per cent) and 2 (33 per cent)). The overall average score for all respondents was 2.3, which can be interpreted as suggesting that on average members of councils and governing bodies are in favour of universities being funded primarily from public funds. The statistical means were compared for differences between internal and external governors. Internal members scored a 1.9 average while external members averaged 2.5, indicating that internal members have a stronger preference for funding from taxes than do the external members. Figure 3.8 provides a clear picture of the differences between types of member on this variable.

Figure 3.8 How universities should be funded, by type of member.

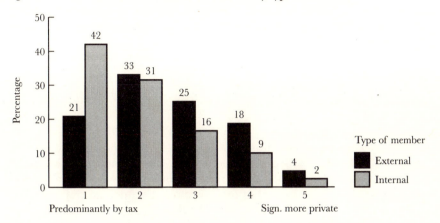

Table 3.4 How universities should be funded, by vote (percentages)

How universities should be funded	Party voted for in last general election			
	Conservative	Labour	Liberal Democrat	Total
Public	41.1	88.3	72.7	62.9
Equal public and private	29.2	6.3	13.6	18.5
Private	29.8	5.4	13.6	18.5
Total number	168	111	88	367

Pearsons chi-square 0.00000, d.f.4, correlation 0.305, no. missing 127.
Note: Column percentages do not all sum to 100 because of rounding.

The largest proportion (42 per cent) of internal members favoured scale option 1, which indicated a system with the greatest reliance on taxes, whereas only the third largest (21 per cent) proportion of external members favoured this option. The largest proportion of external members favoured the next scale option (2), which indicates a system still primarily reliant on taxes but with slightly more private funds. As can be seen, a greater proportion of external members also preferred scale option 3 to 1. Therefore, although external members had a greater likelihood than internal members of preferring a system with significantly more reliance on private funds, their overall preference – like that of internal members – was for a system funded primarily by the state.

A relationship between attitudes to funding and political affiliation was found. However, owing to small cell sizes at the higher scale, it was necessary to collapse categories into three sections.[4] Table 3.4 shows how those voting for different political parties differed in their attitude towards this question.

Although the greatest proportion of members voting for the three main parties preferred a funding system based predominantly on public funding, it is evident that Labour and Liberal Democrat voters are far more likely than Conservative voters to favour this option. Conservative voters are more likely than Labour and Liberal Democrat voters to prefer a system whereby funding is provided from either an equal mix of public and private funding or predominantly private funds; and as may be expected, Labour voters are least likely to favour either of these two options.

Methods of private funding
Governors were provided with a list of seven methods of private funding and asked to indicate which three methods they most favoured by order of preference. Table 3.5 lists the seven methods ordered by the mean for each method. Analysis by mean takes into account the first, second and third ratings on each funding method. (The final column also provides a count of the number respondents rating this method as their first most favoured.) From the mean scores we have a result which places loans for tuition and graduate tax equal first most favoured methods of private funding. Top up fees, employer surcharge and private sponsorship came equal second. Alumni appeals and overseas students were the third and least favoured methods.

Public funding and growth

Governors were asked to indicate whether they agreed or disagreed with two statements regarding funding of higher education institutions.

Current levels of public funding are adequate to fund the present system
Overall, the majority (79 per cent) of respondents disagreed with this statement. There were no differences between the old and new universities and the majority of both types of member also disagreed with the statement. However, internal members were more likely than external members to disagree (96 per cent of internal members disagreed as opposed to 71 per cent of external members), and almost 30 per cent of external members agreed compared with only 4 per cent of internal members. The differences between members were of a greater magnitude in the new universities than the old. This was mainly owing to a lesser proportion of independent members (64 per cent) in the new universities and a greater proportion of lay members (75 per cent) in the old universities disagreeing with the statement.

Attitudes to the sufficiency of current levels of public funding were examined in relation to political affiliation. Unsurprisingly, Conservatives were more likely than those voting Labour or Liberal Democrat to agree that current levels are sufficient. However, the greatest proportion of Conservative voters, like Labour and Liberal Democrat voters, disagreed, suggesting that the post-war political consensus on welfare issues may not have

Table 3.5 Most favoured methods of private funding

Method of funding		Mean score (number of respondents)	Number selecting method first (percentage)
Graduate tax	Graduates pay extra income tax regardless of the cost of their HE	1.72 (191)	96 (20.6)
Loans for tuition	Students would be charged for tuition and would be eligible to receive loans to meet extra costs	1.75 (235)	106 (22.7)
Top-up fees	Charging students a premium on top of fees paid by local education authorities	1.90 (162)	64 (13.7)
Employer surcharge	Employers of graduates would have to pay, perhaps through a NI charge	1.94 (121)	40 (8.6)
Private sponsorship	Academic posts, courses, buildings etc. should be paid for by private sponsors	1.95 (239)	86 (18.5)
Alumni appeals	Universities should redouble their efforts to persuade alumni to contribute	2.13 (157)	40 (8.6)
More overseas students	The proportion of full fee-paying overseas students should be increased, i.e. non-EU	2.23 (145)	34 (7.3)
Total			466

disappeared among certain sections of the community. Labour voters were the highest proportion of members to disagree, at 92 per cent, compared with 85 per cent of Liberal Democrat and 67 per cent of Conservative voters.

Projected growth can be paid for out of productivity gains
Again the majority of respondents (over three-quarters) disagreed with this statement. Members in the new universities (26 per cent) were more likely than those in the old universities (15 per cent) and colleges (19 per cent) to agree with this statement. Again internal members (93 per cent) were

more likely than external members (74 per cent) to disagree that projected growth could be paid for out of productivity gains. Political affiliation was also examined in relation to this variable, and a relatively low association was found. Political consensus was again found among respondents, since the greatest proportion of members favouring each of the three main parties disagreed that projected growth can be paid for out of productivity gains. However, Conservative Party supporters were more likely (27 per cent) than Labour (11 per cent) or Liberal Democrat (10 per cent) supporters to agree.

Future student numbers

Governors were asked to indicate which option was closest to their preference for future student numbers in the forthcoming years. The options were as follows: (a) a reduction; (b) no further increase; (c) a period of consolidation with only moderate growth; and (d) continued rapid growth.

Overall, the majority of respondents (83 per cent) preferred a period of consolidation. Differences were found between types of member, but these were only small differences in members' second preferred choice. Over 80 per cent of both external and internal members preferred consolidation. However, internal members' second choice (10 per cent) was no further increase in student numbers, while external members (11 per cent) preferred a period of continued rapid growth. No significant differences were found between different types of institution.

Admissions policies

When asked to indicate which admission policy they thought institutions should place greater emphasis upon, governors were again given a dichotomized choice between (a) academic achievement (top A level grades) and (b) measures to widen access for under-represented groups. Overall, members were almost equally divided. The majority (54 per cent) thought that institutions should place greater emphasis on academic achievement, while 45 per cent chose the second option of widening access and 1 per cent of respondents chose both options.

Differences were found between members of different types of institution. The greatest proportion of old university members (64 per cent) and higher education college members (52 per cent) favoured placing greater emphasis on academic achievement, while the majority (56 per cent) of new university members preferred measures to widen access. Interestingly, internal members were more likely than external members to favour widening access (a difference of 20 per cent; see Figure 3.9).

When the influence of type of institution is eliminated, the differences between types of member lessen in the old universities and strengthen in the new universities and colleges of higher education. In the old universities both more external (68 per cent) and more internal (55 per cent)

Figure 3.9 Admission policies, by type of member.

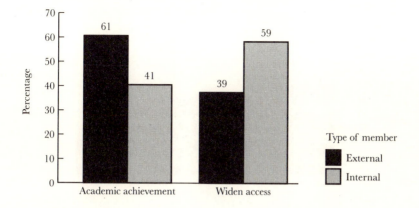

Pearson chi-square 0.00006, d.f.1, correlation 0.187, no. missing 29, total no. 465.

Figure 3.10 Admission policies, by type of member: 'old' university.

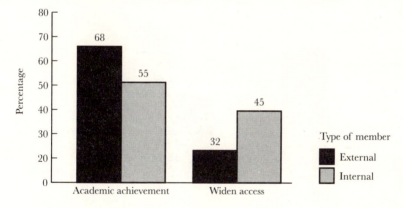

Pearson chi-square 0.04394, d.f.1, correlation 0.129, total no. 241.

members are in favour of placing greater emphasis on academic achievement. In the new universities the greatest proportion of independent members still preferred to place greater emphasis on academic achievement but
this number reduced to 53 per cent, and a far greater proportion (81 per
cent) of internal members preferred to place greater emphasis on measures
to widen access. In the colleges of higher education about the same proportion of external members (60 per cent) preferred academic achievement.
However, as with the new universities, a greater proportion (71 per cent)
of internal members preferred placing emphasis on widening access (see
Figures 3.10, 3.11 and 3.12). Thus, in old universities the majority of both

Figure 3.11   Admission policies, by type of member: 'new' university.

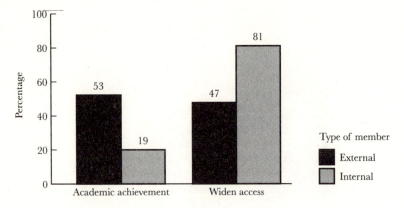

Pearson chi-square 0.00007, d.f.1, correlation 0.302, no. 172.

Figure 3.12   Admission policies, by type of member: higher education college.

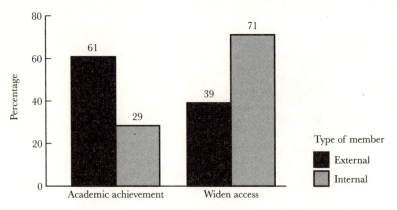

Pearson chi-square 0.04079, d.f.1, correlation 0.283, no. 52.

academic and lay members agreed that greater emphasis should be placed on academic achievement. In the new universities and colleges there is much greater division of opinion, with most academic members preferring to widen access and the majority of independent members placing emphasis on academic achievement.

The relationship between political affiliation and this variable was also examined. The majority of those voting for Labour (84 per cent) or the Liberal Democrats (52 per cent) preferred measures to widen access. However, the majority of those members voting Conservative (76 per cent) preferred greater emphasis to be placed on academic achievement.

Academic standards

Opinions were sought from governors regarding academic standards over the past five years. Respondents were asked whether they thought academic standards had improved, stayed the same or declined. Replies to this question were almost equally distributed between the three choices, in itself a worrying divergence of opinion among those directly involved in university leadership and direction. The majority of respondents (35 per cent) believed that standards had stayed the same, 33 per cent felt standards had declined and 31 per cent thought standards had improved.

No significant differences were found between members from different sectors. However, significant differences were found between types of member. Overall, just over half of internal members (53 per cent) thought that standards had declined, whereas only 23 per cent of external members were of this opinion. The largest proportion of external members (39 per cent) believed that standards had improved, while only 17 per cent of internal members thought that this was the case. In old universities, a greater proportion of both internal members (57 per cent) and external members (27 per cent) believed that standards had declined, although the highest proportion of lay members of council (39 per cent) thought that standards had stayed the same. In the new universities, although the largest proportion of internal members still believed that standards had declined, this proportion was lower, at 48 per cent. The largest proportion of external members (43 per cent) believed that standards had improved and a larger proportion of internal members (22 per cent) compared with those of the old universities (15 per cent) thought that this was the case. No significant differences were found between members in higher education colleges (probably owing to the small sample size; see Appendix 2 for details). To summarize, lay members of old universities were inclined to think that standards had stayed the same, while their counterparts in the new universities tended to believe that standards had improved. Academics from both old and new universities took a bleaker view, believing that standards had declined over the previous five years.

Perceptions of students

Governors' views in this area were sought as to the extent to which they agreed or disagreed with two statements.

Students should be viewed as clients with 'consumer rights'
Overall, the majority of respondents (72 per cent) were in agreement with this statement. Just less than a fifth of governors (19 per cent) disagreed. A small proportion (9 per cent) had no opinion. No significant differences were found between types of member, types of institution or members voting patterns.

*The implementation of the Student's Charter will result in better education
for all students*

The largest proportion of all respondents (40 per cent) had no opinion
regarding this statement, while a larger proportion agreed (32 per cent)
than disagreed (27 per cent) with the statement. Differences were found
between types of member: the largest proportion (43 per cent) of internal
members disagreed, compared to only 19 per cent of external members.
The largest proportion of external members (47 per cent) had no opinion
and the second largest proportion (34 per cent) agreed with this statement,
compared to 30 per cent of internal members.

A relationship between this variable and voting propensity was found.
The majority of Conservative (43 per cent) and Liberal Democrat (46 per
cent) voters had no opinion regarding the improved effects of the implementation of the Student's Charter. The largest proportion of Labour voters (38 per cent) disagreed with the statement. Conservative voters were
most likely to agree, at 38 per cent, compared with 28 per cent of those
voting Labour and 20 per cent of those voting Liberal Democrat.

Conclusion

In this chapter we have focused on the social and cultural identities of
those who participate in university governance, the educational and work
experiences they bring to the task and the reasons why they decided to
become governors. Our findings indicate that university governance does
not offer significant opportunities for the practice of citizenship among a
wide cross-section of the population. Although the thrust of recent reforms
has enhanced the role of lay participation in university governance, in
practice both formally and informally this has tended to focus on members
of the business community, particularly in the new universities. Because
university governing bodies have a far greater antiquity than modern conceptions of citizenship, the effect has been to graft on to existing patterns
of participation a new layer that has probably done little to alter the fundamental balance of governing bodies. While the concept of lay participation, therefore, offers undeniable opportunities for wider community
involvement in the running of a major public service, it would be unwise to
place the typical university governing body neatly into modern theory of
participatory democracy.

Instead, the research revealed just how atypical of the wider population
university governing bodies are. The majority of members are aged between
46 and 65, male, white, qualified to first degree, Conservative voters, in full-
time employment and with professional backgrounds. Over half are also
members of other public bodies and most usually these were schools or
other higher education institutions. These findings suggest that opportunities to participate in university governance are extremely constrained, and
factors of social class, gender and race may act as substantial barriers to

entry by certain social groups. The distribution of such opportunities along these lines reflects broader inequalities in access to material and cultural resources within the population as a whole. It is also significant that just over half of the university governors in our survey were also members of other public bodies, further suggesting the domination of certain social and cultural characteristics in new models of active citizenship.

However, among the university governors surveyed there are important differences between types of institution and types of members. Old universities were more likely to have a greater number of retired members and members who had local authority backgrounds or were still members of local authorities. Given the break with local authority structures enforced by statute on the former polytechnics, the absence of such links among the new universities is hardly surprising. Given this background, new universities and colleges of higher education had more external members than old universities from commercial and professional backgrounds, and a greater proportion of members belonging to Training and Enterprise Councils. New universities also had more likelihood than old universities and colleges of having a larger proportion of members from NHS trusts and more self-employed members.

The survey also established extreme polarity between internal and external members in their political inclinations. The general pattern is for a majority of internal members to vote Labour, while lay or external members vote Conservative. This effect is slightly modified in the old universities, where rather more internal members admitted to voting for the Liberal Democrats or Labour, while a greater number of external members tended to vote Liberal Democrat rather than Conservative. In the new universities, the voting polarity between external and internal members was exaggerated, and this was primarily owing to a greater number of internal members voting Labour and slightly more external members voting Conservative.

In the higher education sector as a whole, differences were also found between external and internal members' motives for becoming members of governing bodies. While lay or external members identified their personal attributes as a prime reason for becoming involved in governance – in that they had the requisite skills and experience – internal members were more inclined to relate to 'political' motivations: they were elected and/or they wanted to participate in changing the institution. The existence of fault lines between internal and lay or external members in this and other aspects of the governance process is a theme that runs through the rest of the analysis.

Despite debates about participation and active citizenship, the present configuration of membership of university governing bodies therefore favours certain citizens over others. Social and cultural identities are heavily aligned with professional and commercial occupations, with high levels of academic achievement and with older white males. This suggests that those schooled in these backgrounds are likely to be considered as most likely to possess the necessary skills, value positions and, perhaps the political beliefs to participate in 'successful' governance. In fact, our survey did confirm a fairly high degree of consensus among governors about some major areas of higher education policy and practice.

Over two-thirds of governors surveyed favour a unified system of higher education in which institutions are funded on the same basis by a single agency. Over half favoured a modularized degree programme rather than a traditional three- or four-year single honours programme. The majority of respondents agreed that all institutions should engage in research and a majority was opposed to the establishment of separate 'research universities'. There was also a general resistance to the idea that a majority of staff should concentrate exclusively on teaching. On progress towards a mass system of higher education, most governors indicated that they would prefer a period of consolidation, with only moderate growth in student numbers. A majority of all respondents thought that greater emphasis should be placed on academic achievement rather than measures to widen access for under-represented groups. A majority were in favour of universities and colleges being supported predominantly by taxation rather than private funds. A majority of governors, irrespective of their political affiliations as indicated by voting propensity in the last general election, also favoured a system predominantly reliant on state funding. To reinforce the point, almost 80 per cent of respondents disagreed that 'current levels of public funding are adequate to fund the present system'.

Despite the consensus displayed by governors on these key issues, however, the survey did detect evidence to suggest that the educational philosophies and values of lay governors may be at odds with those of internal governors. For example, across the sector academic members tended to favour traditional programmes, while lay members were more inclined to support modularization. Members were almost equally divided between thinking that academic standards had improved, stayed the same or declined over the past five years. The two types of member differed in their views on standards, with the majority of internal members believing that standards had declined, whereas the majority of external members thought that standards had improved. Finally, differences were found between types of member, where the majority of internal members disagreed with and the majority of external members had no opinion regarding the positive educational effects of the students charter.

Differences between governors were structured along different lines. In particular, the type of institution to which governors belonged and individual voting propensities demonstrated the complicated influences that might be brought to bear on members of all types. However, the importance of the internal–external divide stood out, even if on many key issues there was a good deal of unanimity between the professionals on the governing body and those brought in to represent the broader lay community. The possibility that the involvement of lay citizens in university governance may produce alternative perspectives is, of course, precisely one of the principal arguments in favour of lay participation. However, in itself the existence of divergent views structured on these lines does not tell us anything about how they are played out in specific institutional settings. Nor does it indicate whether the views of lay governors are sufficiently coherent or strong to exert any degree of control over the professionals in the organization. Evidence of these relationships and the broader power flows within the governing body and wider institutions provided by the case studies is introduced and discussed in subsequent chapters.

Notes

1. Percentages do not total 100 per cent because respondents could indicate more than one background.
2. These differences were examined by use of multiple response sets which do not allow for significance tests or measures of association. Thus we cannot assert (a) whether these differences are likely to hold in the population or (b) the strength of such relationships.
3. For ease of interpretation, when using cross-tabulation, the categories have been collapsed into agree, no opinion and disagree; however, before recoding it was checked that such an operation did not serve to disguise any relationships between variables.
4. Details of recoding of variable 'How do you think universities should be funded?' From a 1 (predominantly public) to 5 (predominantly private) scale: three categories were produced: 1 to 2 = 1 (public), 3 = 2 (equal public and private), 4 to 5 = 3 (private).

4

People Like Us? The Selection and Appointment of University Governors

Although the origins of governing bodies are firmly rooted in the history, culture and organizational structures of universities, their existence is far from unproblematic. The representative role enshrined in the principle of lay administration implies at the very least some form of alliance in leadership, direction and management of universities between the 'internal' professional academics and the 'external' or lay elements whose interests and ideas may relate to and derive from very different constituencies. In their early history many universities, particularly the Victorian 'civic' foundations, exemplified the domination of the lay community over the academic in governance. The rise of donnish over lay dominion in the twentieth-century university reversed these historical relationships.

However, inspired by New Right critiques of public policy and the emergence of new emphases on markets and managerialism, recent government reforms of governance structures in higher education and elsewhere in the public sector produced a renaissance of the principle of lay participation in arenas of public life once thought the preserve of the professional. In the former polytechnics in particular there was a clear attempt to vest newfound corporate powers in the hands of unicameral governing bodies with lay majorities strongly infused by members selected from the business community. The legislation which converted the former polytechnics into freestanding independent corporations deliberately eschewed the principle of universities as self-governing communities of scholars. In its place the legislation stipulated a clear 'independent' or lay majority on governing bodies, with these governors being drawn from those who 'have experience of and ... have shown capacity in industrial, commercial or employment matters.' Although the statute does provide that there must be members who have experience of education, the statutory provision made no allowance for a balanced representation of alternative political views or sectional interests from either the lay community or within the university itself.

Fears that these governance arrangements were flawed precisely because they sought to promote one form of sectional interest over all others were fuelled by rising concerns about accountability and standards of conduct across a broad range of public activities. In the case of higher education, they were ignited by the well publicized cases of governance failures at Huddersfield and Portsmouth universities. As the Nolan Committee made clear in its deliberations, local bodies such as universities possess considerable freedom to set their own priorities, yet their decisions are inextricably bound up with wider public policy (Nolan, 1995b: para. 4). Since the operations of universities can have far-reaching implications for the communities they serve, however the latter are defined, the constitution of their governing bodies must be a major concern of public policy and confidence. In particular, how these bodies are assembled and maintained in terms of selection and appointment of governors is a critical factor in their legitimation and operation. Focusing on the issue of securing representation on governing bodies, the present chapter first considers the issue of securing lay participation on governing bodies and the principles which inform governance procedures. The second section presents empirical evidence collected during the course of our research project, which sheds light on how university governors are actually selected and appointed.

Conceptualizing lay governance

Lay or independent governors have been accorded a primary role under the present framework of university governance. In the 'old' (pre-1992) universities it is a basic principle that the council, as the governing body, has a majority of members who are neither staff nor students of the university: a so-called lay majority. Their equivalents in the 'new' (post-1992) universities, the independent members, also have a primary place in membership terms. It is a statutory duty for boards of governors in new universities to ensure that at least half of their membership are independent members (Council of University Chairmen (CUC), 1995: 10, 15).

It was envisaged that independent governors in the new universities would act as the equivalent to unpaid non-executive directors of companies. In terms of their statutory powers and obligations and their predominance in numbers they are the most important governors on the governing body. Provisions in the instruments and articles of government ensure that independent governors are given the decisive voice in decision-making. Included in their 'powers' are approval of any appointment of independent governors and the right to defer decisions if a board meeting does not consist of at least half of the independent members.[1] In addition, the right to exclude other types of member from certain committees of the governing body ensures their involvement in key decisions.

In old universities, lay members of the council, although they must constitute a majority of the governing body, do not possess quite the same importance. Part of the reason lies in the emphasis historically placed on staff and student representation in governing body membership. Endorsing this emphasis in its *Guide for Members of Governing Bodies*, the CUC (1995) observed: 'This representation is integral to the nature of governance in those institutions.' In the new universities, it is possible for staff and student members to be excluded by decision of the governing body, even if, as the CUC warns, such exclusion should be approached 'with very great care' (CUC, 1995: 24).

Despite these provisions, however, the concept of lay participation is characterized by two ambiguities. First, it overlaps with and, occasionally, contradicts other notions of democratic participation. Within the membership of the various university governing bodies there is an uneasy alliance between democratic election and co-option. In broad terms, internal members representing academics and students tend to be chosen by success in elections, while external or lay members tend to be co-opted or appointed. Securing of representation of the outside community of interests, therefore, can be highly undemocratic and is open to the accusation that governing bodies can be so constructed that certain politically inspired agendas are more likely to be achieved. This was an accusation which could be, and was, levelled at the former polytechnics during the era of local authority control, when it was not unknown for incoming local ruling parties to make massive changes to governing body personnel on the back of their new political majorities.

Since then, the creation of the polytechnics as free-standing corporations under the constitutional arrangements of 1992, together with the emergence of new market-based discourses based on consumerism and managerialism, have created new opportunities to fill governing bodies with members driven by different concerns. There is little doubt that in the reform of the governance framework of the new, post-1992, universities, the government envisaged governing bodies invigorated and enthused by the selection of external members experienced in decision-making in industry and with value positions in tune with business culture. Through their presence, governing bodies would be well placed to transform the culture of their institutions. Like governing bodies in other arenas, therefore, those in universities tend to be hybrid organizations which exhibit tendencies towards democratic, corporatist and managerialist principles (Deem *et al.*, 1995: 72).

This shift towards greater entrepreneurialism and the adoption of business metaphors, symbolically represented in the emergence of the vice chancellor as the chief executive, is associated with the second ambiguity of governance. The central issue is where the emphasis of governance should be placed. Should it be to encourage governors to act in an entrepreneurial fashion, taking the culture and practice of the university towards the principles of modern corporate business? In this model the governors act as directors, akin to their counterparts in the private sector, taking responsibility for decisions which may occasionally necessitate being amoral in calculations of corporate over public good. Conversely, should governors act more as trustees than directors? In this model the emphasis of governance tends to be on policing and controlling institutions much more than on initiative and innovation. The bewildering array of legislation applicable to universities as organizations, and the increasing complexity of the regulatory regime imposed by the government's funding agencies, imposes considerable burdens on governors to ensure that they serve not just the interests of the institution but the wider tests of good governance and accountability.

University governing bodies have two important sources of advice for good practice with respect to appointments procedures. Both the Cadbury Committee and the CUC recommended that a nominations committee should have a central role in the governance process. For Cadbury, the primary justification for the inclusion of a majority of non-executive directors on governing boards is to ensure the exercise of independent judgement, free from any relationship, financial or otherwise. In order to protect this independence, Cadbury (1992) recommended that a nominations committee, comprising a majority of non-executive directors, be established to ensure that appointments are made on merit and not through any form of patronage. It was also recommended that non-executives should be appointed for fixed terms to prevent loss of the independent edge.

A variant of these recommendations found its way into the CUC's *Guide for Members of Governing Bodies* (1995). According to the CUC, the role of such a committee should be to 'seek out and recommend new lay/independent co-opted members to the appointing body'. The committee should be chaired by the chair of the full governing body and include at least three lay or independent co-opted members, the chief executive of the institution and at least one senior member of academic staff. The CUC advocates a wide trawl for suitable members with due regard to the balance of the governing body and the needs of the institution. Recommendations from a committee, it is further suggested, should be voted upon by the whole governing body in the case of old universities, and by the independent members (after discussion by the whole governing body) in the case of new universities.

Such advice remains, at the time of writing at least, no more than a code of conduct which is not enforceable. Individual governing bodies remain free to decide the procedures that are best suited to their needs, bearing in mind the diverse histories and traditions which inform the governance process. However, in view of the rising concern with issues of accountability and probity already described, the recommendations of Cadbury and the CUC provide a valuable benchmark against which to compare practice in the case study institutions, although it should be noted that the publication of the CUC's recommendations (in June 1995) occurred after the case study research had taken place.

Securing participation: empirical evidence

Whatever the degree of inclusiveness practised in old and new universities, the constitutional importance of both lay and independent membership is well established. Given this importance, our investigations were designed to explore the critical issue of similarities and/or differences in approach to governor appointments in old and new universities. In this section we concentrate on membership of governing bodies and appointment procedures, both formal and informal, adopted by councils and boards in the case study institutions. The intention is to compare and contrast practice to the recommendations of Cadbury and the CUC.

The old universities

Approaches to membership and appointments differed considerably at the two old universities studied. The first contrast was the size of the respective governing bodies. One, the Old University of the South (OUS), was representative of the tendency for university councils to be much larger bodies than their counterparts in the new universities. At the time of the research there were 50 members (recently reduced from 60) on the OUS council, consisting of officers (approximately eight in number), members appointed by the court (not greater than ten), members appointed by local authorities (11), members appointed by senate (approximately nine), non-academic staff members (three), members appointed by council (not greater than three), representatives of convocation (three) and representatives of the union of students (three).

The council of the Old University of the North (OUN), in contrast, had a membership of only 30, smaller than the norm among the old universities. Like the OUS, however, the council retained provision for both local authority representatives (five) and elected members of the court to be included in its membership. Eight members of the council were *ex officio*, namely the chancellor, three pro-chancellors, the vice chancellor, the deputy vice chancellor, the pro vice chancellor and the treasurer.

At the time of the research, the question of reducing the size of the OUS council was continuing to exercise the minds of university leaders. The vice chancellor of the OUS suggested that the main motivation behind reducing council membership was to create a more coherent body in which individuals would acquire a greater feeling of responsibility and commitment. The council was still to have a lay majority, but one class of membership where it was generally agreed that reduction could be made was 'class 3: members appointed by public authorities'. These local authority members, 11 in number, were generally considered as free-riders who more often than not did not come to meetings and when they did had nothing of value to contribute. This view was put forcibly by the OUS registrar:

> What struck me as particularly odd against the background of the history of the old and new universities was that the new universities had had this imperative laid down in terms of the constitution and were prescribed from having local authority members other than by co-option after the governing body was in existence. Yet they came out of

the local authority sector – you look at [our] constitution, it had 11 local authority members out of 50. I mean there was this kind of ludicrous situation – in terms of the histories of the two institutions – and it was particularly looking at the 11 local authority members who quite honestly are pretty useless as far as the university is concerned. They're good folk and all the rest of it but you get the feeling that for most of them it's an odds and sods job after all the useful offices have been handed out within the controlling group.

It was left to a staff member to put the counter argument to the reduction process. Suspicious that the implicit motive behind such a move was to imbue the administration, and in particular the registrar, with more power, he suggested that since council debates or votes rarely affected decisions, it was immaterial whether the council numbered 30 or 50. On the other hand, reducing council numbers risked undermining regional and community perspectives:

Council very seldom has debates, very seldom has a dispute – that is decided on the vote or anything like this. It's normally in the form of a few questions, a few comments and it's put through – so in that sense whether its 60 or 30 people there it does not matter. But there are other ways of involving people – in setting up short-term working groups to make people feel committed and involved. I mean the risk is that the sort of balance of people that will end up on council will be more the business-oriented people that are driven by financial matters, which is important – because we're all short of money – but you'll lose the regional role of the university – looking at other perspectives, perhaps doing things that maybe the community needs but may need a bit of financial help from another area.

Another staff member was less apprehensive than his colleague, arguing that as long as policies remained driven from academic foundations with adequate senate representation, fewer members would result in the role of individuals and council, as a whole, becoming more proactive.

Rather than the size of councils, however, perhaps the more significant difference between the OUS and the OUN lay in the procedures for appointing new members. The mechanism used by the OUN to make appointments to council was a sub-committee known as 'Appointments to Court and Council'. Membership of this sub-committee consists of three senior academic officers (the chair of senate, the pro vice chancellor, the deputy vice chancellor), three pro-chancellors (the chair of council and two others lay members) and the treasurer. This sub-committee also manages the membership of council sub-committees. The committee keeps account of the current composition and expertise of council in order to determine what appointments need to be made to maintain a balanced board; and it generates a list of potential candidates for court and council. It also ensures that it anticipates any vacancies occurring on the main council and its committees and decides, in advance, who is going to serve on its key committees.

In appointing people for council committees, the OUN engaged in a practice not encountered in the other case studies. Its lay members were invited to join certain committees as a kind of 'apprenticeship' before being asked to join council and other (less pedestrian) committees. For example, one lay member told us that he had served for four years on the college and catering committee before being asked to join council, and after one year as a full council member he was asked to join the policy and resources committee. This 'apprenticeship scheme' was seen to have the advantages of a probationary period where both the lay member and the university can assess the candidate's suitability for full council membership; and it also provides the candidate with an induction period before taking on more responsibility. Council has nine sub-committees, and introducing lay 'apprentice' members to certain sub-committees was found to be an effective way of preventing over-stretching council members and 'spreading the (work) load'.

The chair of the council explained why in his opinion the OUN approach to appointments worked:

> Our problems are usually getting enough lay members . . . and spreading them out over the committees. We're increasingly bringing people on to university committees who aren't council members, which has two advantages – one, you obviously spread the load but also you get people, you can establish whether people will fit into the university and you can establish whether they will be happy perhaps later being a member of council . . . And they come on and they – let's say they spend some time on the estates and buildings and they're interested in that or college and catering which are the two biggest . . . As a sort of apprenticeship and it is – it's enabled to get both sides to see how you get on together, and if they don't like it they can drop off; if they do – as fortunately most of them do – they usually come along and say 'can we do more?' And we have quite a number of people saying to me 'can I do more?' And you have to try and find the right role to fit them too. Which is another aspect of what we were talking about earlier – if someone has done three or four years on one of the big committees and he's obviously happy with that then many of them come along and say 'can I do more?' And you say fine. And that's what you want, I mean you do not want people on council who are there frankly for the ride. We want people there who actively want to contribute.

One lay member, who had actually begun on the college and catering committee, said that he would often feel that he was wasting his time, but that on reflection the experience had been useful in providing him with a grounding in university governance. He thought that overall 'the apprentice scheme' was a good idea, in that it tested lay members' reliability and commitment:

It's a 'bottomer'. I don't think I could honestly do that forever because I found it very difficult, and I've spoken to other lay members who are very experienced and capable people, and we have found it difficult to contribute to college and catering. I just don't know what I can say about the price of a pint of beer ... And you just think well this is nonsense, I'm wasting my time. Now I look back on it, it does actually give a little bit of flavour ... the grounding helped ... having this 'bottom-up' early introduction is a bit like an apprenticeship, you wonder why you are doing it at the time, but on reflection it helped.

The vice chancellor, however, did comment that people of high business calibre were usually extremely busy people and often were 'not too keen on being on pedestrian committees – like the building and estates committee or something', but that they were very willing to help. Thus it is not a statutory or conventional requirement that all lay members undergo an apprenticeship before entering the higher ranks of council.

Unlike the OUN, the OUS had neither a nominations committee nor an 'apprenticeship' scheme for lay members of council. It would appear from the constitution that the executive of the OUS had very little control over membership, since only three out of 50 members could be appointed by council. In the registrar's opinion, this restriction made it difficult to engineer a balanced board and recruit people who really 'add value to the working of the university':

What I've been used to is actually being able to harness people – who bring a great variety of experience to bear – people of stature, people who are networked into all sorts of areas that are important to the university. You can achieve that if you can influence the membership. You know to have somebody, for example, who's into banking, somebody else who's into property and somebody else who's a lawyer – all these sorts of things which at the end of the day add value back into the university.

Without a nominations committee, the appointment of lay members at the OUS seemed to rest solely on the judgement of the vice chancellor and registrar. The vice chancellor suggested that appointment was an opportune process in which he heard through informal networks that certain people 'were coming on to the market':

Well, of the people who've been recruited in my time – we recruited usually in an opportune way – you know I've heard that they were coming on to the market. An old friend of mine ... retired from the oil business and wrote to me to say that the personnel director of X International was approaching retirement and was going to be living in Xshire – get him whilst you can, he says. Now nearly all these people I mentioned to you I happen to hear are moving into the neighbourhood or approaching retirement.

It was suggested by the vice chancellor that the OUS had two groups of lay members – those still active in the employment market and retired members – and that the majority resided in the latter camp. A slightly different categorization was used by the registrar: in one camp, there are those 'with real clout' and business experience; and in the other camp are the local great and good, who have been associated with the university for a long period of time. In the latter camp, he put ex-graduates with modest careers and local people who are moving into retirement (such as school teachers) and want to help out. Although he suggested that individually members of this latter group were 'excellent people', they failed, unlike the business group, to bring that 'extra "added value" dimension' to the university.

The registrar emphasized that a substantial number of lay members at the OUS were involved in time-demanding committee work. He felt that the balance of retired members' involvement outweighed the contributions of those still actively employed. Since they had more time, he felt that retired people got 'more involved than is actually sensible in terms of their role'. He felt that in appointing committee members, standing committee of council, the body responsible, encountered a dilemma of trying to involve high-profile employed people with limited time or retired people who have more available time but less up-to-date expertise and interpersonal contacts.

For the registrar, there were clear, if informal, criteria used in trying to recruit these more active members. First, they should be usefully networked to external agencies, so that they can act as 'intelligence bridges' and provide influence outside the university; second, they should be able to act as consultants to the executive:

> They're people with real clout – they've got real experience. I don't think one uses them to persuade people internally as to what we ought to do. I think one is using them in two modes: one, in helping us externally in terms of opening the right doors and getting to know what's going on; and two, in terms of reflecting back internally and helping us to decide issues based on their own wisdom and understanding. They're actually pointing us in the right direction, if you had to pay for that it would cost you an arm and leg and he wouldn't necessarily be detached.

Recent appointments to the council reflected the application of the registrar's criteria. They included the chair of a government regulatory body and director of a national bank (a court appointee), a former senior civil servant (council appointee) and the chair of a public utility (council appointee). Such experience, it was contended, was highly valued because it brought independent judgement to bear on university business.

Selection criteria applied by the nominations committee at the OUN reinforced the emphasis found at the OUS on business experience and networking ability. Although an interest in the university and a willingness to serve on at least one of council's major committees was important, the registrar felt it vital that some members had financial and business acumen. In this category the OUN could claim a chair of a major international company, an ex-finance director of a national building society, a chair of a regional health authority and a chair of a national trade association.

Apart from wanting people who will make active 'business'-related contributions to the university, the chair of council suggested that they also sought people who would be 'sympathetic to academic purposes' and a collegiate managerial style:

> I think anyone who isn't sympathetic to academic points of view or the academic world is going to be uncomfortable on a council anyway. So we would try to find people who would start off with being sympathetic to academic purposes – if what you want to do is to put on someone whose avowed purpose is to sort those academics out then you can get conflicts arising. I wouldn't seek a member of council to do that – I think it's a waste of time and energy to set up conflicts deliberately, I think you do far better working with people. So we have, I suppose, probably self-selected to some degree people who will fit into a collegiate type of way of running the place.

A lay member commented that he felt that one's background in relation to other council members' experience was more important than 'committee style'. For example, someone with engineering or construction experience would complement someone with a legal or an accounting background. He also felt that anyone with a confrontational style would have been eliminated early on and prevented from participating in serious discussions.

The new universities

To what extent did approaches to independent governor appointments in the two new universities studied replicate the models adopted by the old universities? Our two case studies in the former PCFC sector suggest that approaches to appointments do not follow any clear distinction between old and new universities. On the contrary, one new university, the New University of the North (NUN), was much more closely aligned to the Old University of the North. The other, the New University of the South (NUS), was much closer in practice to the Old University of the South, although we do not in any way postulate a regional effect to explain the similarities between old and new in this respect.

Consider the case of the NUS first. As in all new universities, the process of appointing independent members is vested by statute in the hands of that same category of governors. The appointment procedures, however, were clearly still evolving. Just prior to the research the governors had experimented with an electoral system which was intended to introduce a greater semblance of democracy into the system. Under this system independent members put forward nominations, from which three or four key players then selected a dozen or so names. The remaining names were put forward to independent members for election by postal ballot. This process was put to the test but failed, it was claimed, because several individuals elected were unwilling or unavailable to stand as governors. The electoral system, therefore, was deemed impracticable owing to the voluntary nature of governorships. The idea of approaching candidates before an election to investigate their availability was thought untenable because, as one independent member suggested, it was unlikely that potential candidates would be interested in competing for governor positions.

In the wake of this failure, the board had reverted to the previous informal selection system, which by-passed a ballot and relied on a form of recommendation from a few key players. Yet the experimental 'democratic' system and the informal 'recommendation' system have elements in common. Initially, the chair and vice chancellor look at the balance and composition of the current body and identify main characteristics – in terms of gender, ethnicity, experience and expertise – that are missing from the current board. Independent members are then invited to put forward nominations. At the nomination stage, the vice chancellor admitted that he was able to, and did, exert considerable influence: 'I admit, and I think it's quite proper, that I put names up and I wind people up to put names up and I discourage them from putting other people – other names – up. But generally, the board of governors, it is their process.'

The danger of the informal system, as one independent governor admitted, was that it could lead to the rather desperate process of 'picking mates of ours'. In practice, the informal system depends on a few key players, two of whom are the chair and vice chancellor, making a selection, taking soundings and suggesting names to the independent governors. As the vice chancellor noted, this process gives him and the chair considerable influence over the selection procedure. The system, he claimed, remained tenable because it suited the institution and the 'style' of governance:

> The chairman and I negotiate the slate we want to put up and that happens on their [independent members'] blessing. But because of the political style in which we operate . . . we're just being realistic – it will certainly contain no one whom I'm not keen to have – but the names will not all be names that have originated from me.

An independent member suggested that the chair's personal integrity was largely responsible for the success of the informal selection procedure. It had, in his opinion, produced and maintained a very competent and satisfactory heterogeneous board. The vice chancellor admitted that his own views on who would make good governors had changed. In his younger, post-corporate, days he was of the mistaken impression that what were required were 'captains of industry'. He gradually came to the realization that having these 'regional big players' on the board was actually counter-productive, in that, first, they often did not have the necessary time to commit to meetings and other work, and, second, when they did attend they had a tendency to develop a disparaging attitude towards the mechanics of university governance. The fact that the board contained prominent trade union officials (NATFHE and UNISON) as staff members did little to improve this attitude on the part of some members from business backgrounds.

Confirming this problem, one independent governor said that he had experienced a form of 'culture shock' by the transition from attending commercial sector boards to the university board of governors; and he also admitted that initially these differences and the adjustment required to adapt to these differences had made him feel quite anxious:

> You know one is not familiar with the formality of that kind of an intellectual, academic board of governors – you know it's horribly like my worst fears of what the civil service must be like, with numbered papers and paragraph after paragraph with brilliantly written but turgid paperwork. There's no comparison with a board meeting in a commercially working environment in a medium-sized business. So that's very frightening in a funny sort of way.

The chair had been on the original formation committee and told us that he and the vice chancellor had considered candidates very carefully, taking into account that the institution was seeking to be a regional organization, wanted links with the further education sector and in some cases required international links. The chair also expressed a reservation in making selections based purely on business experience/expertise criteria, but felt that people with experience of managerial techniques were very useful:

> You need different skills you see, I don't think higher education is a business and I think it's wrong to regard it as that; on the other hand, I think it's wrong not to run it in a business-like manner. So people who have experience, whether it be trade unionists or big businessmen or whatever, who have experience of managerial techniques can be very valuable in their own right.

It was reiterated by an independent governor that the chair had been instrumental in ensuring that the board was composed of a wide cross-section of independent members who provided different perspectives and balance to ensure effective decision-making:

> It would have been very easy to pick independent members all from industry, all thrusting, sort of, you know, dynamic, cut the people out, we'll make some money stuff. So we didn't get into that trap – we've got a very good mix of people who have understanding, those that have been in the public sector and those that have been in different organizations, and so there is a good cross-section.

Compared to the informal and essentially 'closed' appointments procedure operated by the board of the NUS, the system encountered at the NUN
appeared far more open. All board members, including senior officers, at
the NUN were invited to make nominations. According to the instrument
and articles of government the appointing authority in relation to independent members is: (a) the full board, after approval has been gained from
independent members, if the appointment is made within three months;
and (b) the independent members, should the full board fail to make an
appointment within this duration.

Changes have also been made to the appointments procedure, which, we
were told by the clerk to the board, had previously operated 'behind closed
doors'. The board has now established a 'nominations committee' in order
to replenish the board of independent members. Membership of this committee consists of the chair of the board of governors, the vice-chair and
the principal, and it is served by the clerk to the board of governors. The
clerk notifies the committee when vacancies are coming on stream, and
the committee identifies particular characteristics required of potential
members.

The objective of the nominations committee is to ensure that the membership of the board is well balanced in terms of 'sectoral representation,
gender balance and functional balance' (expertise and experience in specialist areas such as finance, estates, accounts and personnel). These requirements are then put before the main board and ideas for potential
candidates are sought from both governors and senior executives (assistant
principals have been known to make suggestions).

The nomination committee endeavours to identify approximately ten
possible candidates and then attempts to make a selection from these 'nominations' based on the prescribed criteria given to the board. From the
interviews it is not entirely clear how selection decisions are reached, but
the principal told us that 'The chair and myself pick it up and look at them
in terms of the overall balance.' The chair added, somewhat ambiguously:
'we all keep some kind of check list and make it our business over a period
of six months or so to get to know the people on our own private check list
– nobody else sees it. So that we've got people who are being considered
at any time.'

Control of the selection process is retained by this small number of key
governors who make up the nomination committee. The clerk qualified
such a procedure by telling us that although the process was undertaken
'behind closed doors', a record is taken of the deliberations. When the
decision has been made the principal is asked to approach potential candidates informally, to see 'how keen they are, whether they understand the
role, and just what they would have to contribute.' Should candidates agree
to become governors they are then given extensive briefing sessions by the
clerk to the board. These sessions are intended to assist the candidates in
developing some understanding of what is required of them before they
attend their first meeting. It is only after they have agreed, in principle, to

become members that formal proposals for their appointment and details of their curricula vitae are put before the board for approval.

Essentially, although proposals are sought from the board and the senior executives, the final selection decision rests with the nomination committee. As the chair put it, 'It's not their [the board of governors'] decision – sorry it is their decision in a sense, it goes before the nomination group . . . the names then have to be put forward before the board of governors and approved or not approved.' It would seem unlikely, the procedure having advanced so far, that such recommendations received from the nomination committee would be rejected. As two governors noted:

> It's very much on the basis of your objecting or not to this individual. I mean obviously they're not presenting individuals who in themselves are inappropriate to be governors. Yes, proposals are put to the full board, but it would be quite a brave man who turned up and who would stand up and say, I don't think we ought to have X, he's not much use, is he? It's all terribly grab hands and thanks terribly much for your invaluable and wonderful service.

Despite structural arrangements designed to give the board and its independent members authority over appointment, in practice the power of appointment is located elsewhere. When officers were asked whether respondents thought that governors should actually be allowed to vote on these nominations, several objections were raised. It was pointed out, by the clerk to the board, for example, that appointment procedures were a 'delicate' matter, since 'these people are being invited to be on in their own right'. A staff member felt that elections could hinder the deliberate, and from her point of view successful,[2] attempt to achieve a balanced board membership. However, there are no formal legislative requirements to attain a 'balanced' board, since definitions of balance are left solely to the group responsible for selection. Thus, the few members selecting new appointees are given wide discretion over the composition of their governing bodies.

An illustration of the appointments procedure in practice can be gleaned from an independent governor's perceptions of how he came to be on the university's board of governors:

> Let me offer you my theory. Because this says something about how people get on governing bodies. I used to be a director of X, a company that was chaired by Y [also the chair of the university board of governors] . . . It was a company run by the local authority to develop its tourist profile. I was there for about two years. I went to one annual meeting and Y collared me in the corner, very embarrassed, and said, 'Z, I should have spoken to you earlier but you are not going to be a director of this company as from today.' I said, 'Why not?' He said, 'Well, we've had a meeting of a small group of directors and we've

decided to re-jig the company and reduce the number of directors and bring in A to chair it, and I'm resigning as well as you.' So we had a debate, a private conversation to make sure that another trade unionist got on instead of me ... And then Y said to me, very furtively, 'Don't worry, I've got something else in mind for you.' And a month later I was invited by B [the principal] to go and see him. He wouldn't say why he wanted me to go and see him but I guessed correctly that he invited me to become a member of the governing body of the university ... Now that's how you get on to these bodies, not because you represent anything but because some people who have the power to choose believe that you represent something they want. Which a lot of the times will get it right. But is it the right way to do it?

From this account it is clear that informal networks of existing key members are utilized quite extensively in selecting appropriate governors. This conclusion corresponds closely to a finding from a recent study of boards of directors in top British companies, which found that personal recommendation is a prerequisite for non-executives (Hill, 1995). According to another recent study, two-thirds of non-executive director appointments were made because candidates were known personally to the chair or other board members (PA Consulting Group and Sundridge Park Management Centre, cited in Further Education Unit, 1994). The selection procedures may be effective, undertaken with the best intentions and based primarily on rigorous achievement criteria; however, they are conducted in a 'closed' environment and are also clearly based on personal recommendations. Under such circumstances they are vulnerable to charges of subjectivity and prejudice – employing a range of filters that, intentionally or not, tend to assist in the selection of 'people like us'. Selection from these procedures will often be limited by the range of board members' informal networks and may result in a board where certain members are closely linked to each other through previous associations. Indeed, such factors may account for the under-representation of ethnic groups and women on university boards of governors.

In relation to the under-representation of these groups, it was pointed out to us that one of the recurring issues at the NUN concerning appointments is that of gender and ethnicity balance. Attempts have been made to rectify the imbalance, but they have on the whole been unsuccessful. Certain reasons for this relative lack of success were proffered. It was felt that the compilation of the nominations lists, which tend to consist of 'white men', was a reflection of the local business community. This community comprises the main catchment area of university governor candidates, since candidates from further afield would have less 'interest' in becoming a governor and those that did express an interest would probably experience difficulty in attending board and committee meetings. It was also felt by one governor that the issue was not perceived to be of high enough priority by the majority of governors to effect real change.

Conclusion

In order to ensure against patronage and the establishment of self-perpetuating oligarchies, both Cadbury and the CUC favour a system of checks and balances that relies on voluntary self-regulation by individual institutions rather than the imposition of national external legislation. Underlying this preference is a belief that self-regulation allows governing bodies to take account of institutional circumstances and needs and provides sufficient flexibility to allow institutions to adapt to a changing and competitive environment. However, in order for voluntary self-regulation to remain viable, it must, necessarily, be accompanied by the principles of openness and transparency.

These principles clearly apply to the procedures adopted with regard to the appointment of lay and independent members of governing bodies. Indeed, in the opinion of the Cadbury Committee, the establishment of a nominations committee is essential to protect the independent judgement exercised by non-executive directors and to prevent the self-perpetuation of oligarchic bodies.

The case studies provide some clear evidence of how these principles have been interpreted in terms of procedural arrangements and their operationalization. Only two governing bodies, the OUN and the NUN, had established nominations committees. At the former, the relevant committee – appointments to court and council – contained most of the personnel advocated by Cadbury and the CUC. Included in the roles of this committee was ensuring a wide trawl for potential members in the light of maintaining council balance. The NUN had made similar provision for ensuring that as far as possible appointments were made on merit rather than patronage. Here too the nominations committee, in theory at least, made appointment recommendations after due consideration had been given to the balance of the board, the needs of the university and the qualifications of nominees.

In contrast to these formal arrangements, neither the OUS nor the NUS had established nominations committees. In both institutions the evidence suggests that the governing bodies' role in appointing lay/independent members was limited. In effect, responsibility had been delegated to senior managers, led by the vice chancellor. In this informal process, selection of new governors depended on patronage and opportunism.

However, the differences between the two institutions with formal appointments committee and the two without should not be overdrawn. In practice the *processes* of seeking new members were remarkably similar in all four institutions. Even with formal committees in place, extensive use was made of existing members' informal networks via personal recommendations. Nor should it be assumed that without a nominations committee the governing body will inevitably be unbalanced and unrepresentative of a wide range of community interests. The case of the NUS clearly demonstrated the ability of the vice chancellor and chair of the governing body to appoint independent members from a range of backgrounds and so to widen the perspectives available to the board. More importantly perhaps, the processes involved in making lay/independent appointments to the governing bodies in each of the case studies appeared remarkably similar. Overall there was no conclusive evidence from the case studies that transparency is improved simply by the existence of an appointments committee.

Notes

1. To be fully quorate a board meeting must consist of ten members of whom six shall be independent members; and no decision can be deferred more than once under the latter condition.
2. In support of this claim the respondent pointed to the fact that the board had two governors who, although appointed on an individual rather than representational basis, were respectively a TUC delegate and a city councillor.

5

Governing Bodies: Roles and Organizational Structures

Since the mid-1980s the transformation in the scale and culture of British higher education has been extensive. A number of major changes in the way in which universities are organized and funded, together with growing emphasis on competitiveness and entrepreneurialism, have produced some basic shifts in operating patterns and the orientation of universities towards government, employers, students and the broader community. Responsiveness and flexibility, resourcefulness and efficiency have become the watchwords of a new era in which once taken for granted relationships within and without the university have been challenged and, in some cases, broken. As the need to compete and react with flexibility to new environments has increased, so new patterns of organizational authority and control have emerged.

The turbulance of the university environment and the need to implement and, critically, to monitor effectively the new structures being introduced can scarcely be ignored by governing bodies. As we have seen, part of the response at institutional level has been deliberately to increase participation in the governance process by those whose experience in business and commerce is seen as equipping them with the necessary skills to embrace the new cultures and operational imperatives of the mass university. Yet what evidence is there that the structures and cultures of the governance process itself have moved on from previous eras, when universities had far less need to be innovative and competitive or when their identities and reputations were less scrutinized by politicians and the broader society? This question relates to the time, skills and responsibilities required by governors in a period of rapid institutional change and is all the more relevant as the demands on governors themselves increase. Rising expectations from government and the community of what is expected of those who take on the role of governors contribute to the burdens of this form of public office. So too do the statutory responsibilities on governors for the control of public monies.

The need to exercise these responsibilities conscientiously and accept the burdens associated with wider tests of accountability is only part of the governor's task. Institutions increasingly engage in more complex funding and finance arrangements and are expected to develop detailed strategies for corporate, financial, human and physical resources. At the same time, they are becoming more entrepreneurial and market-oriented (Smith *et al.*, 1995). As the complexities of the task of leadership, control and monitoring rise, can it be reasonable to expect the role of governors to remain static? In this new environment, what are the levels of attendance and commitment required by university governors; what levels of 'knowledge' do they require; how and by what channels is the institutional and system-wide information which contributes to that knowledge channelled to them; and how important are the various activities and roles undertaken by governors?

This chapter draws extensively on our research data to aid an exploration of these questions. In the first section we consider the results of our questionnaire survey of governors' activities, roles and perceptions of the activities of university governance. In the second we explore the organizational features of the governing bodies encountered during our case study research. Our intention is both to describe and to explain how organizational structures articulate with the concept of lay participation in the governance process. The important position of the lay element of governing bodies within the statutory framework was emphasized in Chapter 4. Here we switch the focus to explore how the formal structures of university governance accommodate these elements in terms of influence and decision-making.

Certainly, the lay and independent members, by virtue of their majority on the governing body, are allocated a 'controlling' function. But how is this function exercised? To what extent is it mediated by the interventions of other, non-independent, governors? And does the committee system, itself an integral part of the day-to-day functioning of university governance, have the effect of elevating certain governors into key players at the same time as marginalizing others? In exploring these questions, we seek to interpret how university governing bodies handle their activities. In the next chapter we attempt to relate organizational structure to decision-making processes.

Governors' roles and activities

Roles

In attempting to elucidate meaningful information from governors about their roles, we decided to provide respondents to the questionnaire with a range of structured responses. Governors were invited to rank these roles in order of importance. Eight possible roles were identified, which we felt relevant to the task of governance. Five of these – strategic, audit, supervisory, managerial and appeals roles – concern the internal functioning of the organization. Two – representative and negotiating roles – concern the institution's relationship with its external environment. The final role – support – straddles the internal and external environments.

Brief definitions of each role were included for the benefit of respondents. We defined governors' strategic role as taking responsibility for determining the institution's strategic mission. Guaranteeing the institution's financial and organizational integrity relates to their audit role. Governors' supervisory role concerned their relationship with chief executives and other senior managers. A related, but separate, managerial role is also performed by involvement in staff appointments and the fixing of performance-related pay. Governor involvement in hearing appeals and settling disputes appeared to us to represent a further role. Representative roles were taken to mean ensuring that local and regional voices in the broader community are heard, while negotiating involves handling links with external bodies, such as further education colleges, schools and other organizations in the public and private sectors. It involves both the provision of technical advice internally and lobbying on behalf of the institution externally.

Governors were asked to rank these roles in two ways: first, in order of importance; second, in terms of time spent undertaking each role. Comparison of the mean ranking of each role has been used to order these roles according to how governors see them. The results are shown in Figure 5.1.

Figure 5.1 shows clearly that governors rank their roles in the same order for importance and time spent on each role. Governors clearly consider their strategic role as by far the most important, and one that they feel they spend the most time on. Audit stands as the second most important role, with supervision (of management), support (on behalf of the institutions) and representation (of local community and business) considered as fairly equal in terms of both importance and time spent. Managerial, appeal and negotiating roles appeared the three least important and time-consuming as far as governors are concerned.

Given the increasing burdens and responsibilities being placed on governors, we also asked them to indicate whether, in terms of importance, they expected their roles to increase, remain unchanged or diminish. Their responses are illustrated in Figure 5.2.

For six of the eight identified roles, a majority of governors anticipated that their importance would remain unchanged. However, there were two exceptions to this perception. First, the majority, nearly 60 per cent, of governors anticipated that their role in strategic direction would increase. The second exception, where governors were almost equally divided between thinking this role would increase in importance and remain unchanged, was support (equal third in order of importance rankings). The 'internal' representative role was the third most likely to increase in importance (also equal third in ranking order), although a larger proportion of respondents felt that this role was likely to remain unchanged. The fourth role that respondents thought was likely to increase in importance was audit (38 per cent), although almost 60 per cent of respondents felt that this was likely to remain unchanged. Few governors anticipated diminishing importance

Figure 5.1 Ranking of roles (in order of importance and time spent) for all respondents.

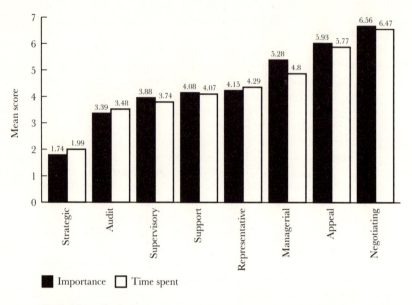

Definition of roles
Strategic: taking responsibility for determining the institution's strategic mission.
Audit: guaranteeing the institution's financial and organizational integrity.
Supervisory: supervising chief executive and other senior managers.
Support: lobbying on behalf of the institution and/or giving technical advice.
Representative: ensuring that local/regional and community/business voices are heard.
Managerial: appointing staff, fixing performance-related pay.
Appeal: settling disputes and hearing appeals.
Negotiating: handling links with other bodies such as the National Health Service,
    Training and Enterprise Councils, further education institutions and schools.

for any of their roles. The role that the largest number of governors thought would diminish was supervisory, 13 per cent indicating that this was likely to be the case. However, a greater proportion (19 per cent) felt that this role was likely to increase in importance and almost 70 per cent felt that it would remain unchanged.

These findings provide some evidence to indicate that governors do not see their role as being confined to institutional monitoring. The prominence of taking an active role in determing the institution's strategic mission suggests that the discourse and practice of strategy has become deeply entrenched in higher education. It also raises important questions about how active a role in this particular area governors actually play. We return to these questions in subsequent chapters. At this stage it is sufficient to note that governor participation in strategy formulation may still be confined to

Figure 5.2 Expected change of importance for governance roles.

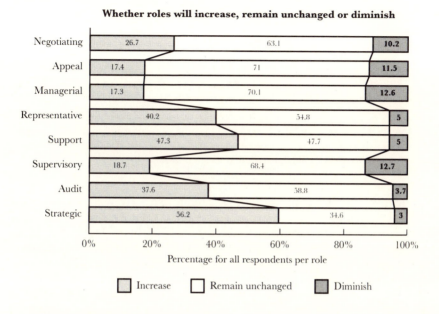

Whether roles will increase, remain unchanged or diminish

Percentage for all respondents per role

☐ Increase   ☐ Remain unchanged   ▨ Diminish

overseeing strategy development rather than devising policy. It also needs stressing that these are governors' perceptions of the relative importance of their own roles. As such, they may not accurately represent the extent of their contribution to each role.

Activities

The performance of governors' roles can take place in two forms. The first is by participation in formal meetings, including both full meetings of the governing body and the meetings, often much less formal, of various sub-committees to which governors may be attached. The second is by participation in activities outside of formally convened meetings. Some of these activities may be formal, such as participation in ceremonies or taking part in deputations and official visits. Others may be informal, such as meeting staff, students or other governors, and involve the development of governors' own personal networks both professionally and socially. By definition, the latter are more difficult to identify and quantify, even if in practice they prove highly influential to the governance process. In this section, however, we concentrate on the formal elements of both meetings and activities outside meetings.

Attendance at meetings
Governors were asked to specify approximately how many meetings of the governing body and its sub-committees they were eligible to attend and

Table 5.1 Attendance level at meetings by type of member (percentages)

Attendance level (per cent)	Type of member		
	External member	Internal member	Total
≤50	7.9	3.1	6.5
51–75	23.2	9.4	19.1
76–99	44.7	23.4	38.4
100	24.2	64.1	36.0
Total no.	302	128	430

Pearson chi-square 0.00000, d.f.3, correlation 0.38, no. missing 64.

actually did attend during the past academic year. From these responses, individual attendance rates were calculated and then aggregated into four categories. Over the whole sector, governors claimed high attendance records, with only 7 per cent of respondents admitting to attending 50 per cent or less of meetings. The largest proportion of governors, almost 40 per cent, claimed an attendance level of between 76 and 99 per cent, while over one-third of members said they had attended all meetings to which they had been invited or were eligible to attend. The remaining one-fifth of members attended between 51 and 75 per cent of meetings.

There were no significant differences in attendance levels between governors of different types of institution. However, internal members had a better attendance level than external members: almost two-thirds of internal members claimed a 100 per cent attendance level, compared with only one-quarter of external members. Almost one-third of external members had an attendance level of 75 per cent or below, compared with just over 10 per cent of internal members (see Table 5.1).

Despite the differences in attendance levels between internal and external governors, the results reveal a picture of fairly conscientious commitment as measured by attendance. Given the voluntary nature of participation in governance, the results confirm the strength of this tradition within civil society. Given also the representational role attached to internal membership of governing bodies, the fact that attendance should be generally higher than among lay governors is perhaps not surprising. However, in order to gauge the level of commitment required by attendance at formal meetings, we asked governors to indicate approximately how many meetings of council/governing body and of its sub-committees they were eligible to attend during the previous academic year. These details are provided in Table 5.2.

Before aggregation into categories, the largest proportion of respondents, at 13 per cent, specified that they were eligible to attend six meetings in the past academic year. These would probably include three meetings of the main governing body, which usually meets once an academic term, and would allow for three meetings of a sub-committee. Categorization of the

Table 5.2 Number of meetings respondents were eligible to attend and actually attended

Number of meetings	Eligible to attend (per cent)	Actually attended (per cent)
≤2	8.3	12.9
3–5	20.3	26.4
6–10	39.7	38.5
11–15	17.6	11.6
16–20	6.5	5.7
21–30	5.0	3.1
>30	2.6	2.6
Number	459	455

data into the groups shown in Table 5.2 revealed that the largest proportion of governors (almost 40 per cent) were eligible to attend between six and ten meetings in the past academic year. From Table 5.2 we can see that almost 86 per cent of members were eligible to attend 15 or fewer meetings and that almost 80 per cent of members actually attended ten meetings or fewer. For most governors, the number of meetings to which they were entitled to attend was about right. A large majority (84 per cent) indicated that they would not change the number of meetings.

In order to assess the amount of time governors devote to their governance role, we asked them to specify how many days in a month, excluding time spent in attendance at formal meetings, they spent on their role as members of the governing body. The largest proportion of governors, just over a quarter, specified that they spend one day a month (excluding time spent in formal meetings) in their role as governing body member. However, another quarter of members said that they spend no extra time on their role outside of formal meetings. Indeed, 70 per cent of respondents spend one extra day or less a month in their role as governor. Of the remaining 30 per cent of members, half spend more than one day and up to two extra days a month. Nearly one-third of old university members spend no extra time outside of meetings, compared with only half that proportion from the new universities and one-quarter from all higher education colleges. New university members were more likely than old university and higher education college members to spend greater amounts of extra time in performing their governing body role.

Activities outside formal meetings

Apart from attendance at meetings, university governors spend their time on at least four other formal activities. These are talking to students and staff, visiting units and departments within the institution, representing the university on other external bodies and engaging in ceremonial work as representatives of the governing body. Governors were asked to rank these

Table 5.3 Activities ranked in order of importance and time spent

Rank in order of importance			Rank in order of time spent		
Ranking	Activity	Mean score	Ranking	Activity	Mean score
1st	Talking to students/staff	1.58	1st	Talking to students/staff	1.63
2nd	Visiting units and departments	1.74	2nd	Visiting units and departments	2.08
3rd	Representing institutions on other bodies	3.05	3rd	Ceremonies	2.71
4th	Ceremonies	3.28	4th	Representing institutions on other bodies	3.32

in order of importance and in order of time spent on each activity. These rankings were analysed by calculating their mean scores and then by placing them in ascending order. The overall results for all respondents are shown in Table 5.3.

There is a correspondence between the first two activities in terms of importance and time spent relative to other activities; that is, the activities of 'talking to students and staff' and 'visiting departments' were considered the two most important and time-consuming. However, the last two activities, representation and ceremony, are ranked inversely in terms of the criteria of importance and time consumption. Although respondents ranked 'representing institutions on other bodies' as the third most important, they felt that they spent less time on this activitiy than the less important one of 'attending ceremonies'.

We examined whether different types of member had ranked these activities in different orders of importance and time spent in conducting them. Results from a non-parametric test allowed us to verify that there were group differences in ranking orders. The means for all sub-groups were calculated, and the results of this analysis are shown in Figure 5.3.

Figure 5.3 reveals differences between external and internal members' views on the importance and time taken over the four activities. In terms of importance, external members paired the four activities, thereby creating only two ranks. That is, 'talking to students/staff' and 'visiting units and departments' were ranked as equally the most important activities, while 'representing the institution on other bodies' and 'ceremonies' were also ranked equally least important. In terms of the amount of time expended on these activities, external members' scores produced three rankings. It would seem that external members spend about the same and most time on 'visiting departments' and 'talking to staff and students', while 'ceremonies' ranked third on time expenditure and the least amount of time was spent 'representing the university/college on other bodies'.

Figure 5.3 Ranking of activities (in order of time and importance), by type of member.

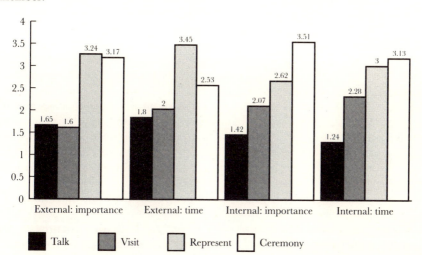

Mean scores for internal members, on the other hand, produced far more segregated rankings in respect of the importance of the four activities. They viewed 'talking to students and staff' as the most important activity. 'Visiting departments' rated second. Unlike external members, internal members thought that 'representing the institution on other bodies' was more important than participation in ceremonies. The rankings on time spent on the four activities mirrored the order of importance, although 'representing the institution' and 'ceremonies' were almost equal in terms of time consumption.

In summary, internal members made a greater distinction between the 'ceremonial' and 'external representative' activities of governors, perceiving the latter activity to be far more important than the former, although both groups agreed that the most important activities were 'talking to staff and students' and 'visiting departments'. The findings may be interpreted as suggesting that more time than is warranted in terms of perceived importance is spent on 'ceremonial' activities; and that, from the perspective of internal members, insufficient time may be given to external liaison functions.

Information: quality and relevance

In previous chapters, reference has been made to the concept, developed by Giddens (1984), of knowledgeable actors. Given the importance attached to lay participation in the governance process, how knowledgeable about higher education institutions and the broader system processes do governors need to be? Analysis of the backgrounds of governors has already revealed their strong associations with business and the professions, and it is safe to assume that they bring with them fairly detailed and specialized bodies of knowledge from their own particular fields. Indeed, our research revealed that in seeking out 'suitable' citizens to recruit as governors, institutional and governing body leaders will apply quite instrumentalist criteria to the selection process which assesses the skills and contacts – in effect, other forms of knowledge – of possible candidates. Testing directly the educational knowledge of governors, particularly those from outside education, was, we felt, inappropriate and quite likely to be misleading. However, we were able to establish some of the views about higher education and its management held by governors, and these are reported separately in Chapter 3. Our concern in this section is to establish members' views about the quality and relevance of the information that is channelled to them by the institution itself. Such information, whatever the particular conduits deployed, is likely to contribute both directly and indirectly to governors' knowledge, and so, in turn, have an important bearing on their ability to perform their various roles.

Respondents were asked questions regarding both the quantity of information they received from senior managers and chief executives and its relevance for dealing with specific issues. Almost 70 per cent of members thought that the amount of information they received was about right. One-fifth of respondents thought that there was too much and just over 10 per cent thought there was too little information. Differences were found between types of member. In both cases, the largest proportion of respondents (over 60 per cent) thought that the information received was about right. However, external members were more likely than internal members to hold this view. External members were more likely than internal members to think that there is too much information and internal members were more likely than external members to think that there is too little information (details are shown in Appendix 2).

Respondents were asked if they were generally satisfied with the relevance of the briefing information provided by the chief executive and senior managers in order to deal with specific issues. Overall, the largest proportion of respondents were satisfied, while 23 per cent were very satisfied. However, a quarter of respondents had mixed feelings and 8 per cent were dissatisfied with the information.

Figure 5.4 reveals differences in attitude between types of member. Although the majority of both types of members were satisfied with the information, external members were more likely than internal members to be satisfied with the information (a percentage difference of 21 per cent). Of those respondents who had mixed feelings or were dissatisfied – these were more likely to be internal than external members.

Organizational styles

The results of the questionnaire survey convey a fairly clear picture of how governors see their roles in terms of importance and time spent on them,

Figure 5.4 Satisfaction with relevance of information, by members.

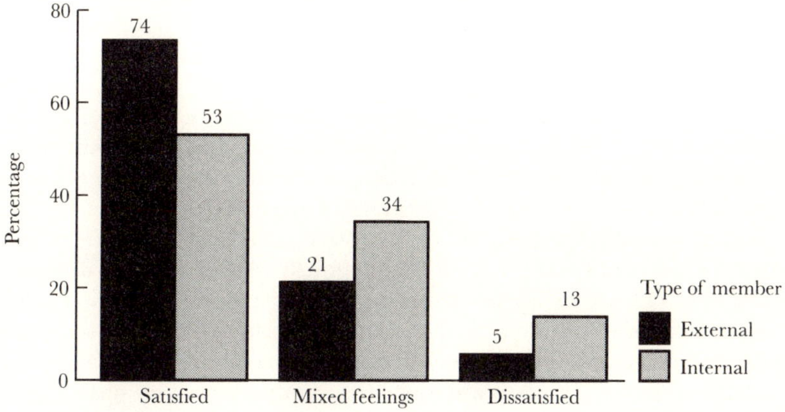

Pearson chi-square 0.00000, d.f.2, correlation 0.225, no. missing 13, total no. 481.

which roles they think are likely to increase in importance in the future and the range of activities, in addition to formal meetings, they engage in as university governors. However, in order to understand more fully how these roles and activities are activated and the work of the governing body accommodated within the broader structures of the university's decision-making processes, we needed to examine in greater depth the organizational arrangements devised for governing bodies. For example, we have already referred to the formal meetings, which, governors indicated, tend to dominate the time allocated to governance work. Yet formal meetings, held several times in the academic year, may offer governors very little real opportunity to become actively involved in the roles that they consider to be important. In this section, therefore, we consider in greater depth the formal organizational structure devised by the universities in our case studies for the purposes of institutional governance. Of particular interest is the part played by the sub-committee structure within the broader decision-making process. From interview data and observation, we have been able to construct reasonably comprehensive accounts of the way in which the committee system works and how decision-making takes place. As in the previous chapter, the analysis attempts to uncover any significant differences between the old and new universities. We begin with the former.

The old universities

In both of the old universities studied, most of the ground work behind the ultimate approval of policies is done at committee stage. Consider the OUS first. Here there were three main committees: the standing committee of council, the planning and resources committee and the university management committee. The latter two committees were joint committees of council and senate and were in the process of being amalgamated into the policy and resources committee. From the committee flowchart, it can be ascertained that all council sub-committees and some joint council and senate sub-committees report to the policy and resources committee, which in turn reports to standing committee of senate and direct to council.

From the point of view of the council, the standing committee is the most important of these committees. As one staff member observed, 'It is really the power.' Standing committee's membership consists of the chair of council, vice-chair of council, vice chancellor, treasurer and two deputy vice chancellors. The three lay members of this committee are effectively the core members of the full council; and this committee pre-digests issues and effectively leads council by making firm policy recommendations. The vice-chancellor was careful to point out that council was not just 'a passive rubber-stamping body': even though standing committee 'always got its way', council could, and sometimes did, give the 'front bench quite a hard time'.

This 'front bench', according to a staff member in the old university council, consisted of the core members mentioned above, with the addition of the finance officer and the registrar. He felt that in full meetings of the council, 'the front bench' were too active in steering debate. In this respect, he thought that the spatial arrangements of council meetings assisted this front bench domination and effectively inhibited debate. Front bench 'members' face the rest of council, who are seated in rows opposite the bench, thus creating a rather hierarchical structure whereby members may feel of lesser status. A member described the arrangements:

> It's a room with a long front bench where all the big wigs sit and then the rest of the council sit in rows behind – facing down to the front bench. It's actually the senate room. It has actually occurred to me that having the senior officers there – given that council is supposed to be the decision-making body – having the officers there gives them a real unfair advantage and that really they should sit and speak when they're spoken to.
>
> I think they should speak when they are spoken to, you know, answer questions but not take such an active role in the debate, because otherwise they are actually steering the debate. And I often wondered how our meetings would be different if it wasn't a top bench model, so it wouldn't be like a one way conversation to the front all the time – there'd actually be more debate because people would be more on an equal level.

Another staff member thought that standing committee of council performed a very necessary and important role in pre-digesting and debating issues. However, he felt that a balance had to be found between a pre-digested, fully structured meeting which tends to stifle debate and one that is so unstructured it ventures on anarchy:

I mean, the standing committee is very necessary and important but can be dangerous – because, of course, they can sort out everything and just present a picture and they can stifle debate and discussion . . . And that's bad – that's not to my mind democracy – you've got to get a two-way dialogue. So it's a matter of having a balance between something which you've pre-digested and partly structured – otherwise it would be anarchy and chaos – as opposed to something which is so well structured that you're just sitting there lecturing to them for one or two hours and then they all go away.

It was also pointed out that should one want to influence an issue in any particular direction then the right people must be approached before it gets to council. In other words, council was not the correct forum for disputing recommendations from standing committee and by the time issues arrive at council there is very little room for manoeuvre:

A number of us try and stand up and make speeches in council and point out various things and in some cases it's taken quite seriously, and in other cases where the chairman of council . . . who is not as bad as he could be, I mean some chairs of council are real strong industrialists, our fellow used to be a labour councillor, for example, . . . but when he chairs those meetings he's very tough from the chair, and he shoots people down – you know, even quite senior professors that have stood up and challenged something that standing committee of council have recommended get shot, in the nicest possible way. So it is actually not a forum for having these debates. I think if there are issues, we have to operate in other ways – you know, lobbying, writing to people, trying to get to senior academics, so that even before it gets to council things have been altered. I don't think council itself is actually all that, you know, it's not really interested in making policy decisions – it's a rubber stamping body, I think.

Respondents interviewed at this old university were clearly of the view that the so-called 'front bench' governors acted as the 'core' members of the governing body. Their status was conferred by membership of the standing committee, which played a pivotal role within the committee structure and in 'controlling' the full council. Respondents also emphasized that in effect council acted essentially as an 'approving' body, rather than one in which policy is initiated and formulated.

To what extent was this model of governance replicated at the second old university? At the OUN the equivalent committee to the OUS's standing committee was the policy and resources committee (PRC). Membership of this committee consisted of five lay governors (including the chair and treasurer of council), five academics and three senior academic officers (vice chancellor, deputy vice chancellor and pro vice chancellor). The terms of reference of the PRC were clear: to be responsible for the formulation and coordination of planning and resource allocation across the whole university. Firm recommendations, which are usually approved, are made by this committee to council. The registrar described arrangements in the following terms:

> You need to take account of the fact that council has a number of absolutely key committees, of which I suppose the most important is the policy and resources committee, which I think the membership is about half and half lay members and academic members. And that's the body that basically determines how the university's resources should be deployed in broad terms – it keeps its vision on the financial policy, it regulates the university's financial situation and it advises council through its minutes as to what it thinks should be the most appropriate strategy. It would be unusual for council to take a different view from the one that was being recommended by the policy and resources committee.

The importance of PRC recommendations at the OUN was, in the registrar's opinion at least, derived from the power and political weight within the institution of its members. He continued:

> In other words, council wouldn't, well that's not to say it couldn't, but thus far it has not said, well, we totally disagree with the view that's been taken by the policy and resources committee on this and our view is that much more money should go into the fabric of the place and less money should go to academic side. I think this is one of the reasons why the system works – because council has got important membership on these key committees. By and large they work very well, their recommendations are clearly sensible.

The vice chancellor, in a separate interview, confirmed the significance of the PRC and the key role played by lay governors:

> The crucial value of the council doesn't actually lie in the council itself, in my judgement – as a new boy. The crucial function of council is that it has on it a number of people who work in lower committees and that isn't window dressing, that isn't nominal representation, they work. And in crucial decision-making committees we nearly always have members of council – the best example is the policy and resources committee, in which we have four senior members of council, all of whom are enormously experienced in business terms . . . Now those four people, five actually, are immensely valuable on that committee and that is the main committee for distributing resources.

The principal concern of the PRC is prioritizing investments rather than scrutinizing the management of accounts (a task undertaken by a sub-committee of the PRC). Decisions are then taken regarding future developments; for example, a choice between more academic staff or promotions. The chair of council felt that most of his and the PRC's time is spent

ensuring that income and expenditure flows are synchronized and that
there is enough room to manoeuvre should income fail to materialize.

The vice chancellor reinforced the chair's view, seeing the PRC as the
'principal source of proposals to council'. The committee functions as a
first line of consideration for proposals, which are properly scrutinized by
experienced people, and if they pass this stage they would be 'well on their
way for approval' (lay member of the PRC). Thus, many proposals from
other committees of council go to the PRC for recommendation to council.
This process was thought to combine the need to accomplish effective
decision-making with the recognition of, and respect for, more traditional
modes of consultation. A lay member of council and the PRC confirmed
custom and practice in this respect:

> Everything comes up to council eventually for the final approval, but
> a lot of things go through the PRC first. For example, certain things
> of college and catering will go through PRC. If the PRC says 'Yes, that's
> a good idea', and recommend it to council, then – it's certainly not a
> rubber stamp at council – but clearly the approval of PRC carries a lot
> of weight. Its the first line of consideration. If it gets through there, I
> wouldn't say it's rubber stamped at all, but it's certainly well on the
> way.

The pre-eminent role of the PRC within the governance process of the
OUN gave it the appearance of an executive body, in effect running the
university. This interpretation was rejected by the chair of the council. In
his view a balance had to be struck between 'a reasonable attempt to get
consensus with a process of actually getting decisions taken.' Academic
membership of this key committee certainly outnumbered lay membership
and, as the chair of council also observed, the committee was chaired by the
vice chancellor. These constitutional arrangements and a less formal reliance on the priority of academic principles in the deliberations of the
committee were held by the chair of the council and other governors to be
instrumental in controlling any excessive executive tendencies.

The new universities

Committee arrangements at both new universities mirrored to a considerable extent those found at the old. Both had developed 'executive' style
committees of council, whose members acted effectively as an inner cabinet
within the governance process. But there were a number of differences
between the case studies. Committee arrangements at one of the new universities, the NUS, resembled those found in the old universities.

Three broad groups of governors were identified by respondents at the
southern new university: internal members (made up of staff and students),
the core of independent members closest to the key players and the remaining independent members. Both explicit and implicit references were

made to these three groups, and they can be briefly described as: (a) a caucus of internal members, consisting of staff and student governors; (b) an inner cabinet or 'in-crowd' of independent members who constituted the chairman's coordinating committee (CCC), consisting of the chair of governors, deputy chair of governors, treasurer and chair of personnel committee (and, mentioned less frequently, the chair of property development committee); and (c) an 'out-crowd' of independent members who were far less involved at the policy formulation/negotiating stages.

One staff governor actually categorized the three sets of governors in almost identical terms:

> I suppose my view of it is that there are three fairly distinct groups of governors. There's the staff governors who . . . tend to act as a little bit of a caucus. There's the in-crowd of independent governors who tend to be chair, vice-chair, chairs of sub-committees. And then there's the out-group of independent governors – who most of the time haven't got a clue what's going on, who turn up at meetings, never say anything and sometimes will say to me afterwards I don't know why I come to this meeting, I've got nothing to contribute.

The 'inner cabinet' of independent governors most closely resembles those lay members on the standing committee of the OUS and the PRC at the OUN. Like their counterparts in the old universities, these core members are formally recognized in constitutional terms, since they are the members of the CCC. 'The real power within the institution', an independent governor observed, 'is with the chairman's coordinating committee – it's not with the board of governors, the board of governors is a rubber stamp.'

The CCC normally meets once a term to deal with industrial relations and confidential financial matters. Neither students nor staff are represented. However, the chair of the board was keen to emphasize that, although the CCC fulfils the legal requirements under the articles to operate a confidential committee, dealing with issues such as contracts and land transactions, every effort was made to operate as openly as possible. To this end the board of governors had two other related committees – the finance committee and the personnel committee – to which both staff and students were admitted. He felt that these committees served an important two-way function of: first, keeping staff and students informed of new policies and the reasoning behind such policies; and, second, acting as a feedback mechanism for staff and students to voice any matters of concern. 'We try to operate as publicly as we can, as openly as we can', the chair remarked:

> We try to keep staff and students informed. I'm very keen on this because I feel it's far better – if you want to do something – it's far better that they know what you're doing and why rather than just impose it on them. So although the act and articles say we've got to have a committee of independent members who are responsible for matters of personnel and finance – that is the CCC, and it carries out

the legal functions – but we also have a finance committee to which staff and students are admitted and a personnel committee, although we're thinking of streamlining that . . . We also have, for example, a student affairs committee, where we meet and all the top brass turn up – myself, deputy vice chancellors and so on – and students can raise anything that can't be dealt with through ordinary channels. And on the whole we have very little trouble with either staff or students, despite the difficulties.

The vice chancellor was also keen to stress that, although the membership of the CCC consisted solely of the key independent governors, it should not be viewed as an executive committee and did not operate as an executive body. In his opinion, if any group could be described as 'the executive committee of the university', then it would have to be the directorate who could be more accurately described as 'the accountable executive'. In the vice chancellor's view, the executive is accountable not only to the governing body but also to elected members of faculty:

The price that the fleet footed executive must pay is to be accountable . . . No member of the executive, a head of department, a dean, can chair a faculty board. The head of the faculty board is an elected heavyweight 'back catcher' and they don't have any executive powers, but they have the powers to call the persons . . . for an explanation, they can put the spotlight on the executive – they do see their role as being to monitor whether the executive is executing the agreed policy. So we do attempt to be fleet footed . . . it's supposed to be reflected in our select committee type of arrangements and so on, and because that's the rhetoric, we never had a problem on almost anything. And the expectation would be that between meetings . . . and the chief route that I look to would be the chairman, the vice chairman the lay treasurer, depending on what type of issue – if it's about terms and conditions and whether to act on a recommendation from the employer's board it's the chair of personnel – but if there's any board of governors laying on of hands in blessing or approval of, its done by a group of four.

From this quote, we can also ascertain that the vice chancellor uses these key members from the CCC (between meetings) as a sounding board to establish the acceptability of following certain policies and strategies of implementation.

For one staff governor, however, the CCC was definitely an executive committee. In his view, the CCC sometimes exceeded its terms of reference when making decisions on issues which should be brought to full governors' meetings. When this view was expressed, the chair of the board reassured him that each issue had been carefully considered with due regard to the terms of reference of the CCC. This particular governor accepted the chair's integrity in policing policy decisions at the CCC. However, he was more perturbed by the informal than formal influence of the CCC:

There's no doubt that it has become an executive, but when I com-
plain, as I have done at about 20 different governors meetings, I am
always assured that the chair looked very carefully at the issues, that
policy decisions were not taken unless they were strictly within their
terms of reference ... But it's undoubtedly used as a sounding board
by the directorate to see what issues will get through governors and
which ones won't, and staff members are excluded from that. I think
the difficulty is that the membership of the coordinating committee,
with all the heavyweight governors on it, means that inevitably if that
group sit down and discuss anything, whether it's with or without a
formal decision, it does then set the tone and the direction for future
decision-making.

This staff governor accepted, however, that in order to avoid untenable
conflicts of interest, staff members should be excluded from discussions
relating to terms and conditions of employment (although he also observed
that, as a dean, his position as a governor could sometimes be compromised
by the knowledge that if he was publicly to make the life of the executive
too difficult, then such action could have repercussions for his faculty).

The clerk to the board felt that other governors listened closely to the
staff and student governors, partly because of their long-standing contributions to the board of governors, their personalities, their knowledge of the
university and mode of articulation of that knowledge, and also, in the case
of the student representative, 'because there are 17,500 individuals behind
that person'. He felt that staff governors were used extensively as 'informal
grapevines' to discover the perspective and strength of feeling of the academic community on certain issues. Moreover, it was clear from the interviews that the chair's role was vital in this respect. There was no evidence
of any discrimination between different types of governor, the chair himself remarking that 'as far as I'm concerned a member's a member's a
member.'

Despite the important differences in constitutional arrangements for
governance between the old and new universities, our analysis of committee
arrangements at the NUS portrays a picture very similar to that found at
both old universities. At all three institutions there is evidence to suggest
the existence of a supreme executive body 'leading' the governance of each
institution. In each case, however, the executive role is tacit rather than
formal, while considerable care is taken to ensure that wider constituencies
within the university community are not ignored. This was true even at the
NUS, where the independent members form a core group on the CCC.
Nevertheless, it is equally clear that the constitutional arrangements of the
new universities in particular allow sharper divisions between independent
(and co-opted) members on the one hand and staff and student members
on the other to be enshrined in committee arrangements. As our final case
study makes clear, where this happens the results can be divisive indeed.

The board of governors at the New University of the North (NUN) had recently revised the committee structure by merging three sub-committees (staff affairs, finance and general purposes, and buildings) into one finance, employment and general purposes committee (FEGP). Henceforth, membership of this new committee was defined 'solely by the exclusion of the internal members'; that is, it was composed of a large sub-group of the board, comprising all the independent members and principal. Staff governors claimed that, with the creation of this committee, the locus of decision-making shifted away from the main board, thereby decreasing their influence and participation in the decision-making process. They now see themselves as non-participants in the wider governance process.

Justifications for the establishment of the FEGP committee have been made in terms of facilitating an 'integrated' approach to planning and development, improving supervision of management and providing space on the main board agenda in order to debate larger strategic issues. Both the secretariat and the chair of governors reasoned that such an approach was necessary because of the inter-relatedness of every item of policy. It was also claimed that the background of most independent members prevented them making decisions on proposals that had not been sufficiently contextualized. The clerk to the board explained the logic behind the changes in the following terms:

> If we go to the governors with ideas for – we've had one recently – an early retirement scheme, they just will not look at an early retirement scheme in isolation. So each item of policy we give them has got to be properly set in the wider context. So early retirement has got to be set in the context of the academic profile we want to achieve, the staff we've got already, the tools we've got at our disposal actually to change that profile, what we think government policy is going to be like, whether we've actually got a chance of increasing our research funding. If you don't give them the information in that comprehensive form, their background won't allow them to make decisions out of context. So very often a policy proposal, if it's not properly contextualized, will be referred back for more work.

Thus, the creation of the FEGP is presented as a rational programme designed to achieve an integrated planning objective. Restructuring of committees was also intended to improve overall board-level effectiveness by creating clear functional distinctions between the board and its committees. The FEGP was to take major responsibility for supervisory activities, which would in turn create agenda space and time for the full board to discuss the larger issues of strategic direction. Initially, the supervision of management performance was carried out by the whole board at full governors' meetings. This practice, it was claimed, had proved inappropriate, since it was discovered that detailed probing of management performance was being impeded by the presence of staff and student governors. The chair of the board was unequivocal that on these grounds alone the changes had been essential:

You find yourself as a lay governor wanting to ask questions of the management which it's rather difficult to ask in the presence of their employees or the students. So that tends to limit how much probing you can do. On the other hand, we had, we tried to avoid that with committees – one of which dealt with finance, one of which dealt with property, one of which dealt with employment – even that didn't work very well because if ever two issues were closely linked, then finance was linked with employment and every financial decision you had has an implication. So what we actually created was a finance, employment and general purposes committee bringing all those things together, which consisted only of the lay governors and they sit with the management team – and they're the ones who ask the detailed pointed questions about the plans for achieving the strategic objectives, what the detailed statistics show. And the aim would be that because we've put that to the FEGP committee we wouldn't need to lumber the governing body with all that detail.

Effectively, therefore, this restructuring removed supervisory responsibility from the whole board and placed it in the hands of the non-executive (or independent) members who constitute membership of the FEGP.

The principal objection to these procedural manoeuvres, voiced by a number of respondents, is that the restructuring has had the effect of shifting the locus of decision-making away from the board to this key committee. These respondents view the committee in a negative light, as an alternative centre of power and the true locus of authority, rather than as a committee operating within the limits of its legitimate delegated responsibility. Under such circumstances, board meetings become nothing more than a rubber-stamping exercise used for approving decisions made elsewhere in powerful committees.

Staff and student governors perceived the committee restructuring as an intentional attempt to exclude them from exercising any real influence over decision-making processes. Their objections were made clear by one staff governor:

The students' union officer and X and myself felt that it was not a proper way to proceed to set up a sub-committee that was defined by exclusion and then shove all the business through it, because previously you had at least had the finance committee and a staffing sub-committee, each of which was chaired by somebody with particular expertise. You could at least take a view that you were using expertise and 'dear, dear the government won't let internal members be members of those', but this is such a blatant attempt to exclude us. But if you then look at the way business is done, the terms of reference still suggest that FEGP is not the authoritative body, that issues of policy come up to the board. But if you look at the way it's operating, the board is being operated as a sort of consultative body on the big issues, like quality or the university strategic plan. But anything that gets anywhere near the 'nitty gritty', where in a way the policy is really shaped up, is dealt with by the sub-committee with confidential papers, so that in fact the internal members actually have very little access to information, and almost no access to issues that may be of concern to them. So what they've done, in my view, as a matter of convenience rather than do what Huddersfield has done – they have created a structure in which the internal members have very little role to play . . . Without formally agreeing they've used the sub-committee device to actually change radically the way that it [the board] functions.

Another staff governor added a rider to this view: 'We had quite a lot of discussion when the FEGP in its current format was established about exactly what their remit was and I don't think it was really ever resolved . . . I still think there is quite a lot of ambiguity about how much devolved power they've got.'

In an attempt to mitigate the perceived exclusionary effects brought about through restructuring, the staff governors had proposed that they be allowed to attend meetings of the FEGP as observers. At first this proposal was accepted as a conciliatory concession. However, after one meeting with staff attending as non-participant observers it was found 'that this compromise actually negated the whole purpose of the thing' (chair). From the chair's point of view, staff observers had the effect of preventing governors properly exercising their supervisory functions:

It didn't work, that was the trouble. The whole purpose was to enable one to probe without causing difficulties or embarrassment or problems for management. Actually the management were getting away with things because the lay governors were restraining themselves in their criticism in the presence of students and staff.

Staff accounts of the observer exercise show that they were in any event excluded from the majority of the meeting; but they did feel that it had been useful in raising the whole question of the legitimate jurisdiction and remit of the FEGP and the criteria of confidentiality used over financial and employment matters.

It was quite interesting what happened over that actually . . . I went along to observe and it was all deeply embarrassing because 95 per cent of the agenda was labelled confidential and they had to kind of say to me, 'well you can listen to the apologies and these three announcements and then we're going to have to ask you to leave' . . . So the current position is that we aren't entitled to observe what goes on at that committee and yet virtually all the real business goes on in that committee.

The exclusion issue also raises some important questions, recently raised nationally after some highly publicized resignations from college governing bodies, regarding the extent to which staff can be deemed culpable and financially liable when they are not privy to discussions leading up to major decisions. As one of the staff governors explained:

> I can understand that there are issues of staffing, well I don't know the legislation around the financial side of it, I'm not quite sure why that should be confidential. It intrigues, I know that we're not excluded in law from culpability and if anything goes wrong; so I think it's intriguing that we're not even being allowed to watch the decision-making process.

Another staff governor echoed this concern: 'I am aware that I have financial responsibility just like any other governor, and yet I don't have access to information and to papers and to the regular business meeting of the board, which is how I view FEGP, it's a device.'

The implications of the NUN's approach to governance had been most graphically demonstrated in connection with a building project requiring the university to borrow £24 million. The project had been cleared through the finance committee but had to be ratified by the whole governing body. According to the principal, staff were under the correct impression that the project was being 'steered through'. He agreed that staff were restricted in their ability to challenge and contribute to the debate, but the reason for these limitations, he believed, lay at their own door through their inexperience and lack of expertise within the substantive field, rather than through lack of access to prior discussions:

> Governors' approval was required to borrow . . . governors would have been personally liable if they, if the due diligence clause hadn't been met. The interesting thing is to where that placed staff and students, because there is a finance committee but it has to be ratified by the whole governing body. And what we used was the finance committee but we also had . . . where the whole governing body, where staff and students could actually ask questions, they felt that it was all just being steered through, and it was, and it was, because they didn't have the experience, they didn't have the competence, in that particular field.

Staff, on the other hand, felt that the constraints on their ability to contribute to discussion were largely owing to their exclusion from this key committee. Exclusion from the committee was accompanied by related aspects, which also contributed to their marginalization. In their view, information coming up from the FEGP was controlled to such an extent that they had very little notion of the context of debate or how decisions had actually been reached, and this deficiency left them unable to make any adequate or valuable contributions to discussion. As one of the staff governors explained,

> We get the minutes and in the executive report there's sometimes reference to things that have been done in consequence, but again because you have so little information about what has gone on there,

again, it's very difficult to know what questions you might sensibly ask. What issues it might have raised that you'd want to pursue in the wider forum of the governors.

This point was reiterated by an independent governor, who said of decisions made at the FEGP:

They don't come up to the governing body in the context in which they've been discussed necessarily. They come up to the full governing body, if they come up at all, as a very cryptic note that gives no clues as to what actually happened in the context of that debate and decision. I know from experience that unless you know exactly how it got to that point and exactly what all those words mean and what the subtext is, you can't respond to it accurately.

Staff governors were perceived by senior managers to have an inherent conflict of interest: as employees they are almost bound to harbour sectional interests which prevent them from completely identifying with wider organizational goals. These interests are thought to be incompatible with managerial control and are liable to jeopardize the efficiency of the enterprise. Two senior members of the governance team expressed views on this problem. First, the clerk to the board:

The reasons why staff put themselves up for election are many and varied – but they aren't generally because they are keen to go in there and do anything which will upset their colleagues back at the ranch. So they put themselves in an enormously invidious position right from the start.

Second, the principal:

I think there are difficulties – because of the nature of the staff representation, because essentially here it is a union representation. It's elected by the whole of the staff but essentially it's on a NATFHE ticket, and because of that they see themselves as representatives of NATFHE rather than governors. And they themselves have difficulty in accepting, for example, that they have a responsibility as governors and that could be a financial responsibility.

As far as we could ascertain, only one staff member could be said to be a NATFHE 'representative'. This governor felt that perceptions of her views as being sectional – in that she was expected to reflect the union line rather than be objective – had led to some of her contributions being discounted, much to the governors' cost:

One of the difficulties of staff representatives and particularly staff representatives like me who are known to be relatively active in NATFHE in the institution – when I say something, I think the immediate reaction is, well she would say that wouldn't she. And sometimes that may be a legitimate reaction but it means that there are times when I would say things that it is important that they listen to and they really dismiss them.

In her opinion, independent governors were also disadvantaged by staff exclusion from the majority of policy discussions. She argued that staff knowledge of higher education would compensate for some independent governors' limited understanding in this area. Questions posed by staff in debate could alert independent members to different dimensions, of which they could be completely oblivious, and thus provide contributions towards governors forming a wider understanding of the issues at hand.

Senior management and the chair of the board expressed awareness of staff governors' disaffection and acknowledged that improvements were required in the availability and quality of communication channels for these minority representative governors. However, the right to reserve certain items from open discussion by the whole governing body remained a prime consideration. In the arrangements devised to activate this right, the governing board of the NUN had brought to the surface a structural conflict in the arrangements for university governance, which pits claims for effective decision-making by the core of independent members against demands from marginalized staff and student members for greater openness and transparency. The signs of this conflict were apparent in all the case studies, but the evidence from our enquiry suggests that it was only at the NUN that it had become explicit and a potential cause of mistrust of the governing body's motives and actions.

Conclusion

This chapter has focused on governors' perceptions of their roles in higher education, the activities that engage their time as members of governing bodies and what they think about the quality and relevance of the information provided by the institution which, to varying degrees, contributes to the accumulation of knowledge of higher education and, in turn, to informed decision-making. Governors ranked eight formal roles that are undertaken by governing bodies in terms of importance and then by the time spent on these roles. Strategic and auditing roles emerged as first and second most important and time-consuming. The strategic role was the only one that the majority of members thought would increase in importance.

In order to perform these roles, most governors attend at least two or three meetings per term. Over 80 per cent of all members attended ten or fewer meetings per academic year, with the largest proportion attending between six and ten meetings. The majority of members reported that they would not change the current number of meetings. Members claim to attend meetings diligently, over one-third of governors having a 100 per cent attendance level and three-quarters of members attending over 75 per cent of meetings. Internal members were likely to have a higher attendance level than external members. Outside of formal meetings, the amount of extra time members spent in their role ranged from none to three days per month. The largest proportion reported that they spent one extra day a month in their role, and 70 per cent of members spent one extra day or less (this figure includes a quarter of all members who indicated that they spent no extra days (or part days) in their role). Old university members were more likely than new university and college members to spend no extra time outside of formal meetings, whereas new university members were the most likely to spend greater amounts of extra time performing their role. The majority of respondents thought that the amount of information they received was 'about right' and were satisfied with the relevance of the briefing information provided by the chief executive/senior managers. External members were more likely than internal members to express satisfaction with the relevance of information.

Governors ranked governance activities undertaken outside formal meetings in terms of their relative importance and the relative amount of time spent on each. There was a correspondence between the first two activities – 'talking to students and staff' and 'visiting departments' – in terms of perceived importance and the amount of time spent on these activities. However, there was a disparity between the last two activities, in that 'representing the institution on other bodies' was ranked third most important, but less time was spent on this activity than 'attending ceremonies', which respondents had ranked least important.

Although these perceptions offer a fairly clear picture of governors' roles and commitment in terms of time, they reveal very little about the organizational arrangements within which these roles are performed. The case studies reveal these arrangements to be complex and, at times, fragmented. According to advice offered by the Committee of University Chairmen, governing bodies should appoint three committees with central roles in the proper conduct of business. One of these, the nominations committee, has already been considered in Chapter 4. The other two, the audit and remuneration committees, clearly have important roles to play in terms of accountability. Appointment of the former is a requirement of the funding councils and is intended as an integral part of a wider system of internal and external financial audit. The remuneration committee is a facet of the governing body's role as the 'employer', and is intended to afford opportunities to determine and review salaries.

Our research did not afford any opportunity to review the work of these, or any other, committees appointed by the governing bodies. However, the interview data provide some clear insights into the way the committee structure works. Three points can be made. First, the committee structure is an essential part of the detailed governance process in specific areas of institutional life. The full council or board is generally not the forum in which policy is initiated or even challenged. Indeed, there is evidence that lay and independent members can feel in awe, if not intimidated, by the dominance of the so-called front bench governors in meetings of the full governing body. In one of the old universities, the physical arrangement of council meetings was felt to contribute to the sense of hierarchy, and perhaps the ability to steer debate.

Second, in all the case study institutions, the committee structure gave to relatively small groups of governors key control of the governance process. These core members, who include all the leading officers of the university and a small number of lay/independent members, play the pivotal role in the committees. Conversely, there are some groups of governors who are effectively marginalized from important arenas of influence.

Third, within the committee structure there is invariably one which acts as the premier committee. Variously described as policy and resources, standing committee, chair's coordinating committee or finance, employment and general purposes committee, these tended to act as the key centres of decision-making and policy development. Within the inner sanctum, issues are frequently debated and digested prior to being referred to the full governing body. The evidence suggested that such committees may effectively act as executive committees, even if this role is informal in strictly constitutional terms. Though they are claimed as essential to the effective prosecution of governance business, the danger is that such committees may be seen to be exclusionary.

6

Processes of Governance:
Roles and Decision-making

Chapter 5 revealed some of the structural antagonisms contained in the system of university governance. These antagonisms reflect the competing ideals of lay control and stronger corporate management on the one hand, and academic self-governance and collegiality on the other. Nevertheless, so far our analysis has tended to reinforce the view that differences in the structures and style of governance are far more complex and less predictable than suggested by a simple 'old'–'new' university dichotomy. The test of this argument, however, lies less in the formal structures for appointing lay/independent governors and committee structures than in the operationalization of those structures: governance in action. Specifically, what roles do governing bodies perform? And, critically, to what extent do they drive institutional policy?

The notion of the governing bodies as essentially reactive rather than proactive is a criticism of governance that has been made of the public sector generally and is not confined to higher education. Addressing this broader governance problem, Carver (1990: 50–1) provides a criticism and definition of reactivity:

> Reactivity involves the board in document approvals which place the board in a reactive position. In that the board is moving after the fact inasmuch as the document has already been created (using criteria the board did not establish). For practical reasons, often little can be done but to approve the measure. Many times, to avoid feeling like rubber stamps, boards nit-pick, particularly in approving the budget. But no matter how much intelligence goes into playing this reactive role, it's clearly not leadership.

Strategic leadership by the governing body is clearly absent in this model. Yet its absence in the context of universities, particularly the old universities, may not be so surprising given the traditional two-tier system of governance, in which the executive body (council) controls finance, leaving academic issues under the almost complete control of academics through senate. In the new universities, however, the governance framework has been designed to facilitate the governing body's 'control', if not ownership, of the core work of the university (teaching and research). Here we might expect to find more proactive boards and evidence of greater strategic drive beyond the traditional governance areas of finance, personnel and estates. Certainly the evidence of staff and student marginalization found at the New University of the North (NUN) suggests that the governing body may well provide the conditions in which the board can be more proactive.

In addressing questions concerning the degree of policy initiative generated by the governing body, one is immediately faced with the dynamics involved in the relationship between the governors and senior managers. Indeed, this dynamic is especially crucial in cases where the governing body, as is possible in the new universities, comprises only one executive member, with a majority of independent or non-executive governors. Under these circumstances the independent members are almost entirely reliant on the executive for supplying the information they require in order to fulfil their statutory duties and be effective in their role. The executive must, therefore, supply not only specific information relevant to individual policies and performance, but also contextual information detailing issues in higher education which will allow members to develop a greater understanding of the nature of the organization they are governing.

It is perhaps inevitable that many novice independent governors will experience what one staff governor called an 'understanding gap', and that the executive faces the difficult task of discovering a 'common ground' on which to work and move forward with its governing body. The executive in this sense is in a pivotal and potentially powerful position, since it effectively controls the content and form of information relayed to the governing body. In this chapter, therefore, we examine the indicators relating to the governing body's performance and any measures which are thought to inhibit or assist it in moving towards a more active role. As in previous chapters, these themes are first examined in the context of the old universities.

Old University of the South

The role of council

Governors at the OUS differed slightly in their perceptions of the role of council. Predictably perhaps, views tended to reflect their position in the power triangle which underpins university governance and management. The chair of council, reflecting the lay perspective, pointed out that the traditional division between senate being responsible for all matters academic and council for all financial decisions was no longer valid, since everything had financial implications. Staff members were less sanguine, tending to the view that the division of responsibilities remained 'a bit grey'. On the whole, the council was still associated with 'finance and input from outside people to help the university in deliberations'. Members of the executive, on the other hand, tended to reflect the approving function of council. The registrar, for example, emphasized the council's role as the body to which the executive was accountable. In this sense, the governor's role was perceived as being similar to that of the non-executive company director. Reflecting the executive position, the vice chancellor was unequivocal about what council's role is and should be:

I don't particularly want council to run the university. I think their role resembles the role of the non-executive directors on a board of a company – and that is to ask questions. And it's the job of the executives to provide the right answers. So I think it's right that the university should be accountable to the council, but I don't see them as our board of directors, quite frankly.

Following the executive leader's position, the registrar was equally forthright:

They shouldn't come in and seek to run the thing, they should certainly by all means give people a hard time – make sure that they're not trying to pull the wool, that they are being challenged and they are being asked to account for what they are doing, kept on their toes – but that's not the same as actually running it.

These comments must be placed alongside awareness of changing roles in the governance process. It was felt, particularly by the executive, that lay members had over recent years become more conscious of their personal financial liability, and that this was an area in which they could detect 'a greater flexing of muscles'. The registrar felt that members on the whole had adequate information to be able to make judgements regarding the financial state of the institution, and pointed out that they could always ask for further details.

The chair of council offered a different perspective. In certain circumstances he felt it was difficult to determine whether management was exercising adequate financial probity, and he gave an example of one lay member expressing concern and challenging the vice chancellor. The point was substantiated in the following terms:

At the end of the day, even with a proper planning system it has really got to be the chairman or treasurer or the vice-chairman who have got to consult each other and come to the conclusion that there is something very wrong, but . . . it can't be self-evident on the papers can it. It is very difficult, we did have a considerable problem not very long ago, not that it got evidenced on a £10 million scale or whatever it was, but in our works department, about the way that responsibility for contracts was handled. And that is the sort of thing that members did get, one or two members got very edgy about indeed. There was one member, who is the ex-senior local government officer, who began to get very firm to the vice chancellor.

Like the chair, a staff member felt that monitoring of the executive did take place, but that its operation lay within the jurisdiction of fewer than a handful of lay members. Another staff member was of the opinion that the executive was not sufficiently monitored by council or senior lay officers, at least not through the imposition of constraints. Rather, he felt that certain members may use their influence to persuade the executive to follow particular procedures or embark on individual projects:

> You never know, of course, because again in the small meeting the chair of council might actually be quite influential – you know, he might say well hang on I don't think you can get away with that, I don't think I can sell that to my council. From what I gather, it works the other way round, that he has particular hobby horses, like he's particularly keen on staff development and the fact that new staff should be treated properly and given guidance and support and trained up properly, and, well, and the equal ops issue, and he's in a sense pushed the executive to take those more seriously, so I think it's worked that way round rather than constraining the executive.

Strategic leadership and planning

There was general agreement that council's role in strategic planning/leadership was largely reactive. Generally, it was felt that council was in the position of responding to policy initiatives, which were at quite advanced stages of development, and thus had little opportunity to exercise a formative role. However, the chair of council and vice chancellor expressed different perspectives on the extent to which council should actually be involved in the planning cycle. The chair believed that council should have the opportunity to contribute to the planning cycle at an earlier stage:

> I would have thought that if it could see itself as a regular part of the process and feel that it did have the opportunity before, as it were, ratifying a finally concluded negotiated budget, like try to lay down some of the constraints, some of the subject matter for the following year at an earlier stage, then their [council's] contribution could be quite significant . . . If we had a proper planning system it would be much easier for council to be asked at least once a year in a more flexible way, where it didn't feel that it was upsetting the board if it had some rather different ideas than those on the table, and if it would be possible for the initiators of that project to put an alternative to it. Now once you have constructed the budget which is terribly late because of government, the idea of actually changing that is almost inconceivable, so at that point of the year it is not possible really to give council very much more, but I think there are a couple of earlier points where you could.

However, the vice-chancellor laid more emphasis on management's need to have sufficient flexibility and scope for opportunism. He pointed out that there were times when income opportunities would arise and that these often occurred between council meetings; at such moments he thought it imperative that management be able to take the initiative. Not that management would act alone: rather, the executive would call the standing committee of council, which is a much smaller body and can be called at very short notice.

> You'll find that lay members – you'll probably get X [the chair] harping on about this – generally are always harping about planning: we must have a planning cycle and an annual plan. Perhaps I'm too *ad hoc* and my full-time colleagues, but in the academic world, especially in the last 10 or 15 years, it seems to me there's been much more scope for opportunism, jumping at chances of funding and initiatives. Now it's very nice to have a rolling plan and we try to do so and we submit to the funding council our plans for the future. But we must always be ready to leap at an opportunity.

Overall, respondents tended to agree that council mostly reacted to initiatives put before them by the executive. The registrar perceived this to be the correct position for council, in that taking strategic initiatives was the executive's role, but he pointed out that they could respond in a way that alters the initiative's direction:

> If you are operating effectively as an executive in a university, as within a company or any other organization, you ought to be the one who's bringing things forward. You oughtn't to have to rely on somebody who is far less enmeshed in what's going on to come along and tell you what you ought to be doing. I would have said you're not doing your job properly if you're having to do that. Now that's not to say that they can't respond to an initiative in a way that alters its direction – simply because of their own experience, wisdom and so forth. You know, you say, well, we really think we need to build a new residence – and an external member who's got probably local experience of these things will say, have you thought about doing a sale and lease back deal with a property developer. Or whatever. So in that sense they're going to alter the agenda – but they oughtn't to be in the position of saying the university ought to build residences. I would regard us as having failed.

However, mostly, governors could not think of any instances where council had significantly modified initiatives presented by the executive. As a lay member observed, 'No, I feel that by the time it gets to council it to a large extent has been thrashed out. I wouldn't describe it as a rubber stamp but certainly council are not inclined to change things very much, that's my impression.' A staff member reinforced this view:

> I have a feeling one or two things are referred back, which isn't the same, because sometimes when things are referred back they just come

back, next time, slightly modified. And the front bench can say we've consulted this and this and we still believe, but I can't think of any actual reverse that has ever taken place in council itself.

That respondents tended to speak in terms of 'feelings' about govern-ance roles reflects the existence, encountered in all the case studies, of sometimes deep ambiguities as to who are the real decision-makers and what are the constitutional and informal powers which they exercise. For example, although the academic community may be thought to be rep-resented by senate at the OUS, another body – the university management committee – also links management and academics. Made up of deans, pro vice chancellors, senior lay members of council and the vice chancellor, this body was perceived by several respondents to be the main decision-making body in the university. Again, however, there was some ambiguity about the relative importance of this body compared to other centres of power. Two comments from respondents illustrate the ambiguity. First, a lay member of council:

> Where does the power lie? Does it lie with the academic body? Where does the academic power lie – senate or the committee of deans or a body of that sort? Or does it in a sense lie with the lay people, or just the administration? I'm making a distinction between the administra-tion and the academic community . . . You can obviously see a type of debate develop as to who really runs the place – the administrators or the academics – but I mean you are talking about a budget of nearly £100 million. And not many industrial companies would be happy to let a budget of £100 million be managed in such a disparate fashion.

The second comment, from a staff member, reveals that even those on the inside find it difficult to understand the university's decision-making structures:

> I think the impression around the place, and it's certainly my impres-sion, is that there's a small group of people – the chair of council, the VC, the deputy chair of council, obviously the deputy vice chancellors (two of those) and the secretary and registrar – I'm not sure if they're all officially on the standing committee. There's also the university management committee – which is the deans – and that's more on the academic side, and there's the policy and resources, which is a joint council/senate committee. But it's ultimately the same sort of people end up on these committees.

It was left to the vice chancellor to interpret the scene from the top. In his view, the past 15 years had seen the administration and senior academics merging into the management structure. The senior academic managers are the two deputy vice chancellors and the deans of faculties. He felt that the deans were in the most difficult position in terms of conflict of interest, since they had to reconcile managerial responsibility with academic leader-ship and departmental interests. He pointed out that even though the deputy vice chancellors 'really are the senior management', they were still firmly embedded in the academic community and context.

The interview data suggest that decisions arising from the university management team would be guided ordinarily by academic rather than lay perspectives. The vice chancellor went some way to confirming this view when he speculated that 'real difficulties could arise if the senior lay members of council were not pulling in the same direction as the senior academics'. When asked what would happen if the differences were found irreconcilable, he suggested that the senior lay members rather than the academics would be changed.

This confident, assertive interpretation of the strength of the executive's hand in university governance suggests that council's role is essentially reactive. In terms of the balance of power, it reveals a tacit alliance, perhaps best termed an 'accommodation', between the academics and the institution's senior managers. Is such an accommodation a feature of governance specific to institutional arrangements at the OUS, or is it something generated by the wider tradition among the old universities that academic staff make up a sizable part of the governing council? Our second old university case study allows us to explore this question further.

Old University of the North

The role of council

In general, the relative strengths and roles of the key interest groups at the OUN provide some support for the notion of an accommodation between academics and the executive. This case study provides further insights into the nature of the accommodation and how it is handled by the executive in order to retain its ascendant role in strategic leadership and planning.

It was generally agreed by governors that council at the OUN is involved in operating decisions through work delegated to its committees. As we have seen in Chapter 5, it is in the committees that the serious debates take place and differences become manifest. Still, both the chair of council and the registrar were keen to emphasize that council could and sometimes did take an active part in the decision-making process. The example both used to illustrate their point was the structural organization of the university's new science park. After being dealt with by a 'working group' over a period of two years, the final opportunity to direct the development was handed to the full council for consideration. According to the chair, council examined every aspect of the proposal before endorsing a recommendation received from the policy and resources committee. In his opinion, this endorsed the ability of council to take an active part in the decision-making process in an area which until then was unfamiliar to the university. The chair explained:

I could ask for any item to be brought to council that I wanted. If I felt that was the best place for it to be dealt with. My difficulty is that in most cases I know it's not the best place for it to be dealt with. The best place for it to be dealt with is in committees and then brought to the council – OK not for rubber stamping in some cases – in things like the science park, where we were taking on an investment on the scale which was substantially larger than we'd done before . . . and risks that some members were unfamiliar with. That was dealt with by a working group which I chaired – this was before I became chairman of council – and that worked on it for two years, reporting back to council what it was doing. And council had an opportunity and did say we'd rather you didn't do that, we'd rather you did this. Then when we came to the final crunch as to how we would organise it – the structure – that is, we would work with X and Y as a partner – a joint venture partner and things like that – that was debated by council twice.

The registrar also believed that council had played a major role in the science park deliberations:

The major debate about the science park took place over a long series of meetings of the policy and resources committee – which made a recommendation to council that this should go ahead. Of course, there were major, major financial implications behind this and council had a long, long debate – it debated it twice in fact and in the end it endorsed the recommendation that it should go ahead. But it only did so after it was satisfied that it had evaluated every single aspect of the proposal – in other words it wanted to make sure it was in the university's widest and best interest to do that.

Even though the science park venture provides an illustration of important issues being debated in council, the developmental procedure for this initiative was still conducted in committees and working groups. Indeed, the vice chancellor used this example to show how governors play a very significant role in identifying and implementing policy through their involvement in committees. He was clear that council was not a 'policy formulating body but a policy approving body', and in terms of both strategic plans and mission statement it responds to proposals formulated lower down in committees.

VC: How far do they set goals? Well, as far as I can see what they do is receive the strategic plan developed by other committees and comment on it wherever appropriate – they don't do it . . . They receive proposals for policy, so in strict terms they decide the policy or the strategy or whatever it might be – strictly speaking that has to be the case – but it would be wrong to suggest they actually formulate it: they don't.

Researcher: And in terms of the broader mission of the institution?

VC: Well, its the same answer ... The formulation of it didn't
come from council. Council was presented with a proposed
mission statement and they discussed it and the majority
adopted it. They didn't prepare it, no, no, and I doubt
whether there is a council in the country that does. It
couldn't – how could it possibly do that?

The registrar was more cautious than the vice chancellor in his reply
regarding formulation of the mission statement, and he denied that its
determination was largely undertaken by management rather than council.
In his eyes, although the council did not formulate and draft the document, in approving the stated aims and objectives it was claiming ownership
and thus must necessarily 'feel that these [goals] are consistent with what
[it] feels the university is aiming for'. He also felt that council did not set
out to strategically steer the institution or determine its overall direction,
but that the committee structure worked to ensure council's input and
ownership of strategic decisions. To this end, it was essential, he felt, that
council have confidence in its key committees.

A similar point of view was expressed by a lay member when asked where
the initiative for strategic decisions came from and who made strategic
decisions. He envisaged a hypothetical scenario, where there was a move to
change from a research- to a numbers-based institution, and suggested that
he would expect the initiative for change to come from members of the
vice chancellor's advisory group and the chair. Justification for this expectation was that, as with any business, those 'highest up the mountain should
be able to see further'; in other words, those in senior positions should be
expected to be the most familiar with economic and social shifts taking
place in their field, and are thus in the best position to be able to determine and predict correct strategic moves. He then anticipated that the next
stage would be to debate the proposal in the policy and resources committee, thus moving the process into consultative stages, before a firm recommendation went to council for consideration. He also defended the
presentation of firm recommendations to council, in that, he believed, the
idea should be thoroughly researched with the funding implications spelt
out in order for council to be able to assess both its feasibility and its
desirability.

Decision-making and consultation

The vice chancellor of the OUN suggested that its approach to decision-
making needed to be understood in terms of a 'bilateral route to the top'.
This approach is characterized by a distinction between decision-making
and discussion or consultation. On the consultative side there is the constitutional academic board, and on the decision-making side there are the
committees, which can short-circuit too lengthy and discursive debates. The
mechanism that links these parallel channels or processes is the senior

management team or executive. It is thought crucial that the relationship between the executive and the academics, represented by the academic board, remains harmonious. Stable relations between these two groups are obtained mainly through the integrity of individual senior officers, particularly the vice chancellor and the pro vice chancellors. The vice chancellor explained this in the following terms:

> You have these two groups really; one is the committee structure group for decision-making and the other is the consultative one and the question is, how do they link? Well of course, they link partly through the individuals – the pro vice chancellors and me, and the system actually depends quite heavily on our integrity ... But it's vital that those two things are kept in harmony when it comes to the ultimate decision-making, and so the test is whether the administration – the advisory group, for example – wants to do something that the professorial board and the academic board don't. I've not had that yet. And the reason we haven't had that is that I've insisted that all these things are moderated through the consultative process. It's not perfect but ... it's very transparent.

Almost hidden in this quote, however, is a reference to the 'the real executive committee'. This is the so-called advisory group. It is an entirely unconstitutional group which meets every week for half a day and consists of the vice chancellor, the pro vice chancellors, the planning officer, the bursar, the registrar and the finance officer. It is here that the policy recommendations are initiated and sifted before going to committee. The vice chancellor expressed the view that, throughout the university, there was an implicit understanding that serious perusal and success of initiatives began at this point in the process.

'The executive committee', the vice chancellor explained, 'is really what I call my advisory group.' He continued:

> It's totally unconstitutional [but] it's a very successful group and totally informal – it has no statutory authority whatsoever. Of course, the university understands that that's where you've got to get something in if you want to have it looked at before it goes to committee ... These things happen because of the need to make speedier decisions simpler. Any decision that is made by the advisory group goes through the committee structure, it doesn't act unilaterally and independently.

The subsequent exchange with the researcher provided further substantiation of the pre-eminent role of the executive and the essentially reactive role of council:

Researcher: We're talking about policy recommendations essentially?
VC: Oh yes, absolutely. Where do you think recommendations come from? They can come from ordinary foot soldiers and they do, but mostly they don't. The elected representatives

on committees tend to be reactive – and that's been true for 20 years in most universities that I know of.

The chair of council pointed out that a similar arrangement to the advisory group found at his university, could be found at most other old universities. In his experience, it was 'the way vice chancellors have chosen to organize their affairs'.

As noted, the advisory 'group' is unconstitutional and has no members on council within its ranks, although all issues it deals with are moderated through the consultative process. To reiterate, the moderation mechanism appears to be subject to the integrity of senior individual administrators/managers presenting issues to the academic boards. The vice chancellor gave an example of a confidential issue that he had chosen to open up to the academic boards for debate, but pointed out that constitutionally he was under no obligation to bring this to their attention:

> There's an issue today which is a very difficult one, which is highly confidential and I didn't have to take to the academic board or the professorial board at all, but I did – I enclosed agenda, I opened it up for debate, I said look this is the problem, these are the issues and so on, I'd like to know what you think. And of course they weren't slow in telling me, and that was very helpful, because it means that I can go to council this afternoon knowing fully what I've been told by those two boards – even though it didn't need to go through that consultative process at all. Nobody could have stopped me if I'd have wanted to do it – constitutionally. So it's a question of how the individual like me and the other people involved in the senior management see the relationship between the management process and the consultative process. Vitally important, haven't resolved it yet – we're going to actually have a review, but that seems to be the essence of it.

Although there are no members of council on the advisory group, the chair of council was quite at ease with its role and contribution to the decision-making process. He affirmed that the group, through the vice chancellor, would informally consult him on issues and always kept him up to date on current developments.

The New University of the South

Unlike in the old universities, the articles of government laid down by the secretaries of state for the new universities make explicit that the governing board is responsible for determining the educational character and mission of the institution. However, the vice chancellor of the NUS was very clear on the division of responsibility between himself and governors regarding the mission statement. Although, by the articles, the governors are responsible for the general educational character of the institution,

The obligation is laid on the vice chancellor to propose what the mission is – and if I proposed a mission which the governors faulted, I would expect the governors and would quite rightly say to the governors, that they quite rightly should send me away with some words of guidance and steer, but they should never write an alternative. That's my job, and if in the end I can't – to their satisfaction – they should consider whether they've got the right leader.

The chair was in agreement that, once the general philosophy of the institution had been agreed, and the various faculties and departments had contributed their own input, responsibility for drafting the document went to the vice chancellor. The clerk to the board of governors was more informative about the actual process of producing the mission. The overall strategy was mostly drafted by the directorate and after many amendments and reiterations it goes to the governors in draft form. The governors usually have two meetings: at the first they comment on the draft and their views are then incorporated by the directorate into the final draft, which at the second governors' meeting is usually approved. He also suggested that certain parts of the mission and strategic plan may from time to time call for review, and in such cases a working group of the governors may be established for this precise purpose. Examples he gave were of research and quality issues where working parties would be or had been established:

After the research assessment exercise and the HEFCE policy . . . we've had to review the research strategy and that again as a result of a group of partly governors and staff here looking at it and coming up with ideas. This particular audit that is coming up, we've decided as a result of our preparations for that, that we really need to review our mission and strategy statement chapter on quality. That is coming up through the academic board but when it gets from academic board to the governing body, then again the governing body input there will probably be a group of members who are particularly interested in that aspect.

Independent members felt that the governing board tended to be reactive rather than proactive. Nevertheless, there were different perspectives on how extensive the board's role should be in managerial decisions. In strategic planning, one governor thought that a mainly 'reactive' position was to be expected:

I think only in the monitoring of the strategic plan. I don't think as a governing body we would ever expect to sit down and prepare them. I don't think we would have the competence or the day-to-day requirements to actually sit down and say this is what our strategy is going to be – so we would expect somebody to present a strategic plan to us then we would with our (a) native wit, (b) knowledge of the institution and (c) as outsiders looking at it, change it. So we really are responders to what people give us rather than originators.

Another independent governor pointed out that although opportunity was limited for governors to engage in the development of institutional mission and strategy, they could, through their involvement in advisory committees, have significant influence on particular departmental strategies. For example, in his role on the advisory committee of the business school, he felt that his input had been 'seminal to the development of the strategy'. However, for the most part the independent governors accepted that theirs was a largely reactive role, which, for the moment at least, suited the needs of both the academics and the directorate.

Implicitly, the role of governors was negatively correlated with the perceived benevolence of the directorate. That is, as long as the directorate is perceived by the staff as leading in a relatively benevolent fashion, they are content to have a reactive board of governors. The converse, of course, is that should staff be concerned over the managerial style and direction of the directorate, then allegiance against the executive would be sought from the governors, whose position would be expected to become far more prominent and proactive. This view was articulated by one of the staff governors:

> The staff governors have confidence in the directorate as well. I think we're an extremely well run university, managed by pretty enlightened humanitarian bosses, and as long as that situation prevails, a lot of the concerns I might have about the governing body – who it is, how it functions – are not that important. If things were of a different order, the role of governors would become very much more important, and I'm sure that not just the staff governors but the staff in the university would start to look to the staff governors much more to represent their position and to try to swing governors against some of the positions of the directorate . . . Most of the time the governing body is simply not part of the consciousness of the staff – governors are insignificant, along with the governing body . . . As long as the governors are rubber-stamping a benevolent directorate, nobody particularly bothers about it. If they were rubber-stamping a malevolent directorate they would take a lot more interest.

The directorate's autonomy and influence over strategy and policy decisions are not in doubt in this view. The chair of the board concurred, preferring to emphasize the importance of appointing senior officers who had the same kind of educational philosophy and would 'fit into the ethos of the institution'. Indeed, selection of 'like-minded' senior post-holders was thought to be an essential element for successful development of the institution – since it served to engender the assumption that across the top tiers of management and government there is a broad identity of values or a shared normative framework from which to progress.

The confidence in the directorate expressed by staff and independent governors alike was, in our view, a reflection of the leadership style of the vice chancellor. By his own assessment the vice chancellor adopted a 'very political' style, geared to giving the board of governors a sense of ownership of both strategic and policy decisions. To this end he had to let the governors bring on board their business experience of issues encountered elsewhere, even if these issues proved sensitive within the institution.

The issue of early retirements provides a clear illustration of the approach. One of the independent governors had raised this subject in committee. In his own words:

> I've seen this coming – that the age profile is changing, that we're going to have lots of old people comparatively. It's a gross comment but what are we doing to maintain excellence, what are we doing to attract the bright new young things who will be the academics of to-morrow? How does that affect our research strategy, because funding is now increasingly related to research – and what are we going to do to get rid of the old buggers who are going to be very expensive to boot out? And you know I've been in the situation of running a £50 million business. I know that the difficult thing to do is to get rid of the people with long service, because they're expensive, and what you end up doing is not promoting your youngsters, and you end up com-pounding the problem, because you lose the young bucks because they go somewhere else and ultimately you compromise your excellence. So I've started to make the point.

Handling the controversial and politically sensitive views of independent governors is a major test of governance style. The vice chancellor took the view that it was his responsibility to avoid confrontation:

> I like to have a very content board of governors, which feels some ownership – so it isn't sufficient just to shut them up or avoid them talking. In fact I admit that there are issues or remarks – if I let some of the business members loose on this sensitive industrial relations . . .
> [So] I plan very carefully how we're going to handle it.

The clerk to the board of governors confirmed that on issues such as the high age profile of the university staff, governors did have important insights, gleaned from managing large organizations, which could be transferred to an academic setting. However, those insights had to be 'adapted and fine-tuned', since even public sector managerial experience differed to quite a large extent from higher education management. For this reason the uni-versity tried to apply governors' expertise to specific 'problem' situations. For example, two had been drafted into an *ad hoc* working group to assist the faculty of engineering develop a new staff recruitment strategy.

For the most part, therefore, control is firmly vested in the hands of the directorate. Agenda items originate here, the registrar producing a first draft which is subsequently amended by the vice chancellor, two deputy vice chancellors and two assistant vice chancellors. No governors (including the chair) are formally involved in agenda production, although there is 'an understanding' that individual members can put forward suggestions for inclusion. In addition, the chair has a standing item known as the chair's announcements, where topics can be raised at the chair's discretion.

In practice, most items are generated in preceding committee meetings and reports. One independent governor, who was also chair of the finance committee, felt that he had exercised the right to raise items, but these had effectively been generated through the committee structure, and he felt it unlikely that a 'non-involved' governor would raise agenda items. On the whole, he felt that the committee structure and reporting was an effective mechanism for raising items. However, like non-executive governors and directors in most organizations, the governors were almost entirely dependent on the executive for information. The directorate, therefore, is in a very powerful position, since it is able to control the content and form of how issues are presented to governors.

It can be very difficult for governors to be able to discern whether, or how much, managers are 'leading them by the nose'. The vice chancellor accepted this predicament but felt that safeguards were in place – giving the example of the dual duties of the clerk to the board of governors, who had a line management responsibility directly to the vice chancellor but also had responsibilities to the chair. He was convinced that should the circumstances arise where the clerk thought that the vice chancellor was exceeding his managerial responsibilities, then he would inform the chair of governors:

> X is clerk to the board of governors and he has a line management responsibility to me – he has a relationship to the chairman. And in certain circumstances, which hopefully never arise, he blows the whistle on me or says sorry I don't agree with you on that issue and I need to draw the chairman's attention to that; not that it ever happens, but I'm quite clear sometimes I will say to X, I'll tell you what to do but you are allowed to tell me that I'm wrong.

The chair was unconcerned about the supply of information from the directorate to governors. Having been chair for many years, he had networks to other information sources and was satisfied that the information governors received provided an adequate overall perspective of developments in the institution. A staff governor felt that much of the significant policy debate was actually initiated by staff governors, and that, with the exception of the CCC members, independent governors would expect staff governors to take the lead on such debates because staff would be better informed of the current issues. Although, in his opinion, members of the CCC were better informed than other independent governors, even so their knowledge would often be restricted to the narrow confines of a particular committee. Overall, he felt the directorate was 'quite good at giving information to the governors', and stressed that there was no evidence of a 'conspiracy culture'. Nevertheless, it was admitted that directorate reports to governors were structured with firm recommendations, as opposed to the presentation of a choice between several options and their subsequent implications.

The New University of the North

The shift from LEA control to corporate independence created opportunities, enshrined in the framework of governance of the new universities, for the development of more effective and active governing bodies. The principal of the NUN, however, was of the view that the governing board was still experiencing transitional difficulties or, more accurately, transferral of ownership difficulties. Still most comfortable with matters relating to finance, personnel and estates, he felt that the governing body had yet to take ownership of core areas of the university, particularly with regard to the curriculum and teaching. 'I think it is appropriate and right that they should take ownership', the principal observed. He continued:

> We've been essentially trying to find our way as to how you'd give that ownership, and particularly how you'd give it over issues which governors you feel want ownership – which are not the finance, and the personnel and the estates stuff. I mean finance, personnel and estates they feel they know something, they feel they can contribute something, they feel happy with that – but that's really not what they're there for, they don't see themselves as being necessarily there for that. And where we've not, I think, yet been particularly successful is to get an ownership of the core work of the university. Of the issues around the curriculum, teaching and learning – the core business as distinct from its financial solvency or personnel related issues.

The secretariat, it was claimed, had not yet discovered ways in which to make optimum use of the governing body, in that the governors were effective in monitoring executive performance but were limited in the extent to which they could make further contributions regarding the general nature of the institution. In order to rectify this situation, the principal felt that it was necessary to find a 'common ground' or commensurable foundation upon which to build further understanding between the two perspectives and engage in productive debate:

> We're still finding that we don't really know how to get the most out of our governing body. And they're still finding they don't know really the points to push on where they can add value as distinct from just check that we're behaving in a competent fashion ... Independent members don't want to be there as free consultants, they want to actually make a contribution. But it's a contribution about the general nature of the institution, some curriculum issues, and in those areas, I think, they are well aware of their limitations, but they want to enter into a debate with us and a dialogue – they don't want to be told that they're limited and they haven't got experience so keep out, they want to

discuss that . . . I think the problem, there is a problem within the sector of trying to keep governors out. I think you have to engage them you have to involve them and it has to be done, not just on their terms and certainly not just on our terms – we have to find a way of working forward on that.

Independent members from a business culture found difficulty with the absence of fixed performance criteria, such as profit and loss statements, and thus no indisputable measure with which to monitor performance. The clerk to the board felt that without such criteria there was no 'bottom line' for the commercially minded to grasp and judge whether something had been a success. Nor were debates much consolation, for, as the principal observed, some governors have difficulty with the academic style of debate. Instead they tended to rely on the executive to sort it all out first, which reduces the opportunities to challenge.

Despite their inexperience in debating performance criteria, it was generally agreed that the presence of independent governors had forced the executive to provide more effective demonstrations of their competence and performance, and thereby to improve management's monitoring system. The clerk to the board confirmed:

As we've got our management act together over the last few years they've started now to be more critical and more demanding in terms of information and answers to the question 'why?' I don't think they're uncomfortable with the overall direction but they have started to test us more . . . 'This is all very nice and it sounds great and I'm sure it's right but how do you know that you're succeeding, how do you know it's of that quality, how do you know you are meeting your targets, have you got any targets'? That kind of thing, so they're getting more demanding.

An illustration of the decision-making process and how independent members influence that process is provided by the NUN's approach to the recent imposition of efficiency gains and declining units of resource for undergraduate provision by the funding council. Two strategic issues were at stake: first, how to implement greater efficiency into the undergraduate teaching programme; second, how to attract funds from sources other than the Higher Education Funding Council for England (HEFCE).

Both issues had been discussed at meetings of the academic board and the governing body. The outcome was 'Cycle 3' – a strategy to develop research and post-graduate recruitment. In the development of Cycle 3, individual targets for each school were devised by the directors of the school and endorsed by the academic board. The governing body was then to endorse Cycle 3, after which it was to receive regular progress reports against these targets. This form of strategic performance monitoring against precise targets was thought to be revolutionary within the university sector.

The policy was not without controversy, however. The academic community feared the imposition by the governing body of pre-established criteria devised without proper consultation or due regard to academic opinion. Extensive discussions took place to establish a consensus within the institution about the proposed direction and projected five-year objectives. The principal felt able to express satisfaction at the outcome in terms of the balance of power between the academics and the governors:

> We are now moving it through in a much more constructive way with governors – having got a degree of consensus from the academic community about where we want to be in four or five years time. Rather than have governors say this is where we want you to be and telling the institution.

The measurement and evaluation of achievement against declared objectives is a commercial management technique. Its introduction, albeit after extensive discussion, provides a clear example of how the business or independent governors have influenced managerial strategy in alliance with the university's executive. The chair of the board clearly suggested joint ownership of the strategy:

> We're putting a plan, a vision statement, to the governing body, of where we want the university to be in five years' time. The governing body will debate, discuss that and probably agree that's where we want to be in five years' time. What then will happen is that the executive will need to work out how to get there and will need to work out which of the various options for getting there are the most effective, likely to be the most effective – or whatever. It's in that second process that the committees of the governing body take a turn – because their job is to question the executive on how they plan to achieve the objectives that have been set by the governing body.

It will be in the inner sanctum governing body – the FEGP – that the executive will be challenged on the plans for implementation and progress towards meeting targets and achieving strategic ends. The principal endorsed the value of the process:

> The FEGP is . . . where the non-executives can challenge the executive and it would be unlikely to happen in the presence of teaching staff or students . . . [It is] healthy, I think, if we got to a position where we could have papers where you would get people saying I'm just not happy about this I don't agree with this, your reserves are far too low, the degree of risk is far too high, go away and think again and if it means cutting staff and if it means chopping a department then fine. Or where you could actually put up performance of a department and you could get some very brutal exchange.

Governors are clearly expecting increasingly to challenge the executive and, in turn, become more proactive in areas of governance once thought the preserve of academics. Their assertiveness is partly a consequence of the introduction of numerical targets for each school, which will allow judgements by both governors and the executive about whether actual performance matches the pre-established criteria. If performance is not matching expectations, then governors can probe into the reasons behind any lack of progress and demand that the principal takes corrective action to ensure on-target delivery. But governor assertiveness is also a reflection of 'time-served' independent governors beginning to reject their mostly reactive role and take a more proactive part in corporate affairs.

A staff governor speculated that the establishment of the FEGP not only allowed the executive to be challenged without embarrassment in front of staff, but also facilitated a forum where assistant principals could be put on the front line and have their proposals criticized and tested by governors. She noted a change in the organizational style of meetings of the FEGP (which is also the case in board meetings), where all assistant principals are now required to be in attendance on the governors, whereas in the previous 'three committee' system appropriate executives were called as and when required. This procedure, she thought, may assist the principal in justifying demands made on assistant principals for efficient turn-around on revisions to proposals. Nevertheless, this staff governor felt that while the governors may be making substantial modifications to proposals, it was the executive that remained in the driving seat of policy, since the executive and not the governing body maintained effective control over the agenda.

It is in this context that the FEGP has come to play an essential role as an 'executive committee'. The chair of the board admitted this, citing the example of library contracts to illustrate its importance:

> It's early days – it's still only been in place about nine months or so – but yes, I do see some signs of the finance, employment and general purposes committee really working like a proper executive board and I do see some signs that we are giving ourselves rather more time to debate the bigger issues in the governing body. It's the nature of the board that you will get debate. People approach things from different angles. You would often find more pointed discussion in the FEGP committee, where in the past we've actually changed recommendations. There was something to do with the way in which we were going to handle the contracts for the library. At what stage we got a tender for different things – there are some quite considerable experience in the property market among the lay governors. They debated it and the lay governors convinced the finance director that the way that he was proposing was the wrong way and it should be done a different way.

This illustrates how independent governors are able to make input into policy implementation, although the initiative in strategic leadership resides mainly with the executive rather than governors. Through control of the agenda, policy initiation and supply of information, senior managers are able to exercise a considerable influence on the procedures and outcomes of board and FEGP meetings. Agenda items are originally generated by the senior management team. A draft agenda is then prepared by the secretariat for discussion and approval by the principal and subsequent discussion with the chair. The principal noted that it was a recent development that the secretariat discussed agenda items with the chair, and that this development arose from a mutual desire for the chair to 'get more involved' and 'to feel some ownership over the agenda'. Prior to main board meetings, the chair and clerk to the board of governors meet to discuss the timing and balance of items and to ensure that the meeting has some element of strategic form by giving 'due time to weighty items'.

Governors are also allowed to put forward items for inclusion and staff governors had been known to use this option. However, it was considered that recourse to such an option was unnecessary, since, as the principal observed, 'normally agenda items are so broad that, if they've got specific issues, they can raise them under a broad item.' A staff governor made the general observation that agendas were flexible tools that can be used, by those with control over their content and design (in this case she pinpointed the principal), to raise items that they want either approved or rejected. In her opinion it is often difficult to decipher, *in situ*, what the executive's intentions are in raising particular items and, consequently, how contrived are the subsequent outcomes.

Policy development was also perceived to be driven by the executive. One independent governor thought that the executive did not encourage governors to think of themselves as leaders of strategy and policy, but rather providers of guidance on specific pre-formulated proposals. In this respect, he was critical of the executive's formulation of policy proposals since the committee (FEGP) was being presented with only one option, rather than a choice between policy alternatives and their implications. Rather than debate and consider a range of options, they were being asked to provide advice or make minor adjustments to an almost finalized proposal before giving formal endorsement. This governor observed:

> It doesn't seem that we are encouraged by the officers to view ourselves as making policy, but rather guiding the policy of the professional officers . . . If you analyse what's in those papers [FEGP], it's not actually asking you for an opinion, it's not guiding you towards a debate about what policy ought to be. I'll tell you what they've done. It's making a recommendation and it's asking you to support it. And the other thing they're asking you for on top of that is your individual expertise in helping to develop policy in the future. So they will say to me, at the moment in our university we're in the middle of an early retirement scheme. The rationale behind it is that they want to replace two for one and they want to open up the career structures because they've got this age band of people stuck in there, not going anywhere. So then they turn to me and say, now how do you feel about that, how do you feel the responses of the trade unions will be to that, and is there anything we've missed out that you think we ought to put in? Now that's great, I was able to contribute to that and that's fine. But

my point of contact with that was when you've got an already framed document and all they're asking you for is some amendments or additions or some off-the-cuff responses to it. Now if you look at a school governing body . . . policy developments are driven by the governors, not by the professional officers. And it's completely the other way round in higher education institutions.

This governor was also under the impression that an insufficient distinction had been drawn between governors' strategic responsibilities and the executive's day-to-day managerial responsibilities. He contrasted governors' lack of involvement in developing a ten-year strategic plan and his detailed probing of the much narrower issue of the early retirement scheme. In his opinion governors had contributed very little to the development of the strategic plan, while, in retrospect, he considered that he had become too embroiled in the managerial task of finalizing implementation details of one strategic element.

Such comment left us to speculate that the extent to which independent governors are able to initiate strategic proposals will depend on their background knowledge of higher educational issues and their degree of self-confidence to express and volunteer ideas in the company of seasoned executive professionals. One independent member referred to the ambiguous status of governors within the institution and contrasted this position with that of the executive:

> They're [the executive] quite high-powered people to take on, actually, because they're very positive, well informed, they've got their status within the organization, which as a governor I don't have. Governor status is a curious thing. Governor status is that somebody runs out and gives you a car parking space and treats you like somebody special. But that's a different kind of relationship to the one he has with the boss. I can't tell him to do anything, but he will treat me with respect because I am a governor. It's rather like being the Queen of England, isn't it, instead of the Prime Minister, it's that kind of difference.

Challenge to the executive was also thought to be restricted in terms of information dependency on the executive. One independent member verified this dependency and the limitations of his own perspective. This respondent was concerned that after careful perusal of executive papers and presentations at meetings, he was often unable to formulate any questions. This inability left him in doubt as to whether he had sufficient knowledge of all sides of the argument or whether all the questions had already been addressed. In the latter case he thought that such a procedure was unhealthy, in that it would seem to eliminate the need for debate; and in the former case, should it transpire that he was in fact only in possession of a part of the argument, then he was troubled as to whether he had been acting with due regard to his duties.

In a bid to address these problems, the executive provides governors with briefing sessions after board meetings on different aspects of higher education, and has organized regular departmental visits. Members are also provided with documentary information regarding current issues in higher education and the principal provides an executive summary of such issues at each board meeting. The visits in particular were perceived by the chair and independent governors to be very useful in terms of generating better understanding and improving strategic decision-making. However, staff governors were rather sceptical regarding these visits, suggesting that many of the departments viewed these occasions as an opportunity for 'senior staff to present the spectacular bits' and that they were nothing much more than a 'kind of PR show'. Their impression was that governors were subjected to a 'good news culture' and that a general perception held by ordinary staff members was that there were no adequate mechanisms in place by which to relay their views to independent governors.

Conclusion

The case studies have emphasized two common characteristics in old and new universities relating to the roles performed by councils and the wider issues of decision-making, particularly with regard to strategic leadership and planning. The first is the essentially reactive role of full council. Councils and boards of governors tend to work as 'backdrops', helping to shape the executive's policy ideas. The evidence suggests that executives are generally aware of and take into account the (implicit) normative framework adopted by their councils or boards when drafting strategy and policy documents. However, it is within the committee structure of each institution that governors, or at least a core group of them, have most opportunity for more detailed consideration of policy issues.

Second, the formulation of policy matters lies elsewhere within the governance process. In both old and new universities the evidence suggests that it is the executive, the senior management team, which takes the 'efficient' or most proactive role in the governance process. There is also evidence to suggest that the academics are incorporated into the process. In theory, the executive might be able to lead without consultation, sidestepping the academics. In practice, an accommodation between the academics and the executive ensures that this has not taken place. This is owing not just to the constitutional arrangement of collegiality, which retains for the academics an important role in the governance process. It is also owing to the custom and practice of collegiality, the incorporation of the academic into the managerial existence of the university. The latter, of course, depends, as the vice chancellor of the Old University of the North remarked, on the personal integrity of members of the executive, not least the vice chancellor, a point to which we return in the next chapter.

The case studies also demonstrate some differences in perceptions of governing body roles. In the new universities, particularly the NUN, the lay governors seemed much more prepared to engage in debate over academic issues. In these universities there was also some evidence to suggest that independent governors were more impatient of university decision-making structures, the penchant of the academic for debate and the absence of measures to monitor performance and judge 'success'. For some, the notion of 'worker' governors on the board was seen as a 'fairly unnatural state of affairs'. In one new university, the NUN, the alignment between the executive and the governors had gone further than elsewhere and had been enshrined in the committee structure. Here there is no doubt that staff governors felt a sense of exclusion from important areas of the governance process.

However, we should be cautious of any suggestion that arrangements at the NUN signify a broad divide between practice in the old and new universities. Certainly, the New University of the South followed a far less 'executive' pattern in its governance arrangements, with practice very much in line with that found in the two old universities. Moreover, even in the old universities the ability of the executive to drive ahead with policy should not be underestimated. As the case of the Old University of the North demonstrated, a small caucus of senior managers meeting informally and without any constitutional existence can provide the vital source of strategic and policy development. In this sense, the key task facing the executive is persuading the various constituencies in the governance process to react positively to its initiatives.

In all the case study institutions, the control held by the executive over agendas and strategy initiation remains substantially intact. The facade of governance enshrined in the committee system, where, nominally, decisions are made, has been substantially strengthened by recent reforms. But the case studies reveal that roles in this sense remain more symbolic than real. To be sure, in one of the new universities there was clear evidence that the governing body, influenced by the infusion of external or 'business' governors, had begun actively to engage with other interest groups in a struggle for ownership of core areas of the university in relation to teaching and learning. It was in this institution that academic and business cultures had already clashed over the development and use of fixed performance data with which to measure and evaluate achievements against declared objectives.

Yet the extent of challenge to the supremacy of the executive, even in this new university, should not be exaggerated. Evidence from all the institutions studied accumulated to confirm the limitations to governor influence over decision-making. The sifting of policy recommendations by informal or, in a strictly technical sense, 'unconstitutional' executive groups restricted the opportunities for governor involvement. Further inhibitors to governor proactivity were suggested by their information dependency, particularly on the executive. The extent to which governors are able to initiate policy is critically dependent on their knowledge of higher education issues and of their institution. As several independent governors admitted, their knowledge was often incomplete and fragmented, particularly in relation to the extensive and coherent grasp of the issues exhibited by members of the executive.

The professional knowledge base of the executive was in normal circumstances sufficiently robust to prevent individual governors, let alone governing bodies, from mounting serious challenges to the initiatives of the executive. But this is not to say that discussion or consultation with governors did not take place, or that initiatives were never referred back for modification. However, despite the challenge to existing facades and practices of governance mounted by New Right critiques of the public services and notions of new managerialism, market and business cultures, the evidence of the case studies suggests that the ambiguous status of governing bodies remains a powerful inhibitor to more proactive styles of governance. For the most part, governing bodies remain far more comfortable dealing with allocative resources, especially the classic ones of estates, personnel and finances, than they do authoritative resources. Within present structures, surveillance and control, key facets of authoritative resources, remain firmly the preserve of the executive, particularly in relation to core areas of organizational activities. Nevertheless, traditional modes of control are mediated by the power relations that exist between sub-groupings of the governing body and the executive. Within these relations there are a number of key interpersonal relationships, which are instrumental to the process of 'getting things done' within a framework of discussion and consultation. The nature of these key relationships in the governance process is an area investigated in the next chapter.

7

Key Agents and Relationships: Vice Chancellors and Chairs of Governing Bodies

This chapter investigates the 'informal processes' of university governance. By this we mean those aspects of governance which depend on the existence of relationships between key players in the system, which, by their nature, are beyond the formal or constitutional framework of governance arrangements. Our decision to try to investigate this area was influenced both by *a priori* thinking about the nature of governance and by our empirical research, which demonstrated that the system in any institution cannot be understood on the basis of constitutional arrangements alone. Essentially a political process, the system depends for its effective functioning on the day-to-day interaction between certain key players.

By its very nature, however, the informal can be opaque, and it presents certain difficulties in constructing a perspicuous account. Without detailed observation to corroborate the interview data, the evidence presented to support our conclusions must be treated with a degree of caution. Many of the informal processes are merely alluded to by respondents or are to be inferred from implication. Within the discussion, however, we are also focusing on elements of formal authority, the role of key players in the decision-making process and their relations with each other. It is hoped that this final analytical section will help to embellish the emerging picture of governing body decision-making in the case study universities and will contribute to a greater understanding of some of the issues underlying this process.

Vice chancellors and chairs of governing bodies

The two key agents in the governance process, in constitutional terms at least, are the chief executive (the terms vice chancellor, institutional head and chief executive are used interchangeably in the following discussion) and the chair of the governing body. Significantly, the CUC *Guide for Members of Governing Bodies* (1995: 18) observes: 'A critical element in the effectiveness of the governing body and of the institution as a whole is a constructive relationship between the chair and the head of the institution.' Before we consider the nature of the relationship in each of the case studies it is necessary to say something about the formal role of each player.

The head of the institution is vested with the largest degree of individual formal authority and responsibility within the university. In the new universities, the instruments and articles of government stipulate that she or he is directly responsible for the day-to-day management of the university, which includes directing and leading the university and its staff, determining academic activities (in consultation with the academic board) and managing the budget and resources (as approved by the governors). As chief accounting officer, the head is responsible to governors and the funding council for ensuring compliance with the terms and conditions of the HEFCE's Financial Memorandum. The head is also academic leader of the university, being chair of the academic board, and is responsible for representing academic interests internally to the board of governors and externally at local, regional and national level.

The roles and responsibilities of vice chancellors in the old universities are normally defined in the university statutes. Like the heads of the new universities, they are in effect the chief executives of their institutions, with ultimate responsibility for executive management and the day-to-day direction of the institution. The proper use of funds from the funding council is, likewise, the responsibility of the vice chancellor. The vice chancellor will also be chair of the senate, the equivalent academic body in the old universities to the academic board in the new.

In contrast to the chief executives, who are appointed to their (salaried) posts, the chairs of governing bodies in both the old and new universities are elected to their (unpaid) offices by the lay/independent members. The chair takes responsibility for the leadership of the governing body and is intended to have a distinct role from that of the chief executive. Indeed, the Cadbury Report (1992: 21) recommended that the chair's role be separate from that of chief executive in order to 'ensure a balance of power and authority, such that no one individual has unfettered powers of decision'. The relationship between the chair and vice chancellor is crucial to the successful management of the institution.

The Old University of the South

Informal procedures and agreements underpinned the relationship between the vice chancellor and chair at the OUS. The vice chancellor recalled that at the time of his appointment, ten years ago, the then chair of council had agreed (in his capacity as chair of the appointing committee) to remain as chair of council until the vice chancellor was established in post. He would then relinquish the chair but remain on the council, a move designed to allow the vice chancellor the opportunity to 'appoint' his own chair. Selection of the new chair was undertaken by the vice chancellor, the two deputy vice chancellors and two senior lay members of council. This is a 'procedure' which the vice chancellor hoped would be adopted by the present chair for the future vice chancellor.

The importance of allowing the vice chancellor to 'appoint' the chair is underscored by the feeling expressed by both that, if one were not pulling in the same direction as the other, then one of them would have to go. The comments of two staff members provided insights into the nature of the relationship. First, how it worked:

> I've never observed an occasion when they've [chair and vice chancellor] been in disagreement. I think the chair sees his job as getting through what the university wants to get through, and what the university wants to get through is really determined by the vice chancellor and registrar.

Second, why it was important:

> I think council could or should have a very important role and clearly defined role different from senate and that the two need to talk. So I think its important that the two parts of the university do talk to each other ... It depends on the key figures – the vice chancellor and secretary and registrar and chair of council – providing that they can interact. As far as I'm aware here more or less they have.

The registrar added a further reason why it was essential that the relationships between chair and chief executive were effective:

> If you are the secretary to council you have a duty to serve the council and it's not utterly inconceivable that council could want to take a view which differed from the view of the VC and senior team. And I think that puts the registrar in a very odd position – because you do have this sort of company secretary role where you do have responsibility for the board and yet you're obviously in line management terms responsible to the chief executive. I always hope that will never emerge and clearly if you've got the right personal relationships going between the chair of council, the vice chancellor and the secretary and registrar one would hope one would never get to that point.

As we have seen in Chapter 6, in at least one area of governance – strategic leadership and planning – the vice chancellor and chair of council expressed rather different views. Their differences had crystallized around the issue of the university's mission statement. The problem originated in the formulation stage, when it appears that the mission statement was conceived not as a planning but as an academic document. Consequently the subject had by-passed the planning and resources committee and gone straight to senate for debate. Senate, supported by the vice chancellor, took the view that since the university is comprised of extremely diverse units, or departments, whose own missions may differ drastically, then it is not really possible to formulate an overall institutional mission statement capturing all the diversity. The chair of council found the argument unconvincing:

Somehow it wasn't regarded as a planning document, but a document that some people outside, like the quality people, were asking for. So it hadn't actually come up through planning committee at all, amazingly, it had emerged, it had gone to senate and I became extremely restless at standing committee's council . . . The argument at senate was that our activities are so wide and so different from each other that what would be acceptable as a mission statement at one department would be the antithesis in another, therefore we can't have one. I just think that is naive.

The vice chancellor was evidently unmoved, choosing a seafaring metaphor to justify his stance:

A broad based university like this . . . we're not like a naval fleet with a battle ship with the admiral on board and cruisers and destroyers and frigates – all sailing in the same direction, all with the same objective. We're more like a merchant line with a couple of luxury liners running tours in the Med and Caribbean and we have a few crummy old merchant ships buying rice from India and selling it to China. And all their captains meet twice a term in a body that's called senate, and they have quite different missions, and I think that sort of diversity is the strength of a traditional university. So the idea of a single mission statement is an anathema to me, I'm afraid.

In the event, the vice chancellor's initial draft mission was all but rejected:

Council said well, it's just bearable as an interim but it is not specific enough, there's nothing distinctive, it could have been for . . . anywhere . . . The chair of council got terribly worked up about it. He said the most important thing the university can do is produce its mission statement.

'Bland beyond belief', in the chair's words, the draft mission was referred to the planning committee and subsequently to the deans and departments on the basis, as the vice chancellor observed, that 'the heart of the mission statement should come from the ground upwards and not be something written in this office'.

Was this issue evidence of a wider clash of values between an out-going vice chancellor representing the traditional diversity and strength of academic collegiality, on the one hand, and a chair representing the growing trend towards managerial values and public accountability, on the other? Certainly we have already pointed to the chair's expression of regret that the university did not have a proper planning system and his sense of frustration that council was generally denied opportunities to be more proactive in planning and policy. It is also more than coincidental that the university has been undergoing a number of changes in the size of the council and a restructuring of its committee system. But the evidence of deeper fissures within the system of governance is suggestive rather than conclusive.

The Old University of the North

Unlike at the OUS, the chair of council at the OUN was a longer standing member of the university than the vice chancellor. He was in his second term of three years as chair and was previously a member of council. An experienced businessman and chair of a multinational corporation, the chair had an excellent grounding in higher education through his membership of a national quality council. The vice chancellor commented that the chair contributes a great deal of time and work to the institution and 'really knows what's going on'.

The chair perceived himself to be a non-executive who has an influence on the council, and thus on the strategy and direction of the institution. He felt that his office put him in a reasonable position to monitor, and act as a barometer of, the general attitude of council:

> It would be a non-executive chair, someone who comes in one day a week perhaps, or perhaps even less in some cases – who is not taking day-to-day decisions, who is not preparing the strategy documents but certainly has an influence in what they say. So I don't regard myself as running the university in any way at all, but I do regard myself as having a significant influence on the direction the university pursues. Influence, that is, with the council, but inevitably the chair of the council has to influence it in relation to his own beliefs – I mean I don't go round before I make a statement and counting all the council members' heads to see that they would agree with me, because they may or may not. But I feel that I am reasonably close to the sense in which the council would want to go and one can test that, of course, as you proceed in meetings – you have a fair idea of what the general attitude of the council is.

He noted that other opportunities arise where he can gauge the general feeling of council on specific strategic issues. For example, the funding council's annual review of strategy documents brought to the fore a review of the institutional direction and a reassessment of established priorities:

> Discussion of strategy documents . . . gives one opportunities again to test how people feel about the direction the university is taking and the balance it's putting between one thing and another. So say in relation to provision of accommodation, for example, or in relation to research and teaching priorities or in relation to new buildings against staff, and all these kind of issues that are, I suppose, resource issues. They can be called resource issues but in a sense they're much more than resource issues, they're actually strategic issues which have resource consequences. So one has to have a sense of that and keep that in one's mind as chair.

The chair felt that his role was to shift the analytical focus from detailed issues to a wider perspective of the general purpose of the institution. The general purpose as he saw it was to function for academic objectives, rather than commercial profit motives; and he felt that it was his responsibility as chair to assist in keeping that general purpose clear and preventing what can sometimes be imperceptible drifts into intrinsic money-making ventures. He also gave high priority among his responsibilities to assisting the vice chancellor. The vice chancellor had only been in post for a short period, and the chair considered that the opportunity of being able to probe the chair of council on certain issues rather than ask (subordinate) colleagues has proved very useful to the vice chancellor.

Since the vice chancellor was new to his appointment, he had only attended three council meetings at the OUN. He saw his role within council meetings as transmitting the institutional view and presenting decisions made further down to council. He also saw himself as a moderator between 'the university' and council:

> I see my role really as carrying lower-level decisions into the council forum for debate and decision – they rely on me to transmit the feeling from down below. There are other people there who speak to issues – by and large they will take the lead from me. My job is a sort of midman between the university and council. There are students on the council as well as academic staff and the pro vice chancellors, so they can all contribute, but normally the chair would ask me to say what I perceive to be an institutional view on an issue – say it and then the council will react accordingly. I think that's fair comment, I think, others may not see it like that.

By 'institutional view', the vice chancellor meant a perspective which had been gleaned through undergoing the consultative process and, therefore, one that reflected both an executive and academic perspective. It was, he thought, highly unlikely that he would express a view 'which was contrary to that of the academic board', and should this situation arise he would make council aware that this was the case. In terms of accountability, the vice chancellor also pointed out that the position of vice chancellor rather than that of council member was the 'accountable office'. In this respect he seemed to be making a distinction between responsibility and accountability (although at points he seemed to be using the terms synonymously):

> They [the council] are not accountable to shareholders obviously, but they have a similar role to a board of directors and the accountability, therefore, is essentially internal, I have to say. The external members of the panel of the council no doubt see their role ... in terms of public responsibility. The clients of the university are, as you know, numerous and we are responsible not to shareholders but to parents, to students, to employers, to ... a list of different constituencies which we're responsible to ... I personally include myself accountable to all those monarchies if you like. But they don't have any public responsibility other than to ensure that the system runs honestly and that there is not a misuse of public funds. But even if there is a misuse of public

funds, I am responsible, personally responsible, aren't I – I carry the can. The council doesn't resign *en masse* if there's over-expenditure; as far as I know, it's me who gets sacked. The accountable person is the vice chancellor and the senior academic is a vice chancellor too. That's in the statutes – I think I'm right about that.

In this interpretation of accountability, a serious case of maladministration would force the vice chancellor to resign, rather than council *en masse*. In this way, a vice chancellor's accountability is similar to ministerial responsibility, but differs in that ministerial responsibility relies for its original effectiveness on the convention that a minister will resign (Davies, 1979: 28). The vice chancellor, on the other hand, is also held directly accountable for his or her actions by council. As the vice chancellor pointed out, council has no corresponding direct accountability to external bodies, except, in broader financial solvency terms, to the Secretary of State via the funding council. It does have 'responsibility' to the public in the form of client groups, but council is not held directly to account by such groups.

These statements of roles and responsibilities by the two key players involved, however reflective, reveal little of the personal dynamics between the two offices. As at the OUS, members understood the importance of the relationship between chair and vice chancellor for achieving effective governance. 'That relationship is absolutely vital', the vice-chancellor observed. 'I think you could say that the whole system actually depends on that relationship – get it wrong and the sorts of problems that you're anticipating would come up, and the agenda would collapse and so on.' One of the lay governors, pursuing a further maritime metaphor, agreed:

> It's exactly the same in business, or it's the same running a hospital, or whatever – you can have all the procedures and guidelines and mechanisms that you like, but at the end of the day it comes down to how the chair of council organizes things and how the vice chancellor runs the university and how those two get on. If those two want to go off and do their own thing and keep it absolutely quiet and just give *fait accomplit* to everybody, it's very difficult for council to know really what's happening ... You can have all the non-executive directors in the world, if the chair and MD don't get on, or decide that they are going to do it this way, then basically that is how it would be. I know the non-executives and other members of the board have the ultimate decision, but the fact is, the ship's sunk by then. It's no good having a debate saying we are going to sack the captain when the ship's at the bottom of the sea and the crew are drowned.

Both the vice chancellor and the chair agreed that they had a good informal working relationship. The chair informed us that where possible he looked for a 'natural affinity' in close working relationships; and he was adamant that he could not work with a vice chancellor who would manipulate the relationship to his or her advantage by being over-selective in the choice of information passed on to the chair. The chair was satisfied that the vice chancellor kept him up to date with current events:

> If there is something that X [the vice chancellor] wants to talk to me about we go and talk about it. I see him regularly anyway for one reason and another. If there are things that he's doing that involve new people – who might be associated with the university – I'd come in and meet them and have lunch with them. Within the last three weeks I've probably had four or five lunches and dinners here where we're talk-ing to people from outside – where he thought I should know what was happening. So the chairman of council must get on with the vice chancellor at some level. It mustn't be one of I'll tell you what I think you need to know, it would be very difficult. I couldn't work with a vice chancellor who really was only going to tell me what he chose to tell me. And I can think of several of the present 100 vice chancellors that I would have nothing to do with whatsoever.

The chair also informed us that, when they were appointing the new vice chancellor, he had met each candidate (eight in total) on an individual basis over dinner, in order 'to make certain that we could live together'. As in the other case studies, the chair felt that it was important for this relationship to embody the attributes of mutual trust and influence, and to avoid conflict.

Should there be significant disagreement between the chair and vice chancellor, then a lay member positioned the lay treasurer as the check behind these two key players. The treasurer was important, he reasoned, because any new developments invariably require financial input; and he believed that if the treasurer was backing the vice chancellor and chair on a new idea, then this would hold tremendous sway with council. However, should the two main players 'fall out', then if the treasurer backed the chair that would be an end to the issue; but if he or she backed the vice chan-cellor, rather than the chair, other key members (the pro chancellors and then the pro vice chancellors) would have to be drawn into the dispute.

The New University of the South

Drawing comparisons between the leadership styles of the vice chancellors in the case study institutions is difficult and possibly unproductive. However, there is little doubt that the relationship between the vice chancellor of the NUS and other key players in the governing body was distinctly individual. As we have seen, the vice chancellor's political and consensual style was respected among governors. He was also perceived by independent governors to have good commercial and business credibility, and overall governors had strong confidence in his competence and ability. The clerk to the gov-ernors also felt that the vice chancellor helped to set the tone of governing body meetings and saw himself as playing a leading role in that body. One of the independent members described the approach vividly:

I have very high regard for X [vice chancellor] but he has effectively chosen everybody around him – one way or the other. So has he stacked the board, has he loaded the dice? Well he probably has. It's interesting to see him, he's a very smooth operator, and he will jump hard on anybody who tries to outflank him and at the governors' meeting. I've seen him do it once or twice and he's awesome, which is what you need – you can't have a committee type board, that's going to tie you up into intellectual knots and try and trip you up and he's awesome when he's dealing with rebellious students, academics or, well, primarily academics and students. But that's fine while it's going well but the guy's omnipotent.

The clerk to the governors, rather less awed, nevertheless agreed that the vice chancellor was very powerful. But ultimately it was power contained effectively by the governors:

This show is run very substantially by a very powerful vice chancellor who is very active and very energetic and the governing body has confidence in what he has done and is quite content to give him his lead, allow him to operate so long as they know what he's up to – which they do – and so long as they are satisfied that what he is doing is in accordance with the mission and strategy which they have approved.

In the clerk's view, the smooth operational running of the system was substantially because of 'the personalities and the mutual respect that operates' and also because of the historical dynamics of the governing body. The chair played a vital role in the process. A chair of some experience, he was liked and respected within the university, having invested an enormous amount of personal energy and time in the institution. The clerk to the board continued:

The chairman of the governors is held in great affection. He was in at the birth of the polytechnic, he was in at the choice of this site, he has seen it grow, he has always taken a personal interest in it, he gave up his membership of the local authority – in case that might have disqualified him from being appointed to the governing body here and becoming its chairman. He is very identified with the institution, we have given him an honorary degree to universal acclaim. He is so liked that so long as he and the VC are on the same wave length ...

A retired general practitioner and former Labour councillor and chair of the local education authority, the chair was effectively 'full-time' in his university role. The time commitment of the chair, including attendance at all committee meetings, was seen by the vice chancellor as an essential ingredient in the prominent role played by the board of governors. In his view, a change of chair to someone who had less time available would impact severely on the influence of the board. It would also deprive the university of the chair's values, values which had strongly influenced the NUS's development and overall ethos. The vice chancellor admitted that he almost unreflectingly accommodated his chair's values, since he knew that if he chose to disregard the chair's views the chair would confront him. The chair stressed that when differences did occur between himself and the vice chancellor, they negotiated informally until a consensus on what to recommend to the board had been reached. In contrast to the situation at the OUS, where differences had become public, the chair was unequivocal on the need to keep differences private, although he could not think of any occasion where he and the vice chancellor had gone to the governors with differing points of view.

From the perspective of one of the staff governors, however, the chair's approach was possibly too conciliatory. Although he had absolute confidence in the chair's personal integrity, he would prefer him to be more public in holding the vice chancellor to account. In this respect he felt that the chair had considerable influence over the style of the governing body:

> I suppose I would say . . . the relationship between the governors and the executive is a good one – it's a friendly one, it's one that tends to work on a consensus rather than a conflict basis. Although sometimes I would like the directorate to be more challenged, it's not that I actually think what they do is wrong – I would just like to feel that the directorate, when they came to the governors, didn't have it all quite so much in the bag as they do.

Although it is in the new university sector, the style of governance at the NUS clearly reflected the strong working relationship between its two leading office holders. The apparent dominance of the vice chancellor is clearly made possible by the role and style of the chair. The vice chancellor's managerial responsibilities and those of governor automatically force him into a position of having to 'wear two hats'. As chief executive and the most senior paid officer, he is individually – as employee – responsible to the board for the proper discharge of his duties, implementation of the board's decisions and providing the board with professional advice. As a governor, he shares collective responsibility with the remaining board members for the overall direction of the institution and supervision of the institution's management. The assumption underlying the duality of these roles is that the separation of these two functions can be achieved under the appropriate circumstances. The evidence of the NUS suggests that without the chair's support and, critically, without the general respect held throughout the governing body for the chair, the role of any vice chancellor could well become untenable.

The New University of the North

In contrast to the dominant governance style of the previous vice chancellor, the vice chancellor of the NUS tended to take a very low key, back seat stance in board meetings. The clerk felt that the vice chancellor, in taking this stance, was consciously acting in order 'to allow the governors to be a body in their own right' and also to position himself as a member of that body rather than as a leader playing a controlling part. In theory at least, by avoiding an overt leadership role in the governing body, the vice chancellor would contribute to the process of giving the governors greater ownership of the essential work of the university. In practice, the picture was more complicated.

The vice chancellor alluded to a relatively recent change of style and presentation at meetings, which had altered his role from fronting management proposals to vetting them. Prior to this change he would have fronted most of the management proposals and fielded all questions regarding them. However, over the past few years there was a move to treat the senior management tier as 'executive directors', and this has effectively meant that all assistant principals and directors of estates and finance were now required to be in attendance at board and FEGP meetings. They are now the ones who present and front management proposals, while the vice chancellor's role has been moderated to one of vetting papers by alerting his colleagues to issues that governors might raise. These senior officers meet before each meeting in order to rehearse their overall presentations and positions, and they then come in on cue, during the meetings, following the layout of the executive report.

The role of senior managers has become far more prominent, thereby allowing the vice chancellor to balance his collective governor role with the individual responsibilities of managerial leadership. The advantage from the vice chancellor's perspective is that certain managerial tasks can be delegated and, although nominal responsibility is retained by the vice chancellor, a critical distance between the vice chancellor and the detailed intricacies of each proposal can be created. This distance allows governors to challenge and probe the individual manager with working responsibility for formulation and implementation of policy proposals, without necessarily confronting the vice chancellor.

The vice chancellor recognized that he had an important responsibility to the academic community. In some ways he saw himself as a bridge between the academic board and governing body, providing advice and interpretations to both bodies on the respective positions taken by the other. In this sense he hoped to avoid a direct confrontational situation ever occurring between these boards:

> In the same way as I would hope that we would never get into a position where there was a stand off between what the governors say and what the academic board says. It makes sense, given I chair the academic board, for me to advise the academic board that they will never get certain things through the governing body in that tone or whatever. And similarly to advise the governing body that the academic board would never accept certain things.

From one perspective, therefore, the vice chancellor can be seen to be moulding apparent consensus by accommodating or eliminating differences of opinion that may otherwise split the groups over proposal changes. Unsurprisingly, perhaps, a staff governor was sceptical over this 'brokerage' role and saw the vice chancellor's dual academic/governor role as being potentially damaging to academic community interests: 'If he doesn't like what the academic board says, it can be sabotaged, can't it?' The observation may well be a valid criticism of the potentially manipulative power of the duality of role, but it should be pointed out that the opposite corollary is equally feasible. Indeed, further speculations made by this governor indicate that the vice chancellor could use the duality of role with equanimity in his treatment of the two boards. It was thought that the vice chancellor had, by his 'fleet-footedness', prevented governors wielding the full might of their 'unbridled power', and thus had also prevented damaging relations between governors and the academic community. Through the use of his 'extraordinary political and manipulative skills' (which were 'second to none'), he was seen, by this staff governor, as having 'spent three years actually keeping the governors at arm's length'.

In the light of these speculations, it may be valid to suggest that the duality of role could be skilfully used as a mechanism not only to distance certain groups from the decision-making process, but also to curb the excessive use of power by one dominant group over another.

During informal conversations between governors, an independent member raised the issue of the drive on policy being initiated by professional officers rather than governors. He was of the opinion that his colleagues recognized their reactive condition and mostly accepted it, since it was assumed that all higher educational institutions must operate in a similar fashion and also that these governors, as lead players in their own organizations, would run their businesses in the same way. That is, as lead players they would ensure that the issues going to meetings and subsequent outcomes were generally aligned with their own plans:

> But I'm sure as individual businessmen and company directors, they probably do it like that as well in their companies where they are the lead player. They might be the director of a company but they make damned sure that what goes to the board is what they want and that the outcomes are what they want, and I suspect that they're on a body where they are on the receiving end of that but they understand it because that's the way they work.

In other words, he felt that the vice chancellor was operating a model of decision-making very similar to that used in business, which allows him extensive control over final outcomes. However, it seems that the vice chancellor's control over decision-making is not necessarily a recent phenomenon brought about through corporate innovations. This governor also suggested that, although under the old LEA system the chair of governors 'thought he was running the place because everything went to him', in fact the vice chancellor 'was running it exactly the way then as he does now'.

The present chair is the second since incorporation and at the time of interview had served almost a year in this position. Since the vice chancellor's position is permanent (in this case, the current vice chancellor had been in post for approximately 13 years), in contrast to the normal fixed-term nature of the chair, it might be expected, given the crucial nature of the relationship, that the vice chancellor exercises a fair degree of influence over selection of the chair. A staff governor confirmed that 'the chair of governors is effectively selected by the vice chancellor'. This caused the staff governor some consternation, since a collusive relationship between the two key players, cemented by their effective control over the selection process of other independent governors, could lead to a breakdown of efficient scrutiny.

Nevertheless, a close working relationship between the two leading office holders was referred to by the chair as essential for the efficient running of any institution. This chair had extensive experience of corporate governance, being also chair of a company, vice-chair and chief executive of one of the major regional companies and director on a number of other boards. In his view, he runs the university board in much the same way as a private sector board. It is in the nature of a good working relationship between chair and chief executive, he observed, that any differences of opinion are ironed out informally without reaching the stage of being aired formally in board meetings:

> The way I have described running a board is no different from the way I run a private sector board – with my own company. Again I would expect to have discussed issues with the chief executive before a board, and if there is a fundamental difference between us on anything I would expect to have bottomed that privately. It is, however, in the nature of good relationships between chief executives and chairmen that you don't very often get those kind of things ... We will sometimes in debate address issues from a different direction – I will sometimes ask questions that reveal that perhaps I don't entirely endorse what the vice chancellor says. But we're back to style again, it would not be my style to go for confrontation between myself and the vice chancellor, it would be self-defeating, it would leave the whole board in a state of terrible confusion. It's far better, if there is a fundamental disagreement, to have had it before hand or to leave it to afterwards.

The vice chancellor confirmed that he and his present chair may have differences of view regarding methods of implementation, but 'no disagreements about the outcome'; and that therefore these differences would not concern the board of governors. He could not envisage a serious disagreement between himself and the chair ever reaching the board of governors, but could accept the possibility of a significant disagreement arising at the committee stage. At this stage, if the governors seriously disagreed with an executive proposal, the executive had two options: to pursue their recommendation regardless of governors' comments or modify it in the light of these comments. He pointed out that in such cases the chair has an important mechanism whereby he can block any proposals that have not been endorsed by the committee concerned – in that he can refuse to let it proceed to governors. Conversely, if the chair allows the proposal to proceed, in most circumstances this would indicate his and the committee's support.

In the opinion of the vice chancellor, the chair may well contribute his individual opinion (which may differ from the vice chancellor's) over an issue, but his main role is communicating the collectively negotiated perspective of the board or, more likely, the committees:

> I could not envisage it getting to that stage and if it were a very serious disagreement one of us would have to walk away and it would probably be me. I would not envisage our ever having a chairman of governors who was so dogmatic – that it was his view and not a governing body view and therefore I have to take that into account. The role of the chairman of governors and the responsibility of the chairman of governors is to advise me of the view of governors, not to advise me of his view. If it's just a personal thing, then that's fine – he can say, look, I disagree with you, we'll put it to governors. But if he says I disagree with you and I don't think the governors will agree with you, then he is telling me not to push it, and if I push it and it's very serious then – if I pushed it then I would think it's serious – so I can either persuade them or I can't.

In the relationship between chair and vice chancellor the dominant behavioural norm of the 'avoidance of conflict' is consciously observed – especially in formal board meetings. The chair suggested that observance of this norm by all co-participants in board meetings was also influenced by the particular chair's style, in that some chairs may prefer to generate confrontation in order to reach conclusions, whereas others, such as himself, preferred an approach which built consensus from progressive points of agreement. The chair also consciously avoided intruding into the vice chancellor's domain of executive responsibilities, and in this respect he perceived that his role was to ask questions and make suggestions. 'You see in the end – looking at it from the point of view of the chairman – it's the chief executive who has the responsibility of delivering. If the chairman gets too involved in saying how he thinks it should be delivered then he's starting to do the chief executive's job.'

The chair of the NUN board was clear that he was not there to take executive action or to take responsibility for the executive action taken. However, the working relationship between the chair and chief executive was such that individual ideas were routinely exchanged in private before emerging for more open scrutiny by other members. Where the ideas of one after private discussions subsequently reappeared as those of the other, then, in the chair's opinion, the process of governance had clearly worked.

Conclusion

The relationship between the two key office holders in the governance process, chief executive and chair of governors, has been seen as an essential element in the political and operational dimensions of decision-making in the four universities. It serves as a channel for key players to exchange and communicate ideas and differences of opinion between participating groups. It acts as an aid in the negotiation of outcomes. The effective operation of this communication channel is dependent on the maintenance of trust and good will between these two main players.

One-to-one meetings, off the record and unminuted, are an integral part of the 'relationship'. Vice chancellors use this forum to sound out certain ideas on the chair, and will then sometimes incorporate the chair's suggestions in revising these ideas. Vice chancellors, in discharging their executive duties, are responsible for the operationalization and interpretation of policy objectives or end goals. Even if these end goals are stated so broadly as to be acceptable to a majority in the university, how they are to be interpreted and achieved could prove a major source of conflict between different interest groups. Vice chancellors, by incorporating difference and objections obtained from key advisors and power-holders into original recommendations, can be seen to be accommodating or defusing potential conflicting perspectives while simultaneously consolidating influence by building support for and governor consensus over recommendations. A further example of this process may be found in the vice chancellor utilizing individual governors as expert advisors on specific issues.

However, these interpersonal relations with executive officers were difficult for independent governors to negotiate, since governors have no individual authority. It is inevitable that interpersonal processes will have a powerful influence on governance. In all the cases reviewed the interpersonal dynamics between certain influential governors and other key players created an informal core of governors, led by the chair, who could exert considerable influence over the remaining independent governors.

The dependency of 'effective' governance on interpersonal and largely informal relationships rather than on constitutional arrangements contains the best and worst of the governance process. At its best, the system allows the highly political process of managing the creative enterprise of the university to balance the often competing and contradictory interests of its constituents. The relative informality allows lay and independent perspectives to shed light on the management of change with sensitivity and discretion. At its worst, it leaves the process obscure and difficult to monitor. Light is shed, but only by those chosen by the caucus of governors. As one of the case study respondents observed, 'There's a lot going on under the stone, but I haven't got the power to lift it.' In the end it is difficult, even for governors, to ascertain the extent of informal influence on the governance process.

8

Clashes of Culture?
Comparative Perspectives on
University Governance

The changes in the governance culture of universities, described in preceding chapters, have not taken place in a vacuum. They are part of a larger story – in three main respects. First, governance has become both a contested arena and, more significantly, a problematical category. Second, the government of universities has been profoundly influenced by wider shifts in both corporate and public sector cultures, in the former case towards increased accountability and higher standards of conduct and in the latter towards greater enterprise. Higher education institutions, certainly the 'old' universities, have tended to be laggards rather than leaders in this process of corporate re-engineering and public sector reform. Third, changing governance structures, and ideologies, are key components of the worldwide transformation of higher education: from elite systems regulated by public policy to mass systems driven by 'market' imperatives; and from selective (and autonomous) institutions to open (and reflexive) ones.

The first issue was discussed in the introductory chapter. This chapter will consider the second and third: the changing shape of corporate and public sector governance (and, in particular, the reform of the National Health Service); and the evolution of university government in the rest of Europe and the United States. The former constitutes the political and managerial environment in which the recent development of university government in Britain has taken place; the latter reveals the deeper affinities between all modern higher education systems in their governance cultures. Together they serve to place the detailed findings of this research in a wider theoretical and public policy context.

The reform of corporate governance

The corporate system of the late twentieth century is characterized by globalization (successful companies are no longer 'national'), financialization ('instant' capital and cash flows), organizational reconfiguration (downsizing and out-sourcing), institutional volatility (the life-cycle of companies has been radically compressed); the acceleration of production (*sur mesure* manufacturing, just-in-time stock control, the shift to 'symbolic' goods) and new labour patterns ('portfolio' careers, tele-working, freelance contracting). These characteristics are generally taken as evidence of the emergence of a post-Fordist society.

Among the many discussions of post-Fordism, the impact of these changes on corporate governance has received little attention. Most notice, political and academic, has been taken of the emergence of new organizational environments, work cultures and management regimes. But just as traditional patterns of production and distribution, exchange and regulation matched the rhythms of an industrial society dominated by large, hierarchical and comparatively stable corporations, so existing structures of corporate governance tend to reflect the same anachronistic environment. These structures are breaking down because that environment is changing. The strategic and supervisory roles of company directors, essentially medium-term to long-haul responsibilities, are increasingly difficult to reconcile with the acceleration and volatility characteristic of many business organizations. A crisis of corporate control has developed, alongside post-Fordist production and consumption.

It is against this background that the corporate disasters of the past decade, in which boards of directors (especially non-executive directors) appeared unable to check the power, and whim, of charismatic chairs and/or chief executives, and for which shareholders, employees and pensioners paid the price, must be assessed. The collapse of the Maxwell companies and Barings Bank were the most spectacular examples. But there were many others: the Bank of Credit and Commerce International, Polly Peck, Coloroll, Blue Arrow. The cumulative effect of these episodes has been to suggest to some a systematic failure of corporate governance, which in turn can be attributed as much to post-Fordist volatility as old-fashioned piratical fraud.

Arguably, governance structures are the most archaic element within the corporate system. These are often more pre-Fordist than post-Fordist. Some corporate failures can ultimately be traced to this failure to modernize corporate governance. Entrepreneurial managers have been forced to take short cuts in order to maintain business efficiency. Far from policing management, and so preventing inappropriate behaviour, the archaism of corporate governance has provided an incentive, and justification, for bending the rules. According to Professor J. C. Shaw, deputy governor of the Bank of Scotland, late twentieth-century corporate governance perpetuates

a nineteenth-century model of corporate democracy which involves shareholders in general meeting appointing directors and receiving their account of stewardship . . . This model pre-dates the evolution of well-informed securities markets and the emergence of the 'professional' corporate manager. It pre-dates the prevalence of institutionalised savings and investment and, most importantly, pre-dates changing views of 'stakeholder' interests in the corporation beyond those of share-holder ownership.

(Shaw, 1993: 22)

However, the response has been to shore up the traditional model of corporate governance rather than attempt root-and-branch modernization. The open corporate governance culture characteristic of other parts of Europe, based often on a two-tier structure of supervisory and management boards, has not attracted significant support in Britain. The narrower (and shorter-term?) interests of institutional shareholders have been accommodated by encouraging them to develop a sense of 'ownership' in companies at the expense of the wider interests of 'stakeholders', who have been marginalized. The brief of the Cadbury Committee on Financial Aspects of Corporate Governance, which reported in 1992, was confined, as its title indicated, to financial aspects (i.e. how to avoid spectacular business failures and cut out fraud). It was not asked to examine the much broader quasi-constitutional aspects of corporate governance.

As a result, its recommendations were limited (Cadbury 1992). The committee argued: first, that there should be a clear division of responsibility at the head of a company to ensure that no individual had unfettered powers of decision (in other words, that the posts of chair and chief executive should normally be separated); second, that the board should have a sufficient number and quality of non-executive directors, whose views must be given proper weight in reaching board decisions; third, that the structure of the board should highlight the importance of the finance function; fourth, that a clear, and publicly identifiable, distinction must be drawn between a company's directors and its auditors. It can be argued that Cadbury was an attempt to revive the nineteenth-century arrangements which Professor Shaw had found wanting. Certainly, the committee's recommendations made only a modest contribution to resolving the basic flaw, or fissure, in corporate governance as it currently operates, the failure to distinguish properly (and the asymmetrical power relationship) between managers and other directors, still less to confronting the more fundamental dilemmas created by the emergence of the fast-moving, volatile and loosely coupled post-Fordist corporation.

It has been argued, by Professor Shaw (1993: 28) among others, that by recommending an explicit demarcation between executive and non-executive directors, the Cadbury code of good practice implicitly endorsed the eventual emergence of a two-tier corporate structure with governing and management boards. Certainly the report, and code, raised issues of accountability that previously had aroused little interest. They reflected the more thoughtful analyses of the effects of different corporate governance traditions published in the late 1980s. For example, Jonathan Charkham (1989a, b) argued that directors had a key mediating role between managers, the *de facto* corporate owners, and shareholders, the *de jure* owners. If the balance was tilted too much towards the managers and against the share-holders, arguably the effect of current corporate governance arrangements, the latter would attempt to exercise control through short-term buying and selling of shares, particularly in the context of take-over bids, so fuelling the volatility of the corporate system.

However, the political context in which the Cadbury Committee was appointed was of an embarrassing accumulation of corporate scandals, just as two years later the appointment of the Nolan Committee was prompted by 'sleaze'. Inevitably, the emphasis was on controlling excess, rather than analysing the longer-term restructuring issues. Just as the aim of Nolan has been to safeguard standards of conduct in public life, so Cadbury's aim was to raise standards of corporate behaviour. Both, in an important sense, were reactions against the free-wheeling political and business cultures of the late 1980s.

The impact of these changes in corporate governance on the government of universities and colleges has been ambiguous. Perhaps the most powerful message, reinforced more recently by Nolan, has been the need to place the highest value on financial propriety. Lay, or 'independent', members of governing bodies have been encouraged to intensify their scrutiny of management in the financial arena. Audit committees are seen as having a key control role. Next, Cadbury's emphasis on a division of power at the top of companies may have encouraged chairs of governing bodies to be more assertive in their dealings with their chief executives. Material from the case studies tends to support this view.

But the wider debate provoked by the Cadbury Report on the need to distinguish between executive and non-executive directors, and between directors and managers, appears less relevant. In universities and colleges the fundamental demarcation is between lay, or 'independent', members and those governors who are employed by the institution, themselves divided into managers and quasi-representatives of academic and other staff members. Although there is a potential alignment between the two dichotomies, the differences are perhaps more significant. Moreover, in the 'new' universities and colleges the vice chancellor is the only executive director, although other senior managers are likely to be in powerful attendance. In the 'old' universities, pro vice chancellors and other *ex officio* senior academics are council members, but their 'executive' affiliation is weaker.

However, it would be wrong to conclude that debates about, and reforms of, corporate governance have had little influence over the changing patterns of governance in higher education. First, these parallel developments suggest an intriguing synergy between corporate and academic systems, and a deep-rooted secular shift in our construction of notions of governance and accountability. Second, more prosaically, changes in university governance are often seen as having been inspired by corporate examples. So, to the extent that corporate governance is reformed, reverberations are likely to be felt in higher education.

Governing the welfare state

The radical socio-economic changes characterized as post-Fordism are mirrored in an equally radical evolution of the welfare state (a label employed here in its widest sense to embrace not only classic welfare state services, including education, but the wider articulations between state, community and individual citizens). Some commentators have indulged in ideological millenarianism, announcing the death of the welfare state and its replacement by the 'enterprise' society. Most analysts have adopted a more sober approach, arguing that the welfare state is being reformed rather than repudiated. If there is a crisis, they argue, it takes the form of an irresistible force (taxpayer revolt, individualization of social aspirations, marginalization of the 'underclass') meeting an immovable object (vested interests supporting, and deep structural forces influencing, high levels of state expenditure). But even these more sober analysts acknowledge the radicalism of the socio-political trends that have fuelled, and also constitute, the transformation of the welfare state.

These trends include: the undermining of 'welfare' values, the liberal and perhaps paternalistic ideology that conferred legitimacy on state intervention in the social arena; the revival of older collective notions, such as community or civil society, *contra* the welfare state; the downgrading of social justice and upgrading of economic competitiveness among the state's competing purposes; a retreat from 'planning', or public choices made in the political arena, and enthusiasm for 'markets', suitably policed; the rise of the new accountability based on business-like audit rather than democratic responsibility; the erosion of the notion of the state as the guardian of the 'public interest', itself grounded in ideas of national genius and history, and replacement by the contractual state, purchasing services on behalf of tax-payers; the growing fuzziness of the once-sharp demarcation between public and private sectors.

The overall impact of these changes on the workings of the state and the functioning of public institutions has been far-reaching, but also full of contradiction. On the one hand, there is political centralization, for example, by imposing value-for-money audits; on the other, operational disaggregation (even disintegration) by establishing quasi-markets, notably in the health service, which will be discussed below. On the one hand, there is politicization of previously 'neutral' arenas, of which the 'old' universities were perhaps the best example; on the other, increased room for functional manoeuvre for institutions previously constrained by bureaucratic regulation, which has benefited the 'new' universities. On the one hand, there is the end of government, especially in the social policy sphere; on the other, a new political activism, in particular to enhance national competitiveness. Their detailed impact on higher education can easily be traced. The porousness of the public–private frontier has been reflected in the pressure on universities to acquire 'alternative' (i.e. non-state) funding and the growth of privatized niches within public institutions; the thrust towards competitiveness in Technology Foresight and similar efforts to target research; the contractual state in the detailed relations between funding councils and institutions; the rise of the audit society in teaching quality and research assessment.

Although not necessarily well understood, these phenomena have been frequently discussed. However, almost no attention has been paid to the implications of this transformation of the welfare state for the governance of public institutions. In the past two decades, radical changes have taken place in our conception of the welfare state. The institutions and agencies that comprise that state have had to operate in novel environments. They have become different kinds of organization. New discourses, operational as well as rhetorical, have been developed. But, remarkably, the changing role of those bodies legally responsible for public institutions, which are being radically revised in both conceptual and operational terms, has received little consideration as a subject in its own right. To the (limited) extent that governance has become an issue, it has been as a subordinate element within the larger project of introducing a new management culture into the public sector or, as with the reform of the National Health Service, the incorporation of the polytechnics and colleges in 1989 or the establishment of grant maintained schools, a consequential factor, the adjustment of governance to these new arrangements.

As in the corporate sector, the confusion between management and governance has continued. It can be argued that it has become worse. In the unreformed public sector a fairly clear demarcation existed between the role of governing bodies, largely supervisory in their functions and quasi-representative in their composition, and the responsibilities of those in charge of institutions, whose authority was more often derived from their professional status than from their managerial expertise. The reform of the NHS, where this demarcation was more weakly developed than in other parts of the welfare state because of its democratic deficit, has made it more difficult to distinguish between the separate domains of management and governance. Indeed, it is not clear whether, in a decade and a half of reform, the existence of the latter domain was ever properly recognized. Acknowledged itself to be a paradigm shift (Holliday, 1992: 2), the reform of the NHS has also been taken to be the paradigm for the restructuring of the whole public sector. As such, it has exercised a powerful external influence over the evolution of the governance–management of higher education.

NHS reform comprised three phases (Wistow, 1992: 110). The first, from 1979 to 1982, was characterized by an attack on bureaucracy. *Patients First* was the key text (DHSS, 1979). Another important element during this first phase was decentralization. Area health authorities were abolished, and most of their responsibilities devolved to local district health authorities. In the second phase, from 1982 to 1989, decentralization was superseded by renewed centralization. A line management hierarchy stretching from the Department of Health and Social Security down through general managers at regional, district and unit (hospital) levels was created. During the 1980s, increasing emphasis was also placed on efficient management and, more controversially, on managerialism. The report by Sir Roy Griffiths on NHS management was the key text during this second phase (Griffiths, 1983). A powerful NHS policy board and management executive were established within the department to 'run' the health service.

In the third phase, beginning in 1989, an internal market was created. Health authorities ceased to be responsible for providing health care services. Instead they, along with fund-holding general practitioners, purchased services from newly created NHS trusts, which were now responsible for running hospitals ('providers', in the new language of the health service). Currently, 96 per cent of hospital and community health services are provided by trusts and 40 per cent of the population are on the lists of fund-holding GPs. As a result, the role of health authorities has been attenuated. The number of regional health authorities has been cut to six, distancing them still further from the commissioning and delivery of health care, while the purchasing responsibilities of district health authorities have been eroded by the rise of GP fund-holding.

The rise of managerialism within the NHS, and the consequent culture clash with older professional ethics, have reverberated through higher education. The 'marketization' of public policy, of which the NHS reform is perhaps the highest-profile example, has also been a dominant theme of university development, as has been indicated in the introductory chapter. The tension between central direction (in the health service, the NHS management executive; in higher education, the funding councils) and local discretion (in the NHS, hospital trusts and GP fund-holders; in higher education, the incorporation of the former polytechnics and colleges) is also a pervasive theme. Managed 'markets' are full of contradictions. But these are not the issues here. The issue is the impact of NHS reforms on the governance culture of hospitals and the health service.

As has already been suggested, issues of governance, as opposed to management, featured little in the to-and-fro arguments about the reform of the health service. To the extent that governance has been directly addressed it is through the debate about accountability (Hunter, 1992: 436–8). Community health councils, which were established in the 1970s to represent both health users and activists, have survived the reforms, although greater emphasis is now placed on their consumer than on their political functions. In any case, they play no part in 'governing' the health service, even according to the widest definition of governance. Health authorities too no longer 'govern' health services, because they no longer manage hospital or other facilities, although they influence health care provision through their commissioning responsibilities. In the commissioning process technical assessment of local needs is emphasized, rather than political articulation of local demands for health services. Consequently, it is not felt that the (non-executive) members of health authorities should be representative.

Apart from the Department of Health, the NHS management executive and various off-shoot NHS trusts are the key institutions in the reformed health service. As health care providers they manage hospitals and other units. Trusts, like higher education institutions, employ their staff and 'own' their buildings (although with greater restriction on disposal). In some regards they are freer than universities and colleges; they are able to determine the salaries of their employees and the structure of their workforce without necessary regard to national agreements, which explains why skill mix has become such a controversial issue in the NHS. In other regards, trusts have considerably less freedom for manoeuvre: they are obliged to earn a 6 per cent return on assets in use, break even taking one year with another and stay within their external financing limits (House of Commons Health Committee, 1992). So there are important differences between universities and hospitals which make comparisons between their patterns of governance difficult.

However, trust boards are broadly analogous to university and college governing bodies in their status, powers and responsibilities. But they are smaller and their make-up is significantly more 'corporate'. They have equal numbers of executive and non-executive directors, five of each. Superficially, some 'old' university councils, although much larger, have a similar balance between lay and academic members, but it would be a great mistake to assume any affinity between their governance cultures. In 'new' universities and colleges, governing bodies include only one 'executive' member (the vice chancellor or principal) and have a majority of 'independent' members, the rough equivalent of non-executive members of trust boards.

These fundamental differences in size and composition suggest that NHS trust boards and higher education governing bodies are very different animals. The former are significantly more executive in their ethos; governance has effectively been elided into management, with non-executive board members playing a similar role to non-executive directors in the private sector, despite arguments that 'the challenge will be to balance the business interests of trusts with public sector values' (Rosen and McKee, 1995: 704). The latter, despite the impact of incorporation on the government of the 'new' universities and colleges and pressure to modernize 'old' university councils, have firmly remained non-executive bodies with supervisory and strategic functions.

A key difference between NHS trusts and higher education institutions is how they receive their income. The most important source of it, virtually all in the case of the health service and the bulk in the case of higher education, is the same, the state. Because higher education has significant sources of non-state income, its governance might be expected to be closer to the corporate model. In fact the reverse is true. The explanation lies in how public resources are channelled to health and higher education. Despite its artificiality, a market-of-sorts exists in the NHS. As a result, trusts must 'trade' with the purchasers of health care. In effect their income comes from the 'prices' they charge for their products. None of this applies to universities and colleges. They receive grants through the funding councils. They are funded differentially not because they have chosen to charge different 'prices' but because the funding councils have chosen to differentiate institutional funding (whether for bad reasons, such as historic costs, or good ones, such as the results of research assessment).

This distinction between NHS trusts and higher education institutions reflects broader conceptual categorizations that have been made of non-profit organizations (The term 'non-profit' is used because much of the literature is American, although analogies can be drawn with public institutions in Britain). According to one categorization, there are four main types of non-profit organizations: donative-mutual, donative-entrepreneurial, commercial-mutual and commercial-entrepreneurial (Hansmann, 1980, 1987). Higher education institutions are clearly 'donative' organizations because they receive grants, while trusts are 'commercial' because they rely on selling their services to health authorities and GP fund-holders. This is the primary distinction.

The secondary distinction, between mutual and entrepreneurial, refers partly to the ethos of organizations and partly, which is why it is relevant here, to their governance. Mutual organizations are governed by elected or, at any rate, representative directors, while entrepreneurial organizations are governed along corporate lines. In this scheme, NHS trusts are hard to place, although they veer towards the entrepreneurial end of the spectrum because of the lack of accountability of board members (Bartlett and Le Grand, 1994: 55). Higher education institutions are also difficult to categorize. Clearly, all are donative organizations, but in many a significant shift has taken place from the mutual to the entrepreneurial in terms of general orientation and, in the case of the 'new' universities and colleges, their governance. It can be argued that, in Hansmann's categorization, nearly all 'old' universities have remained donative-mutual organizations although some individual institutions are pressing up against the entrepreneurial frontier; while 'new' universities and colleges are donative-entrepreneurial organizations. This distinction not only helps to make sense of the current differences in governance between the two (ex)binary sectors, but may also be relevant to estimates of the likely degree of convergence between them.

University governance in the United States and Europe

A generation ago, only the United States had a truly mass system of higher education. The British system was recognizably elite as late as the mid-1980s, still enrolling fewer than one in five school-leavers, and other European systems, although ostensibly more open, were also constrained by elite academic and scientific traditions, sharp status demarcations between universities and other post-secondary institutions, and post-entry selectivity with large-scale culls of weaker students. Higher education systems in other advanced countries, such as Australia and Japan, although influenced by America's mass paradigm, were similarly constrained. In the mid-1990s, mass systems have become routine. The opening up (and out) of British higher education has been described in the introductory chapter. Across Europe, and the rest of the developed world (and even in the Third World, although the articulations with society and the economy are different), participation has accelerated. 'Binary' distinctions between universities and other institutions have been eroded where they have not been abolished outright. Universities have taken on multiple missions, including 'non-university' roles, while 'university' functions have increasingly been undertaken by other institutions: think-tanks and consultancies in the research arena and the so-called corporate classroom in education and training.

For universities as institutions, and so for university governance, there have been two overarching consequences. First, they have become large and complex organizations that must be managed. The increasing prominence of management, in turn, has upset the quasi-constitutional balance of political and professional interests that sustained traditional patterns of university government. Second, higher education institutions may have to operate in a much more volatile and rivalrous environment. Their own missions have been stretched, perhaps in the process undermining older notions of institutional integrity, and competition is everywhere: within universities, among departments, centres and other units; between universities, as more competitive funding and selective assessment regimes have been developed; and between universities and other 'learning organizations'. These changes too have put pressure on university government. Universities no longer occupy well defined (and well defended) niches. All mass systems in developed countries are subject to similar imperatives. All, therefore, have experienced a similar crisis of governance, despite differences in their legal and/or political status, administrative protocols and conventions and traditions of government. In the final section of this chapter, university governance in the United States and the rest of Europe will be discussed, highlighting these differences and illuminating this general crisis.

The pattern of university governance is shaped by the nature of the relationship between universities and their pay-masters, generally the state. If that relationship is relaxed, the role and responsibilities of university governing bodies are enhanced. If it is prescriptive, they are constrained. As a result, scholars of higher education have tended to draw two important distinctions: between private and public institutions; and, because of the greater weight of private institutions in the American system, between the United States and Europe. Neither is as forceful as has traditionally been argued. First, the public–private frontier has become increasingly porous. Many private universities in the United States are heavily dependent on public money, particularly for research and student aid, while many public institutions raise serious sums of private money (to such an extent, in fact, that some state universities have toyed with the idea of relabelling themselves 'state-assisted'). In Britain, the universities' determination to keep the new funding councils' hands off their non-state income was an important element in their (formally successful, actually vain) campaign against the Education Reform Act.

Private and public institutions alike are promiscuously scattered along the donative-mutual to commercial-entrepreneurial spectrum of non-profit organizations discussed in this chapter. Harvard, with its billion-dollar endowments, is clearly a donative-mutual organization, as is Oxford, although the first is notionally private and the second notionally public. The University of Buckingham, Britain's only private university, fits best perhaps into the commercial-mutual category, arguably along with some 'new' universities. Although no British higher education institution falls into the commercial-entrepreneurial category (some further education colleges may), this categorization is not incompatible with public status, as the example of NHS trusts demonstrates. So the link between the public–private distinction and the character of the institution, and its governance, is far from straightforward.

The second distinction, between Europe and the United States, is equally problematical. A recent study of the level of 'flexibility' in higher education systems in 15 Western European countries and 25 American states found little evidence of trans-Atlantic incommensurability (McDaniel and Buising, 1992). The authors identified seven elements of 'flexibility': the basic legal position of the institution; budgetary flexibility; flexibility to raise its own income; flexibility regarding educational activities; flexibility in determining personnel policy; flexibility regarding administrative structure; and flexibility regarding access capacity. Although governance was not explicitly considered in their study, all these 'flexibilities' are clearly relevant to the character of university government.

The average American state system was more 'flexible' than the average European system. But eight American systems were categorized as either intermediately or predominantly centralized, while six European systems were categorized as decentralized or predominantly decentralized. The most centralized system was Montana; and the most decentralized the United Kingdom. This study, which relied on official information, was not able to assess the actual 'flexibility' enjoyed by higher education institutions. If it had, the trans-Atlantic fuzziness might have been increased. The private and more incestuous administrative culture typical of Europe, arguably, gives universities greater room for manoeuvre than the more public and legalistic culture of the United States. These ambiguities and obscurities need to be borne in mind when considering the evolution of university governance on opposite shores of the Atlantic.

There are broadly four types of governance in the American system. The first is characteristic of the best private universities (Harvard, Stanford, Princeton and the rest) and liberal arts colleges, such as Bryn Mawr and Carleton. Authority is vested in a board of trustees who are distinguished alumni/ae, generous donors to university funds or drawn from the business and civic elite. However, as is the case in the 'old' universities in Britain, they tend to defer to the separate but equal authority of the academic guild. Although fund-raising is an intense preoccupation even in the wealthiest American universities, the emphasis is on increasing endowments as much as securing contracts. Indeed, private 'giving' is directed to endowments; contractual relationships are more likely to be with the federal government and other state agencies. Significant endowments provide a cushion from immediate 'market' pressures, whether to become embroiled in activities that compromise academic freedom or to accept, or solicit, gifts from inappropriate sources. Endowments also allow universities to provide generous scholarships and otherwise discharge their 'public' responsibilities. Although parts of universities may engage in highly entrepreneurial activities and the 'market' for esteem is intense in American higher education, boards see themselves as university trustees, not as company directors.

The second type of governance applies to the rest of the private sector. Here, boards of trustees are able, and obliged, to be more commercial. The comparative lack of prestige weakens the balancing authority of the academic guild. There is no doubt about which is dominant. Trustees hire and fire faculty members. Presidents tend to have short shelf-lives. Most private universities and colleges lack substantial endowments. They must live off their current income. The most important source is tuition fees. Awkward issues arise about targeting student constituencies (affirmative action and all that) and determining affordable levels (high fees are a sensitive political issue for an American middle class struggling to maintain its life-style and life-chances for its children). Other sources include endowment fund-raising but are dominated by contracts. Institutional viability is often an issue. Trustees tend also to be drawn from alumni/ae and local business communities.

The third type prevails in the elite state universities (e.g. California, Michigan, Wisconsin). Typically, boards of regents are appointed by the governor, generally with the concurrence of the state legislature. But, rather like US Supreme Court justices (who, of course, are appointed for life), their long terms of office insulate them from immediate political pressures. Nineteen regents of the University of California are appointed for staggered 12-year terms and seven, including the governor, are *ex officio* regents. The intention is to make it difficult for a particular governor or legislature to determine the composition of the whole board, although they can bring pressure to bear through the budgetary process. But this does not mean that regents are meant to be apolitical, like the old University Grants Committee. Their meetings are often high, and very public, political drama. Celebrated Californian examples were the decision to dismiss the black communist professor Angela Davies in 1968, admittedly under intense pressure from then governor Ronald Reagan, and to scrap existing affirmative action guidelines in 1994, a decision vigorously protested by Jesse Jackson. Most of the famous state universities were established under their state's constitution, which affords them further protection. But again it is misleading to suggest that this denotes a desire for an arm's length relationship. Most also employ lobbyists in their state capitals and in Washington.

The regents of the big state universities and the boards of trustees of the most famous private universities have much in common. Both must contend with powerful academic guilds whom they cannot afford to offend, because there is as active a market for big-hitting professors as there is for football or baseball stars. They are drawn from similar political, business and professional elites. Their institutions have interests in common as large research universities. As such, much of their lobbying effort is directed to influencing the policies of the hydra-headed federal government. Many of the most divisive issues, such as affirmative action, political correctness and sexual harassment, arise from legal obligations that affect public and private universities equally. It is not surprising, therefore, that in practice their governance cultures are broadly similar. Size, not legal status, is the most significant discriminator. Many state universities are multi-campus institutions with hundreds of thousands of students; most private universities are single-site institutions much closer in scale to 'old' universities in Britain.

The fourth type prevails in the bulk of public institutions, whether four-year state universities or two-year community colleges. Although there are important state-by-state variations, a typical pattern is to have a system-wide governing board. Sometimes all state institutions are covered; in other cases all bar the 'flagship' research university; in others again four-year and two-year institutions are governed by different boards. Some states have established coordinating councils while leaving separate governing boards in place. Some councils have budgetary and planning powers; others are confined to advice, coordination and strategic matters. Typically, these boards lack the entrenched safeguards possessed by regents, although the practical effect may be slight. Regents, despite these safeguards, are governing high-profile institutions, expensive to operate and prey to political controversy. Governing bodies, while lacking similar political insulation, are responsible for less contentious institutions.

Another characteristic of this fourth type of governance is that governing boards, and still more coordinating councils, are often responsible for a large number and wide variety of institutions. As such, they are distant bodies, more accurately regarded as part of the state's governance apparatus rather than as representing institutional governance. They cannot be regarded as champions of individual institutions, like the regents of elite state universities or boards of trustees of private universities (or, indeed, the councils of 'old' universities in Britain). Rather, their responsibilities frequently involve them in attempts to restructure whole systems. Their relationship with the academic guild, itself splintered, is weak, more often expressed through the machinery of industrial relations than any collegial links, however, diffuse.

There are many exceptions to, and gradients within, these four types. The world's most developed higher education system, with almost 4000 institutions and 13 million students, is not easily categorized, even on a confined topic such as governance. The variety of American higher education is also its strength. But its constitution possesses certain common underlying characteristics. Clark Kerr, former president of the University of California and uniquely well qualified to comment, has reached the following conclusion: 'The basic governance system of American higher education is, I believe, the best in the world – with great responsibility placed with independent boards of trustees, with comparatively strong presidencies, and with shared governance in academic areas with the faculties' (Kerr, 1994: 36).

The lessons that British higher education might learn from the experience of governance in the American system are probably limited. Political environments and administrative cultures are very different despite shared academic traditions and superficial structural similarities, at least among elite universities in Britain and the United States. The major causes for concern that Kerr identifies reflect the particularities of the American system: political factions within boards of trustees; the domination of boards by faculty unions; the selection of university presidents under 'sunshine' procedures (i.e. open meetings); and the insecurity of flagship campuses within wider state systems. None, with the possible exception of the first, applies in Britain. Yet his list of general problems has more resonance. These include the need to clarify the respective roles of board and president, closer links between boards and the life of the campus, a good understanding between the president and individual trustees and 'careful consideration of the quality of the agenda for each meeting' (Kerr, 1994: 37). Many of these issues have already been touched on in earlier chapters in the context of our research.

University governance in the rest of Europe was once straightforward: it barely existed. Universities were state institutions that, in administrative although not academic terms, could not be distinguished from the rest of the government machine. Their staff were civil servants, enjoying all the benefits in terms of security of employment but also governed by the same regulations as other civil servants. This sometimes produced paradoxical results. For example, in the Federal Republic of Germany professors possessed virtually a freehold title to their chairs but at the same time were subject to the *Berufsverbot*, the ban on the appointment of communists and their sympathizers to civil service positions. In many European countries the appointment of professors had to be confirmed by the ministry. Rectors were often chosen by the government. The maintenance of university buildings was the responsibility of the state, which, in effect, owned them. The internal structure of universities, too, was determined by the state. Faculties and chairs were established by ministries and parliaments, and so could not easily be restructured. It is hardly surprising that, under such conditions, institutional governance was weakly developed. Its functions were essentially symbolic and ceremonial, because oversight of the management of universities remained the responsibility of the state.

In practice, European universities enjoyed considerably greater autonomy than these formal arrangements suggested. First, they enjoyed great prestige both as academic institutions, in terms of their perceived importance in maintaining national greatness and intellectual civilization, and as high-state organizations. Second, the bureaucratic regulations by which they were bound were largely determined by the universities themselves in this latter capacity. They were on the 'inside' of government. Third, the expansion of higher education and student revolt during the 1960s left many European universities with representative organs of self-government. Democratization was more thorough than in British higher education, where older (and opposed) notions of collegiality prevented the growth of a properly democratic culture. Fourth, in any case, far-reaching reforms of state–university relations and of university government have been undertaken in several European countries, notably in Spain during post-Franco reconstruction and more recently in the Netherlands and Sweden as part of a wider liberalization of state structures.

Decentralization was the common theme of all these reforms. Not only were universities granted near-total control over their academic affairs, significant devolution of administrative powers also took place. In some cases new and old regimes were combined. For example, in Sweden the *Rikstag*, through the government, has retained its old power to establish university chairs, but universities are now free to add new chairs within the limits of their budgets. Rectors in all three countries, and many other parts of Europe, are formally appointed by the government but, in effect are elected by a broadly based constituency of staff, non-academic as well as academic, and students. Universities now have much greater influence over student numbers, although in most subjects all qualified students are entitled to places, which makes it difficult for either universities or the state to plan detailed intakes. (Sweden is a prominent exception to open entitlement, and the application of a number clause is becoming more widespread in other countries too.) Typically, university administrations are now responsible for their own buildings, although salary structures are still determined by the state. University companies, and other entrepreneurial mechanisms, are now common.

As a result, more attention has been paid to university governance. Recently, the emphasis has shifted from its symbolic and ceremonial aspects, and its representative functions, which were elaborated during the democratization of the 1960s and 1970s, to its supervisory and strategic responsibilities. Detailed arrangements vary. In France, university councils are large and often politicized bodies, over which the president nervously presides, but effective power is now exercised by executive boards. In Spain, so-called 'social' councils have been established alongside university councils. Their function is to represent external stakeholders, notably in the business community. The rector and the president of the 'social' council form a duopoly. In the Netherlands universities are effectively governed by a *troika*: the rector, the chair of the university council and the university director (equivalent to the registrar in a British university).

A typical case study of how many European universities are governed is provided by the example of Uppsala University, Sweden's oldest. The top decision-making body is the university board (*Konsistoriet*). It is chaired by the rector, who is formally appointed by the government for a five-year term, but after an election in the university. Members of the board are divided into three groups. First, there are seven lay members, again appointed by the government but after extensive consultation inside the university and in the local community. National celebrities mingle with local politicians. Second, three professors are elected by their peers. Third, two students are elected by the students' union. So the council has a seven-to-six lay majority, even when the rector is counted. In addition, trade unions have the right to send observers to the monthly meetings of the board, at which they are allowed to speak. The agenda of board meetings and implementation of board decisions are the responsibility of the rector, assisted by the university's administrative director. The rector also chairs the council of deans (Uppsala University, 1995: 6–7).

The implications of university governance in the rest of Europe for British higher education are intriguing, especially in the light of the wider convergence of institutions within the framework of the European Union. There are important differences, the most important of which is the degree of politicization that many people in Britain would find uncongenial in an academic setting. The councils of many other European universities, in effect, combine the functions of governing bodies and senates (with a quasi-syndicalist role thrown in for good measure). But there are equally important similarities. Particularly interesting is the convergence between the roles of rector and vice chancellor. Both occupy pivotal roles in their institutions: as *primus inter pares* in the academic guild; as head of the administration; and as mediator between the university and its external stakeholders in the community, business and government.

Conclusion

The purpose of this chapter has been to place the condition of governance in British higher education, discussed in earlier chapters, in a wider context. An important element of that wider context is developments in the corporate sector for at least two reasons. First, many lay council and 'independent' governing body members themselves come from the corporate sector, which, rather than the local community or professions, has been the favoured source of new recruits. Second, the government has encouraged the belief that the corporate sector provides the most appropriate model of governance for higher education in the age of massification and marketization. The discussion of recent developments in corporate governance suggests that this second assertion should be treated with considerable caution. It may be that (some) higher education institutions could benefit from a dose of managerialism and entrepreneurship, if only as a corrective to the old donnish culture or municipal regimes. But there is little evidence that the corporate sector has useful models of governance to offer higher education. If this is accepted, the case for giving priority to those from the corporate sector in appointing new governors is perhaps weakened.

The comparison with the National Health Service reforms suggests similar caution. Again, no persuasive models of governance have been generated that might be adapted to higher education – for two main reasons. The first is that, remarkably, issues of governance have barely been touched on in health service reform. The (perhaps obsessive) focus has been on more effective management, which has been interpreted as an elevation of the managerial interest at the expense of professional perspectives. Indeed, it can be argued, the construction of an internal 'market' within the NHS has made issues of governance, as opposed to management, and accountability, as distinct from market transactions, redundant. Time will tell whether that is a valid judgement. The NHS's high political profile, and capacity for headline-grabbing controversy, suggests it may not be. The second is that NHS trusts and higher education institutions, although superficially aligned, are different kinds of institutions. For better or worse, trusts operate in a quasi-commercial environment. Universities and colleges do not, except in terms of fringe entrepreneurial activities. To adopt the terminology used earlier in this chapter, they are 'donative' organizations.

The comparisons with patterns of university governance in the United States and the rest of Europe have produced some intriguing affinities, but also highlighted some significant differences. The USA has an articulate system of higher education, in the sense that regents and boards of trustees are often responsible for multi-campus universities or for whole sectors. As a result, they are largely 'external' to the institutions themselves. In Britain, the standard is single institutions and single governing bodies, a pattern only replicated in the United States in the elite private universities. In the rest of Europe, as has just been pointed out, university government has a politicized, even histrionic, quality alien to the institutional cultures of many British universities. Yet the affinities are equally significant: the pivotal role of the rector, vice chancellor or president; the need to give external stakeholders a sense of genuine 'ownership' while not alienating the academic guild; and conceptualizing, then operationalizing, the separate spheres of management and governance.

Convergence and incompatibility of governance cultures persist in the comparisons made in this chapter: between higher education and other sectors, corporate and private; and between different national higher education systems. Yet, potentially, both are equally illuminating. Through exploration of both similarities and differences, new lights, from opposing directions, are thrown on governance in British higher education, which highlight the dilemmas it faces. At the very least, these comparisons offer some external reference points to open up consideration of university governance.

9

Changing Patterns of Governance?

The governance of higher education is at once crucial and opaque, a key arena and a peripheral topic. It is central to our understanding of the institutional characteristics of universities and colleges; their radically revised (and rapidly revisable) missions; the development of the wider higher education system as it shifts from an elite to a mass configuration; and their, and its, articulation with grand secular themes such as the 'reform' of the welfare state and the emergence of a volatile and reflexive post-industrial society. How universities are governed cannot fail to illuminate these far-reaching changes. But governance is also deeply obscure. Its mechanisms have gone unresearched, in intriguing contrast to the abundance of inquiry into, at the system level, policy formation and, at the level of institutions, managerial responses. More importantly, available accounts of university government oscillate unhelpfully between 'dignified' interpretations that are uninformative about its 'efficient' working and scandalous reports that scream about the invasion of academic space by an alien 'business' culture, the politicization of governance by an unaccountable quango-culture and, in a few instances, sleaze.

The aim of this book, as of the research on which it is based, has been to relieve the opacity and obscurity that has surrounded university governance and unlock its potential for improving our understanding of wider change in higher education and in society. This final chapter is divided into three sections: first, a summary of the arguments and evidence offered in earlier chapters; second, a commentary on the major themes that have emerged; third, a brief discussion of the remaining dilemmas, including an agenda for future action.

Summarizing the arguments

The introductory chapter attempted to place university governance in its larger historical and policy context. That context is far from easy to interpret;

it has many, often opposed, strands. First, a general crisis of governance seems to be engulfing Britain (and perhaps other advanced countries) at the end of the twentieth century. Once-settled constitutional forms are now sharply contested. Second, the development of university governance itself is full of contradiction. The most visible fissure, between 'old' and 'new' universities, is compounded by other subtler differences. The government of higher education embodies many different organizational models and institutional myths. Third, British higher education is in the throes of two revolutions, massification and marketization, that, despite their radicalism, are also characterized by obscure reversions and re-entries. Fourth, the growth of mass higher education has coincided with a root-and-branch 'reform' of the welfare state, in which the mimicking of markets is not only an economizing device but a cultural, even ideological, project.

Chapter 2 reviewed the available conceptualizations, and attendant literature, that potentially illuminate university governance. The contest between professional and managerial ethics offers one interpretative framework, as rival models of the university clash, and coexist – scholarly collegium, bureaucratic organization, political (or cybernetic or entrepreneurial) system. A second, similar, conceptualization looks at power relations within higher education institutions, and how these are related in the principles, and practice, of governance. A third theoretical schema, discussed in Chapter 8 and derived from American studies of non-profit organizations, emphasizes two contrasts: between donative and commercial institutions, the former dependent on gifts or grants and the latter on market transactions; and between mutual and entrepreneurial version of these institutions, the former governed quasi-representatively and the latter in executive mode. Useful as these conceptualizations are, the muddiness of university governance in Britain makes their empirical application far from straightforward.

Governors themselves, as revealed through our research evidence, were the focus of the next two chapters. Three broad topics were addressed. The first was the identity of members of university councils and governing bodies. The results, which will be referred to later in this chapter, were hardly surprising, although discouraging to disciples of democratization or advocates of 'active' citizenship. The second was the views of governors, a key but hitherto uncanvassed group, on a range of higher education policies and issues. Here the outcome was more encouraging. A broad synchronization of opinions emerged, although with intriguing differences. Far from being incommensurable, the views of lay governors (including those from the corporate sector), of senior managers and of the academic guild appeared to be remarkably congruent. The third was the selection and appointment of governors, a sensitive topic that has attracted the interest of the Nolan Committee in its quango hunt. The ambiguous articulation of formal and informal 'searches' opened up revealing, but not always hopeful, perspectives. At issue seemed to be not so much a deliberate attempt to restrict membership of governing bodies to the historically privileged or politically correct, but a narrowness of vision, information and alternative references.

The next part – Chapters 5, 6 and 7 – was about governance-in-action. The first of these chapters dealt with the constitution, written and unwritten, of governing bodies. A key determinant, of course, is how governors interpret their roles and responsibilities, how they perceive the gap (if any) between description, what they actually do, and prescription, what they should do, and how they anticipate these roles and responsibilities changing. As ever, contradictions abounded. Governors stressed both strategy, their most proactive function, and audit, their own most reactive. Clear evidence emerged of how committee structures were used with exclusionary intent, to create separate classes of powerful and powerless governors. The middle chapter examined how decisions get taken – and by whom. Governing bodies emerged as important policy arenas, but the policy initiative was generally taken by the executive management. Resources, not policy, preoccupied lay governors. The third chapter looked at the relationships between key agents, mainly chairs of governing bodies and chief executives (vice chancellors) but also other senior lay officers, notably treasurers, other senior managers and the registrar or secretary. The reliance of good government on these, necessarily serendipitous, personal relationships rather than constitutional protocols tended to highlight the best and worst features of university governance.

The wider context was returned to in Chapter 8. In it, three comparative arenas were explored. The first was the evolution of corporate governance, in which the 1992 Cadbury Report was a key event. Despite the ideologically inspired influence of corporate models, there seemed to be little evidence that the private sector has generated concrete examples of good practice that could be transferred to the government of higher education institutions. Rather, the impression was of a sector struggling to impose anachronistic patterns of governance on increasingly volatile, even anarchic, organizations. The second was the 'reform' of the public sector, of which the reform of the National Health Service has become established as a paradigm. Again, the scope for creative carry-over of good practice seemed limited. In both reform processes, general and specific, attention had been focused on management to the almost complete exclusion of governance. Third, university governance in the United States and the rest of Europe was discussed. Despite deep differences, certain congruities could be observed such as the pivotal role of the chief executive, the need to build networks of local and regional influence, and the difficulty of demarcating the separate domains of managers and governors.

Reflecting on issues

This book is the outcome of research on changing patterns of governance in higher education. The emergence of novel, and increasingly volatile, policy environments, itself the product of the overarching trends towards massification and marketization identified in Chapter 1, led us to expect that the way in which governance was conceptualized (and operationalized) was indeed the subject of rapid change. So, too, did the broader structural and cultural environment within which issues of governance had risen to such prominence. The 'reform' of the public sector, itself both symptom and cause of post-industrial turbulence, has undermined (and even desecrated) once taken-for-granted arrangements for the organization, control and delivery of the 'welfare' needs of society, including the provision of higher education. The links between universities and society, culture, science and innovation led us to expect that the emergence of new principles and patterns, networks and relationships, in the reformed public sector, as well as a new managerialist ethos, would provide all the conditions for the transformation of the environment of governance.

Yet the research evidence points to a more qualified and ambiguous set of conclusions about the changing pattern of university governance. For all the turbulence in universities and colleges, the cumulative effect of these grand secular changes discussed in Chapter 1, they remain in many respects traditional and conservative organizations. In contrast to the position in other sectors, the appeal of corporate models seems to have been qualified by the old academic culture that values intellectual mutuality, organizational collegiality and institutional autonomy and that still strongly persists. The liberal, genteel, even utopian, ideals of the traditional university are not just celebrated rhetorically by, but in many practical ways incorporated into, the modern mass university. Among these values is the notion of 'dignified' lay participation in the control and management of higher education, even if the influence of the academic guild became dominant in most 'old' universities. The two principles, lay participation and academic self-government, were not seen as necessarily in sharp conflict.

The new, and potentially unbalancing, factor is the link that has now been established, or asserted, between lay participation, or predominance, in university governance and the replacement of a traditional public service ethos by a new 'business' orientation as the guiding ideology in the management of higher education institutions. It was, and is, asserted that universities must be less donnish and more commercial, that a change of organizational culture is demanded and that lay governors are the key change agents in this process. Our research was designed to explore that assertion, first by investigating its empirical basis (Do lay governors actually see themselves as entrepreneurial change agents? Are governing bodies, as presently constituted, able to deliver such change?), and second by reflecting on the appropriateness of such culture change to the condition of British higher education.

An obvious starting place was to examine the differences between the governance cultures of the 'old' and 'new' universities. The reform of polytechnic and college government at the time of incorporation, a pattern maintained unchanged by the 'new' universities, was widely interpreted as explicitly designed to produce an instrument – a majority of 'independent' governors mostly from corporate backgrounds – to effect cultural change in these institutions. The characteristics of those who become governors, there-fore, were clearly crucial to the success of this project. So were the mechan-isms of selection and appointment. Because policy circumstances had prevented a parallel reform of the 'old' university councils, it seemed rea-sonable to expect to be able to observe significant differences between the social, political, professional and cultural identities of the two groups of governors. As well as investigating their personal characteristics and identi-ties, our research was also designed to explore the processes of governance in the two sets of institutions: how governing bodies and councils were organized; how their influence over the future direction of their institu-tions was operationalized; how (and which) members of governing bodies became involved in (which) aspects of institutional management. Not all these issues could be easily investigated. In particular, the exploration of all-important power relations, typically informal and volatile, raises serious methodological difficulties. But, despite these difficulties, sufficient evidence was assembled to enable substantive conclusions to be drawn not only about the present state of university governance but also about its likely (and desirable) future direction.

Our findings about the origins and identities of university and college governors influenced our approach to analysing the roles played, by lay governors in particular, in the government of higher education and their broader articulation with notions of citizenship, 'active' or otherwise, and participation. The members of governing bodies and councils are far from typical of the population at large or even of the general population of higher education. They are predominantly middle to older-aged white males employed full-time in professional or business occupations. Most have had first-hand experience of higher education and are educated to at least first degree level. Many are 'active' citizens, in the sense that more than half are members of other public bodies. While overall the majority of governors is inclined to support the Conservative Party, there is a significant (and dis-turbing?) polarization of political allegiance between lay and academic members. The former favour the Conservatives and the latter the Labour Party. The contrast is especially sharp in 'new' university and college gov-erning bodies.

These two phenomena, the tight alignment between professional and business occupations and lay participation in university governance and the political polarization between lay and academic members, might have been thought likely to lead to repeated clashes between members with different value-systems: 'academic' and 'secular', producer and consumer, 'liberal' and 'market'. Indeed, this would be the expected outcome if the link be-tween enhanced lay participation in university governance and institutional culture change were to be substantiated. But our evidence does not reveal such a sharp dichotomy. In fact, the views and attitudes of governors, whether lay or academic, 'old' university or 'new', demonstrate a high degree of consensus over a wide range of policy issues concerning the size, shape and funding of higher education. Perhaps this result is not surprising in the light of the evidence, admittedly largely anecdotal, of a recent softening of the more abrasive and adversarial styles adopted by 'independent' governors of 'new' universities in the immediate post-incorporation (and pre-university) period and the slow but sure development of more assertive attitudes among lay members of 'old' university councils. Nevertheless, it tends to dent the standard assumption that lay governors regard themselves as change agents.

Instead, it suggests that lay governors, even those who lean towards the Conservative Party, do not feel themselves to be political or ideological conscripts. The process of socialization they undergo is too complex and ambivalent to be labelled 'going native'. Instead, they develop a set of allegiances to their institution that, although by no means uncritical, absorb its core values. Like school governors and many other board members of public organizations (Deem *et al.*, 1995: 159), they are unpaid volunteers, which moderates rather than stimulates their critical instincts. Their embroilment in what is unambiguously a voluntary sector rather than commercial environment, which is underlined by the lack of remuneration, may have an important influence over lay governors' attitudes. Paradoxically, paying governors might increase their propensity to act as change agents. This subtle socialization is reinforced by other factors. They are not required to possess particular qualifications or to undergo any form of training to become a university or college governor, although in practice they tend to have relevant experience and skills. Most lay governors identify their suitability in terms of personal attributes (staff and student governors, not surprisingly, see their role in more representative terms). The general effect is to enhance the ties of 'honour' that bind them to their institutions. And these ties may inhibit over-vigorous interventions that could be characterized as disloyal.

These ties are strengthened by the manner in which new governors are selected, whatever objections there may be to the narrow social base from which they are drawn. Governors, in effect, are chosen by institutions, not imposed upon them. So the burden of obligation is increased. In the search for new governors, extensive use is made of informal networks and personal recommendations in 'old' and 'new' universities alike. Lay governors play a subordinate role in these 'searches'; the initiative tends to lie with vice chancellors and other senior managers (such as the registrar or secretary). The overall impression is of pragmatism, even opportunism, rather than of a determination to appoint right-minded governors. The ability to add value, independent judgement and (significantly) sympathy to academic purposes are typical of the selection criteria. It is a process that certainly lacks transparency, and so is open to objection on these grounds. The existence of a formal nominations committee appeared to make little difference to what remains essentially an exercise in patronage; practice in all four case study universities, two with and two without nominations committees, was remarkably similar. But nor is it a process likely to generate critical change agents.

However, although over-critical change-agent governors are unlikely to survive the silent nuances of the selection criteria, the same criteria may inhibit the emergence of active-citizen governors who may wish to play a more positive part in university governance. The careful control exercised by senior managers over the choice of new governors and the subtle interplay of patronage, opportunism and networking are hardly designed to 'empower' governors. The organizational arrangements within which governors perform their duties similarly reinforce the constraints on their freedom of manoeuvre. The full council or board of governors meets infrequently, typically three or four times a year. Its role, although formally sovereign, in practice is secondary. Our evidence suggests that rank-and-file governors, even those occupying leading positions outside the university, may be intimidated by the dominance of inner-circle governors (the chair and other senior officers), by the depth of knowledge displayed by the vice chancellor and other executives and even by the sense of occasion inescapably aroused by the *numen* of the university.

There are further layers of subordination and exclusion. All governing bodies have an inner circle, invariably comprising the vice chancellor and his or her senior colleagues (who may not be members but only 'in attendance') and, perhaps in a subordinate position, the chair and other senior lay officers. Often the distinction between core and other governors is reflected in the council's, or board's, committee structure. It is here that policy is actually initiated, and can be effectively challenged. Invariably there is a key committee which, in practice, constitutes a quasi-executive board and from which certain governors may be excluded. In 'old' university councils exclusion is often self-selected or otherwise informally constituted; in 'new' universities it is sometimes imposed by over-rigid interpretation of rules regulating employee interests in board decisions. As a result, staff governors are generally unable to participate in key decision-making.

A further, and perhaps more decisive, consideration constrains the freedom of manoeuvre enjoyed by governing bodies. The core university and college activities are teaching and research. It is these that generate the fiercest sense of 'ownership', and inform nearly all major issues of strategy and policy development. Our evidence suggests that lay governors feel disempowered, faintly but suggestively, because they regard themselves as excluded from sharing this 'ownership', and inhibited from engaging too proactively in discussions and decisions arising from these teaching and research-related issues. Their inhibition is far from total. The board of governors in one of our case study universities (a 'new' university) had began to spar with other interest groups for ownership of this 'academic' space. And, as was argued in the introductory chapter, the distinction between 'allocative' and 'authoritative' domains has become blurred under the double impact of massification and marketization.

Nevertheless, even in the case study 'new' universities, the willingness and ability of 'independent' governors to engage in academic debates was constrained. They themselves acknowledged the difficulty of mounting serious challenges to recommended policies because of the ambiguous demarcation of formal powers between governing body and executive management, their dependence on senior managers for appropriate information and their own lack of knowledge and insecure grasp of the issues at stake. As a result, they see their main roles as to steer institutional strategy, particularly in terms of financial and estates planning, and to 'audit' the activities of senior managers. Yet their ability to fulfil even these roles is constrained. The sources of strategic planning and policy development, and the capacity to organize (and present) decisions taken elsewhere in the governance structure, remain firmly in the hands of informally constituted groups, or caucuses, of senior managers led by the vice chancellor. Mutual trust and personal integrity, not rules and regulations, are the effective safeguards against abuse of this command over policy formation. Most lay governors acknowledge the frailty of their powers and accept the reality of caucus power, implicitly endorsing the comment of one chair of governors that such groups are 'the way vice chancellors have chosen to organize their affairs'.

Lay governors face other constraints. Sometimes 'accommodations' are negotiated between executive managers and academic governors, which tend to marginalize their influence. This is more likely to happen in 'old' than in 'new' universities, where 'independent' governors have an entrenched status and the academic guild is weaker. A still more serious constraint arises from the nature of university governance itself. Our research suggests that effective power is located not in the formal constitution of councils and governing bodies but in the informal, generally interpersonal, networks that develop in the interstices of these formal arrangements. The ambiguous and evanescent qualities of governing bodies as organizations militate against them becoming effective bodies for initiating strategies, even on key resource issues. To the extent that individual governors, typically the core group, exercise influence over these key strategic and resource decisions, they tend to do so either through their membership of smaller sub-groups or on a one-to-one basis in direct dialogue with other key players, such as the chair of governors or the vice chancellor.

It is precisely such informal exchanges, and the flows of power and influence they constitute, that are most difficult to research. They are highly contingent on the integrity of individual actors and their commitment to maintaining good, and constructive, personal relations. And in their opacity lies the difficulty of both conceptualizing and operationalizing good governance. In fashionable neo-conservative critiques of traditional ways of controlling, managing and delivering public services, the lay (or 'business') element in institutional governance is accorded a key role in producing change, in the process of government and thereby in the institution. To be successful in this task, lay governors must resist the ties of 'honour', the insidious pressures of socialization, discussed earlier. They must be, in an important sense, 'external' to the institution, unsentimental about its existing value systems and management practices. They must even be, to some degree, 'disloyal'. Or, rather, their loyalties must be seen as lying elsewhere. This positioning has been accurately described by Stephen Ball (1994) and others as 'steering at a distance'. In this schema, governing bodies act almost as the sub-contractors or agents of the state, willing to take tough and unpopular decisions that reflect its (rather than their institution's) political agenda and prioritization of resources (even if this damages the interests of their institution). Governors, especially the lay element, are 'agents of the state at a distance' (Deem *et al.*, 1995: 161). An alternative, more benign, account of the role of governors of 'reformed' public institutions emphasizes their responsibilities as 'active citizens', fulfilling their civic duty not in a democratic context but as proxy customers. The reform of the NHS has been constructed on both premises, especially the latter.

Our research offers little support for either in the context of university governance, although elements of both can be identified at a rhetorical rather than operational level. Accounts of governance derived from competing post-modern discourses, which imagine new lay-intensive governing bodies to be simultaneously the antidote to all the ills of (unresponsive) collegiality and (inefficient) bureaucracy and instruments of the new entrepreneurial notions of 'active citizenship', fail to convince in the light of our evidence. True, post-incorporation governance in the polytechnics and colleges, carried over with amendment into the 'new' universities, was explicitly designed to stimulate culture change, from the dead hand of municipal and syndicalist control to the brave new world of institutional enterprise. Although rhetoric is never insignificant, university governance viewed in this ideological perspective is an insubstantial (and unrecognizable) chimera. Viewed through the lens of empirical research, rooted in the temporality of the actual government of universities and colleges, it appears markedly less exotic.

Two questions arise from this discussion of our findings. First, is it more accurate to stress the continuities rather than the disjunctures of university governance? Our answer is yes – but. Second, if continuity of governance is emphasized, does this mean that the deeper continuities of higher education, organizational and epistemological, should be emphasized at the expense of the radical irruption of new social, economic and intellectual imperatives? Our answer is absolutely not. An irreversible transformation of higher education is well advanced. But changes in university governance have only played a subordinate role in that transformation. Both the transformation of higher education and changes in governance are complex phenomena, delayed by the friction that all progressive movement encounters and confused by ceaseless regression and contradiction. As was argued in the introductory chapter, the professionalization of expert society and the academicization of intellectual culture are irresistible trends. They cohabit uneasily with the marketization of institutions and the rise of postmodern doubt. But all four, despite this unease, are elements within a larger movement, the transformation of the modern. Similarly, and more modestly, the tensions persist between the evanescence, and ambiguity, of university governance and the demands placed upon it – whether for greater efficiency, increased accountability or more transparency.

A third question, of course, arises from the first two. If the inner rhythms of university governance have changed less than the outer forms – but, despite this, higher education institutions are being radically transformed by the forces of massification and marketization – it could appear that governance is a peripheral arena. The real action lies elsewhere: in the impact of those forces not simply on what has been termed the 'public' life of institutions but on the 'private' life of disciplines; in the development of senior management; in the restructuring of universities and colleges. The significance of these foci of change cannot be underestimated, but they need not be juxtaposed to the domain of governance. This is not a zero-sum power game, a simplistic calculus of senior managers *or* governing bodies (or, conceptually, executive managerialism *or* corporate governance *or*, for that matter, academic collegiality). The growing importance of university governance lies precisely in what we have observed in the course of our research, its embeddedness in institutional cultures rather than juxtaposition to them. Working from the inside out, governing bodies have a power they could never hope to generate working from the outside in.

One view of the future of higher education distinguishes between the 'core' and the 'distributed' university (Scott, 1995). The 'core' comprises those activities derived from the traditional mission of the university, 'new' as well as 'old', principally undergraduate and postgraduate education and research. The 'distributed' university represents the radical projection of higher education into other domains: further education, the so-called 'corporate classroom', industrial collaboration, community out-reach, even the 'virtual' university. Higher education institutions, of course, will not be divided into these two classes. Instead, individual institutions will comprise 'core' and 'distributed' elements in volatile combinations. If this account is accurate, governing bodies will play a key role: as gate-keepers policing the flow between 'core' and 'distributed' activities; as both-ways interpreters between the university and its proliferating, and increasingly heterogeneous, stakeholders; and as guardians of institutional integrity, normatively as well as logistically. In all three functions they have advantages not possessed by either senior management or the academic guild standing alone.

An agenda for action

It is in these broader terms that we anticipate that governance will become a central concern of the twenty-first-century university, and argue that lay governors should rightly be regarded as a 'rising class' within mass higher education. The present preoccupation, now dwindling, with inducing a long-overdue change in the culture of an anachronistic 'donnish dominion' or, its ideological antithesis, imposing an alien 'business' culture on a liberal academic enterprise appears, in this wider perspective, an uninteresting and unimportant side-show. It is in this wider perspective that an agenda for reforming university governance must be constructed not simply in narrower terms of the swirling debates about detailed mechanisms of accountability.

The latter, of course, are important. On the basis of our research, and reflections upon it, we argue for three key changes.

First, governing bodies should be more representative. As, under the dual impact of massification and marketization, student constituencies become more diverse, stakeholders proliferate and 'markets' for university 'products' multiply, issues of access, responsiveness and representation become conflated. Governing bodies, as presently constituted, are unrepresentative both of the community at large and of their institutions' 'customers' in terms of age, gender, ethnicity, occupational background and cultural capital. If they are to play the key roles we have identified as potentially theirs in the university of the future, they must become more representative of both their civic and 'commercial' stakeholders.

Second, university governance's democratic deficit must be tackled. At present, governing bodies are composed of both elected (staff and student) and co-opted (lay, or 'independent') members. One objection is that this dichotomy produces unhealthily competing legitimacies. A more powerful objection is that co-option leads to reproduction of inward elites. As a result, governing bodies are denied fresh blood and new ideas, and stand accused of being unaccountable quangos stuffed with political placemen (the gendering is generally justified). If co-option is retained (as it probably must be, although American and most other European universities are governed by much more 'political' and democratic systems), it must be opened up: perhaps by requiring lay vacancies on governing bodies to be publicly advertised; perhaps by a much tougher code-of-practice obliging governing bodies to organize the widest possible searches for new members.

Third, the principle, and practices, of open government should be applied to university governance. In many other European countries university council meetings are open to the press and public, as are those of some boards of regents and trustees in the United States. At the very least agendas, reports and minutes should be public documents. There are occasions when confidentiality, whether to protect individual privacy or commercial secrets, should be strictly circumscribed. It follows that the present practice whereby some governors, typically staff members, are routinely excluded, should be proscribed. This is also objectionable because it weakens the collective solidarity, and so authority, of governing bodies.

These reforms are important not in themselves, as attempts to clean up university governance in the context of recent debates about accountability and sleaze, a defensive manoeuvre on the part of governing body elites, *revanche* by syndicalist-minded staff or the donnish dominion restored. Rather, they are designed to increase the relevance, and so promote the effectiveness, of university (and college) councils and governing bodies. Their effect would be to strengthen, not to emasculate, university governance. This is an urgent task, for two reasons. First, mass universities elitely governed will not work. Governance reformed is an essential element in higher education reconfigured. Second, to return to where this book began, government-as-given has been superseded by governance at once active and contested.

Universities and colleges cannot regard themselves as exempt from this grand secular change, this unbundling of established patterns and structures of legitimate authority. It can be observed in our new perceptions of the state, community and civil society; in the crisis of corporate governance; in the erosion of professional privileges; in the reform of public institutions. And it can be observed, surely, in higher education.

Appendix 1: Research Methods

The research on which this book is mainly based was carried out by the authors at the School of Education, University of Leeds, between October 1993 and spring 1995. Two main sets of data were collected, from a questionnaire survey and case studies. The details are given below.

The questionnaire survey

The aims of the questionnaire survey were:

1. To establish a representative overview of the demographic characteristics of members of governing bodies/councils throughout the sector.
2. To gather aggregate information about members' attitudes concerning their role and governance experience.
3. To examine their attitudes towards a number of fundamental issues currently on the higher education agenda.

The sample consisted of 745 governors from 28 higher education institutions: ten 'old' universities, 14 'new' universities and four colleges of higher education. The institutions included in the sample were selected by a two-stage cluster method. The sampling frame included all the universities in Britain (excluding Oxford and Cambridge) and was stratified according to student population between the sectors and then type and/or region within the sectors. It is recognized that use of a cluster sampling method as opposed to a simple random sample reduces precision, because members within the same institution are likely to have similar characteristics. However, a cluster sample was used primarily owing to time restraints and considerations of lengthy procedures involving access negotiations in obtaining sampling lists of governors/council members.

The questionnaire was drafted and a pilot study was conducted with 60 governors in two institutions, one 'new' and one 'old' university. Revisions to the questionnaire were made in the light of this pilot. A postal questionnaire and explanatory letter were then sent to all members of the governing bodies from the selected institutions; after approximately one month a reminder was issued to non-respondents. The overall response was excellent: 533 questionnaires were returned (71.5 per cent). However, 39 questionnaires were excluded on the grounds that they had

Table A1.1   Response rate, by type of institution

Type of institution	Questionnaires despatched	Questionnaires completed	Response (per cent)
'Old' universities	398	252	63.3
'New' universities	272	187	68.7
Colleges of HE	75	55	73.3
Total	745	494	66.3

Table A1.2   Category of member of type of institution

Type of member	Type of institution			
	Old university Number %	New university Number %	HE college Number %	Total Number %
Lay/independent	156	136	39	331
	(62.2)	(73.1)	(73.6)	(67.6)
Academic staff	78	29	7	114
	(31.1)	(15.6)	(13.2)	(23.3)
Non-academic staff	8	9	3	20
	(3.2)	(4.8)	(5.7)	(4.1)
Student	9	12	4	25
	(3.6)	(6.5)	(7.5)	(5.1)
Total number	251	186	53	490
Per cent	51.2	38.0	10.8	100

Number of missing observations: 4

been either not completed or only partly completed. This produced a total of 494 valid responses, or 66.3 per cent. Response rates were similar in the three sectors: 'old' and 'new' universities and colleges of higher education. This suggests that the sample was representative.

Initial analysis was undertaken by examining the overall frequency percentages across the sector as a whole, and the use of cross-tabulation models allowed further exploration of the differences between institutional type and internal/external membership. Thus, two independent variables were primarily used in cross-tabulation analysis. Details of the first, 'type of institution', are outlined in Table A1.1.[1] The second most frequently used independent variable was 'type of member', and this was obtained by recoding 'category of member' (detailed by type of institution in Table A1.2) into a dichotomous variable, which simply divides the membership into external (lay or independent members) and internal (academic staff, non-academic staff and students) members (detailed by type of institution in Table A1.3).

Where appropriate, details of statistically significant differences between 'types of institution' and 'types of member' have been provided in the main text. These bivariate relationships were further explored by the introduction of a control variable (usually by holding one of these variables constant). That is, the original bivariate

Table A1.3 Recode of 'category of member' to 'member' by type of institution

Type of member	Type of institution			
	Old university Number %	New university Number %	HE college Number %	Total Number %
External member	156 (62.2)	136 (73.1)	39 (73.6)	331 (67.6)
Internal member	95 (37.8)	50 (26.9)	14 (26.4)	159 (32.4)
Total Number	251	186	53	490
Per cent	51.2	38.0	10.8	100

Number of missing observations: 4

relationship can be further explored by eliminating the influence of a control variable from the analysis. For example, to increase our understanding of the relationship between voting propensity and type of member, the voting patterns of external and internal governors/members of council from the same type of institution were compared. Thus, the effect of the type of institution was effectively eliminated from the analysis. Copies of the questionnaire are available on request from the Centre for Policy Studies in Education at the University of Leeds.

The case studies

In the second phase of the research project, case studies of governance in four institutions of higher education were undertaken. Selection of the case studies was influenced by two considerations. First, following recent legislative changes, the current higher education sector is much expanded and comprises a diverse range of institutions in terms of origin, size and organization. Second, reflecting this diversity, precise constitutional arrangements vary from institution to institution and governing bodies operate within historical structures developed in line with institutional rather than sectoral needs. However, since the overall aim of the research was to assess the extent to which the 'old' and 'new' universities differ in their governance styles, it was decided to investigate two institutions from each group. Certain institutions were considered to be atypical and were excluded as possible case studies, among them the ancient universities, the federal University of London, the federal colleges of Wales and all the colleges of higher education. The selection from the remaining population of old and new institutions was loosely determined by the need to couple institutions from the respective groups by similar geographic and socio-economic regions. Final selection, as in all case study analysis, rested on the willingness of institutional leaders to participate in the research.

The sample consisted of an old and a new university from the south of England and an old and a new from the north. Within these institutions interviews were conducted with (a) vice chancellors/principals, (b) clerks/secretaries to the board of governors and (c) chairs of council/board of governors. We also interviewed independent/lay and academic staff members. Selection of the latter groups was restricted to those respondents to the questionnaire survey who had indicated willingness to be interviewed. Independent/lay members were interviewed from each institution and academic staff from all but one old university (no staff member who had completed the questionnaire from this university indicated willingness to take part in an interview). In total, 25 in-depth interviews were conducted: four vice chancellors, four clerks/secretaries to the board of governors, four chairs of governing bodies, eight independent/lay members and five staff members. In addition, one of the researchers was able to observe a meeting of the full governing body at one of the new university case studies. Following conventional social science practice, neither institutions nor individual participants are identified by their real names.

Note

1. It should be noted that the small size of the sub-sample of HE college governors makes it difficult to obtain high significance levels and also increases the probability of sampling error. Even where significant levels of equal to or less than 0.05 were obtained, caution should be taken in extrapolating these results to the HE college population.

Appendix 2: Additional Results of the Questionnaire

Chart of mean scores of why respondents became a member, by type of member

Ranking of reasons for becoming member by mean

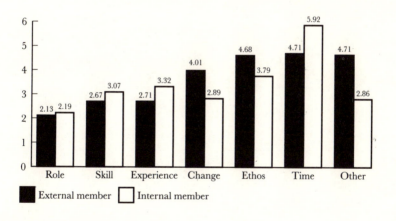

Type of degree programme, by type of member

	Type of member		
	External member (%)	Internal member (%)	Total (%)
Modularization	64.9	44.9	58.3
Traditional	35.1	55.1	41.7
Total (numbers)	229	147	446

Pearson chi-square 0.00006, d.f.1, correlation 0.190, no. missing 48.

Type of degree programme, by type of institution

Type of degree programme	Type of institution			
	Old university (%)	New university (%)	HE college (%)	Total (%)
Modularization	44.1	77.5	58.8	58.4
Traditional	55.9	22.5	41.2	41.6
Total number	229	169	51	449

Pearson chi-square 0.00000, d.f.2, correlation 0.315, no. missing 45.

All HE institutions should engage in research, by type of institution

	Type of institution			
	Old university (%)	New university (%)	HE college (%)	Total (%)
Disagree	42.9	25.0	16.0	33.1
Agree	57.1	75.0	84.0	66.9
Total number	240	184	50	474

Pearson chi-square 0.00001, d.f.2, correlation 0.217, no. missing 20.

Academic standards, by type of member, by type of institution

Academic standards	Old university[a]		New university[b]		Total[c] (includes HE college)	
	External member (%)	Internal member (%)	External member (%)	Internal member (%)	External member (%)	Internal member (%)
Have improved	34.2	14.9	43.2	22.0	38.8	17.1
Stayed the same	39.0	27.7	35.2	30.0	37.9	29.7
Have declined	26.7	57.4	21.6	48.0	23.3	53.2
Total (numbers)	146	94	125	50	309	158

[a] Pearson chi-square 0.00001, d.f.2, correlation 0.316, no. 240. [b] Pearson chi-square 0.00140, d.f.2, correlation 0.274, no. 175. [c] Pearson chi-square 0.00000, d.f.2, correlation 0.312, no. 467.

Opinion regarding the amount of information, by type of member

Amount of information	Type of member		
	External member (%)	Internal member (%)	Total (%)
Too much	22.1	13.5	19.3
About right	70.6	61.9	67.8
Too little	7.4	24.5	24.5
Total (numbers)	326	155	481

Pearson chi-square 0.00000, d.f.2, correlation 0.24594, no. missing 13.

References

Amin, A. (ed.) (1994) *Post-Fordism: a Reader.* Oxford: Blackwell.

Archer, M. (1979) *Social Origins of Educational Systems.* London: Sage.

Baldridge, J. V. (1971) *Power and Conflict in the University.* New York: Wiley.

Ball, S. (1994) *Education Reform: a Critical and Post-Structuralist Approach.* Buckingham: Open University Press.

Bartlett, W. and Le Grand, J. (1994) The performance of trusts, in R. Robinson and J. Le Grand (eds) *Evaluating the NHS Reforms.* London: King's Fund Institute.

Bastin, N. A. (1990) The composition of governing bodies of higher education corporations, *Higher Education Quarterly,* 44, 245–63.

Becher, T. and Kogan, M. (1992) *Process and Structure in Higher Education.* London: Routledge.

Beck, U. (1992) *Risk Society: towards a New Modernity.* London: Sage.

Birnbaum, R. (1989) The cybernetic institution: towards an integration of governance theories, *Higher Education,* 18, 239–53.

Bourdieu, P. (1971) Systems of education and systems of thought, in M. F. D. Young (ed.) *Knowledge and Control.* London: Collier-Macmillan.

Burgess, T., Locke, M., Pratt, J. and Richards, N. (1995) *Degrees East: the Making of the University of East London 1892–1992.* London: Athlone Press.

Cadbury, Sir Adrian (chairman) (1992) *A Report of the Committee on the Financial Aspects of Corporate Governance.* London: Gee.

Carver, J. (1990) *Boards that Make a Difference.* San Francisco: Jossey-Bass.

Charkham, J. (1989a) *Corporate Governance and the Market for Control of Companies.* London: Bank of England (Panel Paper No 25).

Charkham, J. (1989b) *Corporate Governance and the Market for Companies – Aspects of the Shareholders' Role.* London: Bank of England (Discussion Paper 44).

Chell, E., Haworth, J. and Brearley, S. (1991) *The Entrepreneurial Personality. Concepts, Cases and Categories.* London: Routledge.

Clark, B. R. (1983) Governing the higher education system, in M. Shattock (ed.) *The Structure and Governance of Higher Education.* Guildford: SRHE.

Clarke, J., Cochrane, A. and McLauglin, E. (eds) (1994) *Managing Social Policy.* London: Sage.

Cohen, M. D. and March, J. G. (1974) *Leadership and Ambiguity: the American College President.* New York: McGraw-Hill.

Committee of Public Accounts (1994) *Eighth Report. The Proper Conduct of Public Business*. House of Commons. Session 1993–4. London: HMSO.

Committee on Standards in Public Life (1995a) *First Report: Members of Parliament, the Executive (Ministers and Civil Servants) and Executive Non-departmental Public Bodies (Including NHS Trusts) (Nolan Report)*. London: Committee on Standards in Public Life.

Committee on Standards in Public Life (1995b) *Issues and Questions Paper – Local Spending Bodies*. London: Committee on Standards in Public Life.

Committee of University Chairmen (1995) *Guide for Members of Governing Bodies of Universities and Colleges in England and Wales*. Bristol: Higher Education Funding Council for England.

Committee of Vice Chancellors and Principals (1985) *Report of the Steering Group in University Efficiency (Jarratt Report)*. London: CVCP.

Council for Academic Autonomy (1995) *Academic Democracy: a Survey of Current Practice in Universities and Other Institutions of Higher Education*. London: CAA.

Davies, A. (1979) *What's Wrong with Quangos?* London: Outer Circle Policy Unit.

Deem, R., Brehony, K. J. and Heath, S. (1995) *Active Citizenship and the Governing of Schools*. Buckingham: Open University Press.

Department of Education and Science (1965) *Weaver Report*. London: HMSO.

Department of Health and Social Security (1979) *Patients First: Consultative Paper on the Structure and Management of the National Health Service in England and Wales*. London: HMSO.

Ellis, E. L. (1972) *The University College of Wales, Aberystwyth 1872–1972*. Cardiff: University of Wales Press.

Foucault, M. (1977) *Discipline and Punish: the Birth of the Prison*. London: Lane.

Fukuyama, F. (1992) *The End of History and the Last Man*. Harmondsworth: Penguin.

Further Education Unit (FEU) (1994) *Further Education Governors: Supporting the Curriculum*. Blagdon: Staff College.

Gibbons, M., Limoges, C., Nowotny, H., Schwartzman, S., Scott, P. and Trow, M. (1994) *The New Production of Knowledge: the Dynamics of Science and Research in Contemporary Societies*. London: Sage.

Giddens, A. (1984) *The Constitution of Society: Outline of the Theory of Structuration*. Cambridge: Polity Press.

Giddens, A. (1985) *The Nation State and Violence*. Cambridge: Polity Press.

Giddens, A. (1990) *The Consequences of Modernity*. Cambridge: Polity Press.

Graystone, J. (1995) *Governing Bodies and Boards of Management in FE and Sixth Form Colleges: Composition and Membership*. Bristol: FEDA.

Griffiths, R. (1983) *Report of the NHS Management Inquiry*. London: Department of Health and Social Security.

Hall, J. T. (1994) College governors – understanding the checks and balances. Unpublished Paper, Eversheds, London.

Halsey, A. H. (1992) *Decline of Donnish Dominion*. Oxford: Clarendon Press.

Halsey, A. H. and Trow, M. (1971) *The British Academics*. London: Faber.

Hansmann, H. (1980) The role of non-profit enterprise, *The Yale Law Journal*, 89, 835–98.

Hansmann, H. (1987) Economic theories of non-profit organisation, in W. W. Powell (ed.) *The Non-profit Sector: a Research Handbook*. New Haven, CT: Yale University Press.

Hill, S. (1995) The social organisation of boards of directors, *British Journal of Sociology*, 46, 244–78.

Holliday, I. (1992) *The NHS Transformed.* Manchester: Baseline Books.

House of Commons Health Committee (1992) *NHS Trusts: Interim Conclusions and Proposals for Future Inquiries.* London: HMSO.

Hunter, D. (1992) Accountability and the NHS, *British Medical Journal,* 304, 15 February.

Jessop, B. (1994) The transition to post-Fordism and the Schumpeterian workfare state, in R. Burrows and B. Loader (eds) *Towards a Post-Fordist Welfare State.* London: Routledge.

Jones, C. S. (1986) Universities: on becoming what they are not, *Financial Accountability and Management,* 2, 107–19.

Kelly, T. (1981) *For Advancement of Learning: the University of Liverpool 1881–1981.* Liverpool: Liverpool University Press.

Kerr, C. (1994) New focus on leadership, in C. Kerr, *Troubled Times for American Higher Education.* Albany: State University of New York Press.

Keys, W. and Fernandes, C. (1990) *A Survey of School Governing Bodies.* Slough: National Foundation for Educational Research.

Lee, R. A. and Piper, J. A. (1988) Organisational control, differing perspectives: the management of universities, *Financial Accountability and Management,* 2, 113–28.

Le Grand, J. and Bartlett, W. (eds) (1993) *Quasi-markets and Social Policy.* Basingstoke: Macmillan.

Lockwood, G. and Davies, J. (eds) (1985) *Universities: the Management Challenge.* Windsor: SRHE and NFER-Nelson.

McDaniel, O. and Buising, W. (1992) *The Level of Government Influence in Higher Education in the US and Western Europe.* Zoetermeer/Twente: Ministry of Education and Science and Center for Higher Education Policy Studies.

Middlehurst, R. and Elton, L. (1992) Leadership and management in higher education, *Studies in Higher Education,* 17, 251–64.

Middlehurst, R. (1993) *Leading Academics.* Buckingham: SRHE and Open University Press.

Middlehurst, R. (1995) Changing leadership in universities, in T. Schuller (ed.) *The Changing University?* Buckingham: SRHE and Open University Press.

Morgan, G. (1986) *Images of Organisation.* London: Sage.

National Advisory Body for Public Sector Higher Education (1986) *Good Management Practice.* London: NAB.

Nowotny, H. (1994) *Time: the Modern and Postmodern Experience.* Cambridge: Polity Press.

Office of Science and Technology (1995) *Technology Foresight: Progress through Partnership. 14. Leisure and Learning.* London: HMSO.

Osborne, D. and Gaebler, T. (1993) *Reinventing Government.* New York: Plume.

PCFC. (1991) *Guide for Governors.* Bristol: PCFC.

Pearce, F. and Tombs, S. (1990) Ideology, hegemony and empiricism: compliance theories of regulation, *British Journal of Criminology,* 30, 423–43.

Pierson, C. (1991) *Beyond the Welfare State.* Cambridge: Polity Press.

Pollitt, C. (1990) *Managerialism in the Public Sector.* Oxford: Blackwell.

Power, M. (1994) *The Audit Explosion.* London: Demos.

Puxty, A. G., Sikka, P. and Willmott, H. C. (1994) Systems of surveillance and the silencing of UK academic accounting labour, *British Accounting Review,* 26, 137–71.

Rosen, R. and McKee, M. (1995) Short-termism in the NHS, *British Medical Journal,* 311, 16 September.

Scott, P. (1995) *The Meanings of Mass Higher Education.* Buckingham: Open University Press.

Shattock, M. (1994) The UGC and the founding of the new universities in the 1960s: the special case of Warwick, in *The UGC and the Management of British Universities.* Buckingham: Open University Press.

Shaw, J. C. (1993) Governance and accountability. Part 1: corporate governance, in *Universities, Corporate Governance, Deregulation* (Hume Papers on Public Policy. Volume 1, No. 3). Edinburgh: Edinburgh University Press (for the David Hume Institute).

Smith, D. N., Scott, P. and Lynch, J. (1995) *The Role of Marketing in the University and College Sector.* Leeds: Heist.

Stewart, J., Lewis, N. and Longley, D. (1992) *Accountability to the Public.* London: European Policy Forum for British and European Market Studies.

Thompson, E. P. (1969) *Warwick University Ltd.* Harmondsworth: Penguin.

Tricker, R. I. (1984) *Corporate Governance.* Aldershot: Gower.

Trow, M. (1993) Managerialism and the academic profession: the case of England, *Studies of Higher Education and Research,* 4, 2–23.

Weiner, G. (1994) *Feminisms in Education.* Buckingham: Open University Press.

Willmott, H. (1993) Strength is ignorance; slavery is freedom: managing culture in modern organisations, *Journal of Management Studies,* 30, 515–52.

Willmott, H. (1995) Managing the academics: commodification and control in the development of university education in the UK, *Human Relations,* 48, 993–1027.

Wistow, G. (1992) The National Health Service, in D. Marsh and R. A. W. Rhodes (eds) *Implementing Thatcherite Policies: Audit of an Era.* Buckingham: Open University Press.

Index

The Society for Research into Higher Education

The Society for Research into Higher Education exists to stimulate and coordinate research into all aspects of higher education. It aims to improve the quality of higher education through the encouragement of debate and publication on issues of policy, on the organization and management of higher education institutions, and on the curriculum and teaching methods.

The Society's income is derived from subscriptions, sales of its books and journals, conference fees and grants. It receives no subsidies, and is wholly independent. Its individual members include teachers, researchers, managers and students. Its corporate members are institutions of higher education, research institutes, professional, industrial and governmental bodies. Members are not only from the UK, but from elsewhere in Europe, from America, Canada and Australasia, and it regards its international work as among its most important activities.

Under the imprint *SRHE & Open University Press*, the Society is a specialist publisher of research, having some 60 titles in print. The Editorial Board of the Society's Imprint seeks authoritative research or study in the above fields. It offers competitive royalties, a highly recognizable format in both hardback and paperback and the worldwide reputation of the Open University Press.

The Society also publishes *Studies in Higher Education* (three times a year), which is mainly concerned with academic issues, *Higher Education Quarterly* (formerly *Universities Quarterly*), mainly concerned with policy issues, *Research into Higher Education Abstracts* (three times a year), and *SRHE News* (four times a year).

The Society holds a major annual conference in December, jointly with an institution of higher education. In 1993, the topic was 'Governments and the Higher Education Curriculum: Evolving Partnerships' at the University of Sussex in Brighton. In 1994, it was 'The Student Experience' at the University of York and in 1995, 'The Changing University' at Heriot-Watt University in Edinburgh. Conferences in 1996 include 'Working in Higher Education' at Cardiff Institute of Higher Education.

The Society's committees, study groups and branches are run by the members. The groups at present include:

Teacher Education Study Group
Continuing Education Group
Staff Development Group
Excellence in Teaching and Learning

Benefits to members

Individual

Individual members receive:

- *SRHE: News*, the Society's publications list, conference details and other material included in mailings.
- Greatly reduced rates for *Studies in Higher Education* and *Higher Education Quarterly*.
- A 35 per cent discount on all SRHE & Open University Press publications.
- Free copies of the Proceedings – commissioned papers on the theme of the Annual Conference.
- Free copies of *Research into Higher Education Abstracts*.
- Reduced rates for conferences.
- Extensive contacts and scope for facilitating initiatives.
- Reduced reciprocal memberships.
- Free copies of the *Register of Members' Research Interests*.

Corporate

Corporate members receive:

- All benefits of individual members, plus.
- Free copies of *Studies in Higher Education*.
- Unlimited copies of the Society's publications at reduced rates.
- Special rates for its members e.g. to the Annual Conference.
- The right to submit application for the Society's research grants.

Membership details: SRHE, 3 Devonshire Street, London WIN 2BA, UK. Tel: 0171 637 2766. Fax: 0171 637 2781
Catalogue: SRHE & Open University Press, Celtic Court, 22 Ballmoor, Buckingham MK18 1XW. Tel: (01280) 823388.

THE MEANINGS OF MASS HIGHER EDUCATION

Peter Scott

This book is the first systematic attempt to analyse the growth of mass higher education in a specifically British context, while seeking to develop more theoretical perspectives on this transformation of elite university systems into open post-secondary education systems. It is divided into three main sections. The first examines the evolution of British higher education and the development of universities and other institutions. The second explores the political, social and economic context within which mass systems are developing. What are the links between post-industrial society, a post-Fordist economy and the mass university? The third section discusses the links between massification and wider currents in intellectual and scientific culture.

Contents
Preface – Introduction – Structure and institutions – State and society – Science and culture – Understanding mass higher education – Notes – Index.

208pp   0 335 19442 7 (Paperback)   0 335 19443 5 (Hardback)

MISSION AND CHANGE
INSTITUTIONAL MISSION AND ITS APPLICATION TO THE MANAGEMENT
OF FURTHER AND HIGHER EDUCATION

Graham Peeke

Graham Peeke reviews critically the concept of institutional mission in higher and
further education, and evaluates the claims made for its use. Through case studies
he analyses different methods of establishing objectives, provides guidance on how
to operationalize missions so that they are more than just rhetoric, and links institutional change with the development of a strategic perspective in education management. He argues that it is essential to adopt participative methods in mission
development, that procedures for operationalization are crucial, and that broad
dimensions of mission need to be agreed with the core of the organization. However, given the plurality of educational organizations, he also argues that autonomy
is necessary for significant groupings throughout the institutions. This is essential
reading for all policy-makers and managers in higher and further education, and
for researchers into the management of higher education.

Contents
Introduction – Part 1: Context and claims – Mission: definition and claims – Mission and
change – Mission in practice – Assessing the claims for mission – Part 2: Methods of mission
establishment – Methods of mission establishment 1: interest groups – Methods of mission
establishment 2: surveying constituent groups – Methods of mission establishment 3: workshops
– Part 3: Towards a strategic perspective – Operationalizing mission – Implications for
management – References – Index.

160pp   0 335 19338 2 (Paperback)   0 335 19337 4 (Hardback)

LEADING ACADEMICS

Robin Middlehurst

At a time of major change in higher education, the quality of university leadership is an issue of key importance. Whether heading a research team, planning curriculum innovations, managing a department or running an institution, effective leadership is required. Yet how well is the idea of leadership understood? How is leadership practised in the academic world? What special characteristics are needed to lead autonomous professionals?

This book, based on research in universities, is the first comprehensive examination of leadership in British higher education. Robin Middlehurst critiques contemporary ideas of leadership and examines their relevance to academe. She explores the relationship between models of leadership and practice at different levels of the institution. She argues for a better balance between leadership and management in universities in order to increase the responsiveness and creativity of higher education.

Contents

Part 1: Thinking about leadership – What is leadership? – The new leadership – Organizational images – Leadership and academe: traditions and change – Part 2: Practising leadership – Institutional leaders – Collective leadership – Leading departments – Individuals and leadership – Part 3: Developing leadership – Leadership learning – Endings and beginnings – Bibliography – Index.

c.192pp   0 335 09988 2 (Paperback)   0 335 09989 0 (Hardback)